COOL SHADES

COOL SHADES

The History and Meaning of Sunglasses

VANESSA BROWN

B L O O M S B U R Y

LONDON • NEW DELHI • NEW YORK • SYDNEY

Bloomsbury Academic

An imprint of Bloomsbury Publishing Plc

50 Bedford Square
London
WC1B 3DP
UK

1385 Broadway
New York
NY 10018
USA

www.bloomsbury.com

Bloomsbury is a registered trade mark of Bloomsbury Publishing Plc

First published 2015

British Library Cataloguing-in-Publication Data
A catalogue record for this book is available from the British Library.

ISBN HB: 978-0-8578-5444-5
PB: 978-0-8578-5445-2
ePDF: 978-0-8578-5463-6
ePub: 978-08578-5464-3

Library of Congress Cataloging-in-Publication Data
Gill-Brown, Vanessa, 1970-
Cool shades : the history and meaning of sunglasses / Vanessa Brown.
pages cm
Includes bibliographical references and index.
ISBN 978-0-85785-445-2 (paperback)-- ISBN 978-0-85785-444-5 (hardback) 1. Sunglasses.
2. Fashion. 3. Popular culture--History--20th century. I. Title.
GT2370.G55 2014
391.4'4–dc23
2014021549

Typeset by Fakenham Prepress Solutions, Fakenham, Norfolk NR21 8NN
Printed and bound in India

CONTENTS

LIST OF CAPTIONS

ACKNOWLEDGMENTS

First I must acknowledge a debt to Neil Handley, curator of the British Optical Association museum, whose knowledge and willingness to help explore the archives informed and supported the development of this study significantly. There are many others: everyone involved at Bloomsbury, Chris Rojek (who kept me convinced it was a good idea for a PhD all those years ago), Julie Pinches and the research team at Nottingham Trent who helped me find the time and—crucially—extra money for pictures; my fellow visually-curious and right-brain thinking "dcc" people, my magnificent sister, my supercool daughter, my wonderful husband (who wears sunglasses, but only because he has sensitive eyes); all of whom have been patient and encouraging well beyond the call of duty. I should also acknowledge my baby son, who was waiting to be born, or asleep while I was finishing the manuscript.

My previous project—about the image of the housewife—was dedicated to my mother, Anne Brown, who equipped me with the confidence to have ideas and express them. But this book is dedicated to the memory of my father, Kenneth George Brown. He encouraged me to view the world with curiosity and respect, and his own "cool composure" remains legendary among those who knew him.

Facing me, the other exposes to me the defenselessness of his or her eyes...when they turn to me, their direction wavers and their objectives disappear. They turn to me a liquid pool waiting for unforeseeable disturbances. They are more naked than the flesh without pelt or hide, without clothing, divested even of their initiative and position. They are more naked than things can be, than walls bared of their adornments and revolvers stripped of their camouflage; they bare a substance susceptible and vulnerable... Their nudity exposes them to whatever message I may want to impose, whatever offense I can contrive. Exposing to me what is most naked, most vulnerable – the liquid disquiet of the eyes...

ALPHONSO LINGIS, 1994:171

1

INTRODUCTION—WHY WRITE A BOOK ABOUT SUNGLASSES?

Sunglasses are a small thing. They are an accessory, an add-on to life. Some people might question whether such an apparently insignificant thing is worth such study. But Lars Svendsen says that "an understanding of fashion is necessary in order to gain an adequate understanding of the modern world" (2006: 10), and I would like to say something similar about sunglasses in particular. Or, at least, that it might be worth knowing why, in the twentieth century, so many eyes—in images as well as in the "real" world—have been shaded. Sunglasses are usually small in size, but the market for them is massive. At the time of writing, 70 percent of Britons own sunglasses (Mintel 2012: online), in fact since the 1940s it has been claimed that "most people" own a pair (Corson 1967: 225). Most people probably also own umbrellas, but widespread ownership is not the only factor making sunglasses especially significant. The Luxottica group, who own Ray Ban and Oakley, are currently a mighty force in the fashion industry and, perhaps most importantly, sunglasses (and images of them) are everywhere in contemporary popular culture; in fashion, in film, in popular music, in advertising and marketing. Whether "subcultural", "avant-garde", or even aimed at children; the use of sunglasses, certainly in these images, goes way beyond any justification based on a need for protection against dangerous levels of light.

The reason for this is obvious, isn't it? People want to look *cool*! But if this assumption is right, why do they want to be cool and what have sunglasses got to do with it?

This study was partly inspired by a very everyday incident, quite some time ago; on my way home after decorating what was to be my new flat, I stopped at a supermarket to get a pint of milk. I hurriedly got out of the car, grabbing my sunglasses. As I slipped them on, I wondered to myself why I had bothered—it wasn't that sunny, and I really only had a few steps to go. I quickly realized that somehow the sunglasses had made me feel more presentable, and feel less embarrassed about my "scruffy" decorator's appearance. As I approached the entrance, my reflection confirmed to me that, not only was I "more presentable;" to my amusement I actually looked "quite cool"... but of course whether or not I looked cool to anyone else is highly questionable, because cool is well known to be a slippery thing—subjective, elusive, and ever-changing. Whether I *am* cool (or ever was, with or without sunglasses) is irrelevant. This incident got me thinking about how often I had seen sunglasses used in popular culture in just this way, as a sign of some powerful, elusive, desirable quality.

Sunglasses in contemporary culture

As a lecturer in visual culture in a fashion department, I had observed that sunglasses have also been remarkably resilient to changes in fashion and indeed in the sartorial languages of cool. Since sunglasses became fashionable in the early twentieth century, they have remained a powerful component of the fashionable or cool image; in fact, it seems sunglasses are almost synonymous with fashion, underscored by the iconic images of fashion elite like Anna Wintour and Karl Lagerfeld, both recognizable by their tendency to wear shades indoors (film of Lagerfeld even shows him selecting fabrics and evaluating samples in them). Popular frame/lens combinations do get replaced by other styles; and occasionally they have been less ubiquitous, but even then, quite often, other intrusions on the eye (like fringes or hat brims) hold their place. Moments without any form of eye-shade in fashion certainly seem to be short-lived. Every level of the market, every season, every year, from subcultures and street fashion, to couture and luxury branding as well as now the focus of numerous blogs and online articles, sunglasses are an obvious sign of cool which seems to have incredible staying power.

Similarly in film sunglasses have become a cliché of film promotion, for example *Lolita* (1962), *Fear and Loathing in Las Vegas* (1998), *The Matrix* (1999), *Leon* (1994), *The September Issue* (2009) to name a paltry few. Reaching for an image to signify not just the fashion industry but also Hollywood, America, or indeed rock music, hip hop, pop culture, tourism, western culture more generally, sunglasses are a fall-back device in countless graphic designs. Why do sunglasses have such appeal across such wide cultural categories? Could there be something about the *shared* conditions of modern life that makes the appearance of shaded eyes generally—and desirably—meaningful? On T-shirts, necklaces, birthday cakes, children's snacks, and Christmas cards, sunglasses have appeared as a key signifier guaranteeing desirability, an affirmation of desirable social distinction for a mass audience.

Evidently many notorious and beloved twentieth and twenty-first century figures have been known for wearing them, from Miles Davis to Lady Gaga. But

Figure 1.1   Bono of veteran rock group U2, taking up sunglasses initially for his persona as "The Fly" on stage, 1993. (Photograph by Graham Wiltshire. © Getty Images.)

the curious potency of sunglasses in contemporary social life can also be found in news stories about high-profile people who have been unexpectedly photographed wearing sunglasses. A snap of the teenage Prince William "cavorting in wraparound sunglasses" (Greenslade 1999) prompted a debate about "inappropriate" images and, indeed, about the entire role and position of the "modern royals." Quite serious discussions about authenticity and identity were sparked off when the rock "legend" Bono suddenly—and uncharacteristically—began wearing very obvious sunglasses in the 1990s (Sawyer 1997), as they were when the Pope playfully donned the pair given to him by Bono while being filmed for the Jubilee 2000 campaign to write off Third World debt. This moment was allegedly "hastily cut" from the "live" TV coverage from the Vatican (Jelbert 2000). The list goes on but, in all these cases, wearing sunglasses was equated with displaying new or different values, controversial by virtue of their ability to make someone "good" look "bad." On the cover of *The Face* magazine Bono was described as being "defrocked" when he took up the sunglasses, having previously been known for being "messianic," earnest, and depicted as such.

However, these journalistic discussions revealed that, maybe, it was good to look bad, and that this was a complex business. Were the sunglasses an ironic statement of "badness?" Or, did they (embarrassingly) represent "too much effort" to look cool? There was talk of loose morals, hedonism, insincerity, superficiality, but also of "inability to carry off" the cool demeanor. Even more complex was the idea that the sunglasses might reveal a more modest or self-conscious approach to "truth" appropriate to the postmodern world. For some the sunglasses said, "Yes, I know, all I am is a stupid rock star", which somehow made Bono's earnest persona *more* convincing. William's wraparounds helped him "get down with the kids"; but also suggested a "louche, flash" lifestyle too close to fashion and celebrity to be suitable for a respectable future king. When Kanye West and Pdiddy offered Princes William and Harry a try of their

Figure 1.2   Princes William and Harry at the Concert for Diana in 2007 with Kanye West and Sean Coombs (aka Pdiddy). They "jokingly declined" West's offer to try on some shades, but were happy to be snapped with what the *Daily Mail* called "rap royalty." (© Tim Graham Picture Library, Getty Images.)

"ghetto-fabulous" shades at the Concert for Diana several years after the furore over William's wraparounds, they showed caution and "jokingly declined" (*Daily Mail* 2007), knowing the "bad visual copy" this could create. These complexities show there is something interesting here to study.

The book provides a brief history of the emergence of sunglasses specifically as a fashion accessory, but also of the development of their significance within popular culture more broadly, and, most importantly, a detailed investigation of the special relationship between sunglasses and that slippery concept of cool. Often regarded a bit suspiciously by serious fashion writers, cool is nevertheless in common use in popular fashion discourse, and some social theorists have claimed that cool is moving from its roots in black African American culture and the European aristocracy, to become the dominant ethic in western society, supplanting the Protestant work ethic (Pountain and Robins 2000; Poschart in Mentges 2000: 28). Theories of cool will be used along the way to question the meaning and appeal of sunglasses. But perhaps looking at the cultural expressions of cool which make use of sunglasses will also provide further insight into the more general question of what cool might be and why it seems to matter so much.

Existing studies

Some writing and research about sunglasses does already exist; to start with, extensive commentary in fashion blogs and by journalists testifies to their curious power. There are also some useful, heavily illustrated general histories of spectacles and eyeglasses which reference some sunglasses, offering dates and good visual information (although there tends to be a lack of distinction between sunglasses and spectacles). Sunglasses are sometimes treated as a fun but frivolous side-issue in these works; the major exceptions being Handley's *Cult Eyewear* (2011), which details some sunglass-specific brands, and gives more attention to the cultural contexts in which certain brands and models developed their potential meanings; and Moss Lipow's *Eyewear* (2011), which gives some historical context for the invention and development of sunglasses. How and why sunglasses were even invented is often unclear, partly because their current type-form emerged from a variety of reference points (corrective spectacles were in fact often tinted, used to disguise blind or disfigured eyes, and a plethora of goggles and other devices were in use before "sunglasses" became the dominant form). Being "mere accessories" with a technical element, sunglasses have often fallen through the gap between fashion and science; ignored by optical history as too frivolous, by fashion history as somehow not quite the main object of study.

Some short, mainly visual essays by Evans (1996) on sunglasses and Mazza (1996) aspects of the history and poetics relevant to sunglasses have set out brief—but telling—summaries of aspects of the history and poetics of sunglasses, looking at some of the cultural meanings and associations of different styles and forms and their status as "modern metaphors for sight" (Mazza 1996: 19). Sunglasses have also been studied in a number of psychological investigations (for example Edwards 1987; Terry 1989; Terry and Stockton 1993), many of which explore the impact of glasses on physical attractiveness as perceived by others, generally concluding that sunglasses make people more attractive, as opposed to a tendency for corrective glasses to make people seem more intelligent but less sexy (especially female wearers). Another theme emerging from these studies is the perception of authority and honesty, with corrective specs increasing it and sunglasses decreasing it.

None of these studies specifically address these contradictions or attempt to relate them to cool, although sunglasses do often get mentioned by those investigating cool (Pountain and Robins have called them "the sartorial emblem of cool", for example, 2000: 9). Carter and Michael's 2004 essay "Here Comes the Sun" usefully considers sunglasses specifically in terms of their "material-semiotic" relationship to the "cultural body"—identifying some complex potential meanings of the gaze mediated by shades. Influential twentieth century thinkers like Barthes, Goffman, Huxley, McLuhan, and Reyner Banham have also all paused to question the power of shades, but frustratingly none of them have really allowed sunglasses to be a focus.

Studying sunglasses

There are many ways to approach the study of sunglasses, and this book perhaps opens the field for scholars from a variety of disciplines. In this project, my goal was to investigate sunglasses as a signifier in popular culture. Although this project has a design-historical dimension, methodologically it sits within visual and material culture, inspired by the tradition of writers like Walter Benjamin, Siegfried Kracauer, and Georg Simmel, who analyzed the seemingly insignificant "fragments" of modern culture as a way of revealing a complex web of underlying cultural, economic, and ideological values. This tradition is echoed by recent developments in visual and material culture. Where meaning comes from, and how we interpret it, is not located in one place. It is more like a cloud of magnetic dust (which might look different from different angles). The meaning of sunglasses in an advertising or fashion image today is the culmination of decades of design development, technological change, use, representation, and the accumulation of myth in further representations and uses. This necessitates a multi-disciplinary and, in my opinion, a somewhat intuitive approach. This project is informed by some consideration of the material and social "realities" of sunglasses, but it is focused on what sunglasses allow people to dream of being, whether they wear them in real life or consume images of them. The focus of my research was therefore in the collection and analysis of pop cultural imagery featuring sunglasses (mainly from film, advertising, fashion), because these are reproductions of desire and aspiration targeted at the many. Documentary photographs and memoirs indicated how sunglasses were worn by potentially influential figures, and the British Optical Association's archive of British and American journals of the optical industry from the 1890s to the 1960s provided evidence of how products developed and how they were marketed.

The choice of historical and theoretical material was determined by two major things—first the connection with cool suggested a number of starting points (e.g. jazz, other sub-cultures) and secondly, the generic types of sunglass designs and images which suggested certain contexts and connotations (e.g. aviators, novelty frames for beachwear). I looked at hundreds of images initially just seeking patterns and departures, considering the historical and discursive context for them. Themes emerged as starting points for historical or theoretical questions. For example, speed was an important theme both in terms of the "content" of sunglasses' design (many obviously "aerodynamic" forms, e.g. the wraparound) and in the context of imagery featuring them (in cars, on motor-cycles, etc.). Based on the assumption that sunglasses seem to signify cool, I investigated the relevant theory of speed for possible connections with cool and vision. The important thing was to create a conversation between the objects and images and the theory and history, enabling the objects and images to "speak", revealing deeply felt concerns which may otherwise remain uncon-scious. Studying sunglasses tells us more than their own "biography;" here it reveals a novel way to think about coolness, which I hope will be useful to those interested in culture more generally.

The book begins with the cultural context for sunglasses' eventual arrival in visual culture—modernity. Then it proceeds in thematic, roughly chronological chapters about key ideas for the meaning of sunglasses and their connection with cool: speed, technology, light, darkness, shade, and the eclipse. These categories link to a range of cultural and historical contexts in which sunglasses accrued (and continue to accrue) their meanings. The book concludes with a chapter summarizing the development of sunglasses' relationship with cool and concluding on what this might reveal about cool more generally.

Finally, I must state clearly that I am not saying the meaning of sunglasses is fixed. That should be obvious. Neither does this book claim that sunglasses are always perceived as cool by everyone; not now, nor in the past. Indeed, as much popular commentary of sunglass-wearing shows, sunglasses are now a cliché of attempts to look cool—and since making any effort to look cool implies a distinct lack of cool, the person who wishes to look cool should proceed with caution where sunglasses are concerned, paying careful attention to the details of form and context ... Unless of course, they are using the signifiers of being "uncool" as a means to demonstrate their complete lack of concern for others and their rules about cool, which of course, has the potential to make them much cooler than the sort of person who might be afraid of making a sartorial mistake. Ironic and, perhaps, post-ironic forms of cool add another layer of nuance and complexity to the notion of the "meaning" of sunglasses which will, I hope, become apparent through the book. This book explores the *possible*, *shared* meanings of sunglasses primarily in the west, and their emergence as a prime *signifier* of cool in late twentieth and twenty-first century popular culture.

Of course the meanings sunglasses have the potential to suggest will also change in the future. They may become the nostalgic or laughable signifier of an era of clumsy and naïve engagements with technology. Or they might become the sign of a narcissistic, wasteful, and frivolous culture which is unsustainable even for the relative few. They might already arguably be signs of these things for some. But for now, sunglasses are as prevalent in pop culture as ever, they are still packed with powerful allure, and their study makes a fascinating and revealing journey through varying "shades of cool."

2
MODERNITY—AN ONSLAUGHT ON THE EYES

Introduction

Before the twentieth century, sunglasses as we think of them today were not in any kind of widespread use. Tinted glass (green or blue) had been recommended since the eighteenth century—but for *corrective* spectacles (Ayscough in Drewry 1994) intended to be worn indoors. Mid-eighteenth century Venice saw green tinted glasses used against glare from the water (the "Goldoni" type, worn by and named after the leader of the *commedia dell' arte*). At the turn of the nineteenth century, an optical writer does make reference to "those who have the intention of only wearing tinted glasses when they are exposed to the sun's rays or when travelling in the snow" (Scarpa in Hamel 1955), and purely protective "goggles" with tinted lenses were developed for a variety of military and industrial purposes after that, but, even as late as 1867, some optical advisors still felt that a simple "strip of brown crepe" fabric was more fit for purpose (Horne 1867 in Corson 1967). By the beginning of the twentieth century, American manufacturers started to push goggles for the general user, predominantly aiming at men and for driving (*The Keystone Magazine* 1910). By 1925, driving goggles appear on the cover of *Vogue*, but it could be argued that it took until the 1930s for sunglasses to emerge as accessories and become fully accepted (certainly they did not appear in fashion imagery before that time).

Sunglasses are a product of modernity, and perhaps inject a hint of modernity into every image they grace. Even before sunglasses made it into popular use and representations, some important changes relating to appearance and behavior in public were taking place (including the expression of emotion, social power, and other eye-activity) which connect closely with the growth of a modern, urban culture which set the scene for shades, and continues to underpin their meanings. This chapter describes these changes, contextualizing the chapters which follow, starting by considering some of the accessories which pre-date sunglasses but which perhaps demonstrate some similar functional and symbolic uses. A theme running through this chapter is how modernity could be thought of as an "onslaught on the eyes", an explosion of "stuff to see", and of technologies to extend the human capacity to see it. Mass fashion and consumer culture also gave new importance to how things and people *look*. Martin Jay describes modernity as the era in which vision became the dominant sense and in which the visual became a preoccupation of many European thinkers (Jay 1993). Because they are highly visible, and look like eyes, we will see how sunglasses have a wealth of potential not only to protect overloaded eyes, but to mediate the gaze and even to signify vision in the modern context.

The pre-history of sunglasses

The social potential of masking the eyes or in some way nuancing the gaze was understood well before the emergence of sunglasses. At Venetian balls the mask held the frisson of anonymity, temporarily changing the wearer's social role, as did the face-protectors known as "vizzards", which were worn by women in eighteenth century London parks (Heyl 2001). The fan afforded a seductive giving and taking away of access to the gaze, and the ambiguity of showing and hiding associated with conventions of feminine behavior. The quizzing fan, which had a strip of semi-transparent gauze within the fabric, added voyeuristic potential, and the lorgnette (a lens or pair of lenses held up to the face on a decorative handle) allowed a show to be made of the act of looking and inter-rogating. Spectacles could potentially do the same thing, indeed the lorgnette was originally an aid to defective sight; but significantly, the lorgnette's social usefulness and fashionability went well beyond that of spectacles, certainly among women.

    Lorgnettes were made with plano (non-corrective) lenses for those with *good* eyesight (Acerenza 1997), taking the lorgnette firmly into the symbolic territory of fashion. Drewry (1994) comments that because the lorgnette was hand-held, it seemed less like a "prosthetic", and more like jewelry. In fact, the lorgnette was used in noble Venice and at the French court from the late seventeenth century, and continued to be popular in high society well into the twentieth century, despite being functionally surpassed by the kind of glasses we use now, which rest on the ears. A commentator from *The Wellsworth Merchandiser* (an American optical trade journal) stated that "eyewear is rarely socially popular", except for the "scornyette"—a term he uses to highlight the "anti-social" purposes the lorgnette was put to (Wright 1920). This is an early indication of the association between glasses and disregard for others; the fashionable lorgnette was later described by Bennet as "a dirty look on a stick." In the same vein, Bennet also describes the "insolent intent" of the quizzing glass of the regency buck, and the "spurious superiority of the monocle" (1963: 26).

This "insolent" use of the gaze relates to one of the most famous and influential characters of fashion history, and one whose attitude, behavior, and use of eye contact can be seen almost to presage certain twentieth century models of cool—the regency dandy. The dandy is thought to be highly significant to modern fashion because he epitomizes the modern possibilities of achieving social superiority through style alone—clothing, manners, and speech took him beyond the circumstances of birth. Although dandies certainly were not known for having sunglasses, their occasional use of the quizzing glass (and some dandies' use of the monocle) draws attention to way they used various enactments of the gaze to announce their difference. Their defining characteristics were studied detachment and unshakeable emotional calm, which undoubtedly enhanced their social power. The term "dandy" is sometimes used to describe someone (usually a man) who follows fashion to the point of ridiculous extreme. But the original dandies, as discussed by a number of authors, set the pace of fashion, they innovated sartorial styles, many of which were pretty insulting to prevailing ideas of what was "proper" attire, but which would ultimately become trends adopted even by the aristocracy (see Barbey d'Aureville 2002 [1845]; Entwistle 2000; Walden 2002). At one point the dandies even took to distressing their clothes to make them look "threadbare"—this was described by Barbey as an impertinence (2002: 80). They got away with this because of the look of utter self-assurance they wore with it (similar to tactics used by the aristocracy) to establish their distinction from those around them.

Indeed many writers note how dandies used the gaze to anchor their performance of superior status. Barbey (a dandy himself; Jules Barbey d'Aureville) quotes Lister describing Beau Brummel's gaze—"a look of glacial indifference… something superior to the visible world" (2002: 111). Lister goes on:

> Brummel did not pretend to be short-sighted, but when those present were not of sufficient importance to his vanity, he would assume that calm and wandering gaze which examines without recognition, neither fixes itself nor will be fixed, is not interested or diverted by anything. (2002: 111)

Nonchalance or indifference had long been an ideal trait of the European aristocracy (Campbell 1987), and, to some extent, the dandies were cheekily appropriating the aristocratic demeanor. Baudelaire believed the dandies had created "a new sort of aristocracy based on superior indifference and the pursuit of perfection" (Entwistle 2000: 129). But Barbey describes the dandy's cool indifference as demonstrating a superior relationship not only to those people immediately around him, but to the modern world more generally. He says that the dandy's pose was a super-calm response to the "agitations of modernity", demonstrating the blasé mind-set of a person "acquainted with many ideas" but "too disabused to get excited" (2002: 93). The eyes are widely believed to be the ultimate traitor of weakness, emotion, vulnerability; their tiny movements communicating a wealth of information to others (Lingis 1994: 171). In mastering the appearance of indifference or effortless detachment in a time of change and political instability, the dandies showed they were "on top of it." As Walden says, "there is no avoiding the term, in today's parlance, Brummel would be 'cool'" (2002: 16). At its most extreme, the dandy's disdain even extended to himself. The "futile sovereign of a futile world" as Brummel was called by Barbey, affected an ironic "self-cancelling" expression (Walden 2002: 59).

In fact, for a long time, the control of emotion and the display of that control had been emerging as both an advantage in modern life and as a by-product of it (Campbell 1987; Mennell 1989; Stearns 1994) clearly indicating the potential appeal of an accessory which can steady the gaze, and detach the wearer from their surroundings and from other people. Like the lorgnette, the monocle continued to be used into the twentieth century, but as a sign of a detached social and artistic superiority for the avant-garde. Lehmann, in his book *Tigersprung* (2000) discusses the "Dada dandies", who used the monocle to display contempt for immediate opponents (apparently, even during a fist fight, they strove to keep their monocles in) or disrespect for the prevailing order in society. Vaché, a notable "monocular" Dadaist was also noticed for his tendency to use the monocle as a deflection of any "real" emotional involvement or expression, "sav[ing] him from losing distance as well as composure" (2000: 263). These "da-dandies" were immersed in the new upheavals of early twentieth century modernity, indeed the intense shock of the first mechanized war was the backdrop for their art and philosophy, compounding their sense of detachment from the march of so-called rational progress.

So to some extent it is possible to see that in these examples at least, before sunglasses became popular and associated with coolness, intrusions on the eye were already working as a form of social distinction and mediating relationships with others in the modern social world, and they were also potentially poetically suggestive of a more general "attitude" or orientation toward modernity.

The city—a context for the onslaught on the eyes

Although sunglasses did not necessarily gain their initial popularity in the city, it could be argued that the city engendered the necessary mind-set for them to accrue their key values. For most people, and many writers, the ultimate scene for the experience of modern life is the city. The fashion, visual culture, new forms of identity, sociality, communication and information associated with modernity all emerge in the city, and as Robert Park said, as early as 1915;

"the city is a state of mind" (1997: 16). The anonymity of the city, its transport systems, its rules of exchange, and its constantly changing community and environment required new standards of behavior and manners from all of us, not just those in (or on the edges of) high society or the avant-garde. It demanded (and still demands) new survival techniques and affords new pleasures, many of which, though originally located in the city, have, through the twentieth century, been transferred to beach resorts, tourist destinations, and, ultimately, to virtual environments, and become a way of life. In this context, sunglasses were able to develop a whole range of functional and symbolic values. Anyone who has sat in a café or on the Underground in their sunglasses will be conscious of some of this—you can watch others without being seen, you can avoid the unwelcome attention of a street-seller, you can even imagine yourself to be suddenly blessed with the charm of Audrey Hepburn, Steve McQueen, or whoever.

Some of what has been written about the key elements of modern urban life therefore reveals some critical aspects of the appeal of sunglasses, whether in the context of the modern city or beyond it. Here I will go into a bit more detail about some of the main ideas. First, I will consider the city as location of intense and varied visual stimulation and how urban dwellers have adapted to that, including new etiquettes of eye contact, especially in relation to another ideal type who emerged in this context known as the flâneur, who, like the dandy, can be seen as a model for certain aspects of twentieth century cool, and who also has a very particular approach to seeing and being seen. The particular (but now daily) experience of seeing and *being* strangers will also be considered—as it draws attention to the power of outward appearance and the potential to play with that through fashion to alter identity. The influence of film as it emerged as a primary form of urban entertainment is also significant here and will provide a foundation for the discussion of the growth of celebrity in Chapter 5.

In an important sense, the city embodies modernity, focusing and magnifying its features. One of the most significant themes relevant to the appeal of an accessory which protects the eyes is the city's lack of sympathy for the vulnerabilities of the human mind and body. Many twentieth century writers and artists responded to its harsh, unforgiving qualities; the inhuman scale of buildings, the inhuman pace of change. As a center of industry and commerce, cities can be characterized as machine-like, and demanding machine-like obedience to their ruthless systems and rhythms—as in Fritz Lang's *Metropolis* (1927) where the requirement to labor as a "moving part" causes injury, exhaustion, and a slavish existence.

Chaos is another common theme in descriptions of the city—tumultuous, dangerous, and unpredictable, a place of chaotic delight and fear, intense stimulation. Baudelaire celebrates the engulfing potential of the crowd—a crowd of strangers (1964b [1863]). Elizabeth Wilson describes it as a "maelstrom" (1985: 137), and quotes Engels' description of streets in "turmoil" (1985: 135). Frank

Whitford quotes German expressionist Ludwig Meidner, who wanted modern painting to reveal

> wild streets…roaring colours of buses and express locomotives… the harlequinade of advertising pillars, and then night… big city night… battlefields filled with mathematical shapes…triangles, quadrilaterals, polygons… circles rush out at us… straight lines rush past us on all sides. Many pointed shapes stab at us. (Whitford in Timms and Kelly 1985: 48)

Whitford describes Meidner's paintings as "ragged… windswept…splintered… heaving… shuddering… fevered" and "dramatising the insignificance of the individual in the face of the vastness of the urban scene" and its "superhuman forces" (1985: 48). A whole new aesthetic emerged in painting to try to capture the experience of the modern city: exaggeration, distortion, brutal, clashing colors and violent gestural strokes, evoking a "nervy" and "hostile" atmosphere (Whitford in Timms and Kelly 1985: 54).

The idea of the city as a chaotic place in which you might need protection is expounded in Simmel's famous essay "The Metropolis and Mental Life," written in 1903. He describes the "the rapid crowding of changing images, the sharp discontinuity in a single glance, and the unexpectedness of on-rushing impressions," and the "swift and uninterrupted change of inner and outer stimuli" (1964 [1903]: 777). These impressions result not just from the visual landscape, the crowded architecture, and the commercial hubbub, but from the innumerable brief encounters with anonymous others. To engage deeply with every encounter, to give attention to it all, would leave a person in an "unimaginable psychic state" that Simmel terms "neurasthenic" (1964: 782). In fact, around the 1920s there were remedies for (and discussion in women's journals about) the peculiarly modern ailment of "jarred nerves" (Hackney 2003), which was considered to afflict city-dwelling females in particular.

Comment was also made at the time about certain avant-garde urban women, like the bohemians of Greenwich Village and the flappers, whose contrasting nonchalance (literally "lack of heat") was all the more striking in this context (Saville 2005). Simmel had already noted that among urban dwellers, ideally a protective reserve is developed, which he termed a "blasé" attitude to events and people. For Simmel this was compounded by the money economy, where every exchange is reduced to the rational mathematics of cost and profit with an "unmerciful matter-of-factness" (Simmel 1964: 779). Stearns argued in *American Cool* that between the 1920s and the 1960s, this emotional control was increasingly expected, promoted by the growing service sector (1994: 230), and necessary to ensure the smooth running of the capitalist machine.

Simmel describes a "refusal to react" which is the nerves' "last possibility of accommodating to the contents and forms of metropolitan life" (1964: 781).

This is a necessary toughness, but also a kind of numbing. He also observes a general desire to retreat from those others; a "slight aversion, a mutual strangeness and repulsion" (1964: 782).

Amidst this chaos another type emerged whose character and behaviors seem to pave the way for sunglasses' connection with cool in the twentieth century. Like the dandy in society, the "flâneur" of the city (nineteenth century Paris in particular) has inspired both admiration and concern. The French word *flâneur* (meaning "stroller" or "wanderer") was used by Baudelaire in the late nineteenth century, and by Walter Benjamin, to describe certain *heroic* characters, often artists or poets, who inhabited the city with a natural ease and whose behaviors seem to embody the ethos of modern life. The flâneur reveled in the chaos and the anonymity of the crowd, strolling, observing, but, crucially, never getting involved. The flâneur—to some extent—was a voyeur, a "sovereign spectator" whose detached gaze was free to define everything according to his will. Baudelaire described the flâneur as "incognito," "at the very centre of the world, and yet, the unseen of the world" (1972: 400).

Like the dandy, the concept of the flâneur has been taken up by more recent authors as a model for behaviors, which have become more widespread throughout the twentieth century (for example, Bauman in Tester 1994), encouraged by modern conditions and technologies ("surfing" the internet even has a quality of "flânerie" about it). Central to the flâneur is the ability to remain detached; rising above the chaotic scene, not becoming fearful or embroiled. Parkhurst-Ferguson suggests that this detachment was a defence against the potentially distressing levels of change and social upheaval, "reducing...urban diversity to a marvellous show" (1994: 31). The crowds and chaos actually provided the flâneur with an escape; the freedom to roam, nothing demanded, nothing known of him. As Gerard de Nerval, a notable flâneur, said, "What I required was...the freedom to roam ... meeting people when I wished and taking leave of them when I wished" (Tester 1994: 1). Some authors see this detachment as a tragic, anti-social pose far from heroic in reality (Shields in Tester 1994), but this "performance" of self-possession showed a captivating ability to face the pace of urban life and remain unhurried, unflinching. In spite of the idea of being "incognito" and "unseen," and not wishing to engage with others, it would be a mistake to assume that the flâneur was trying to avoid being seen. Far from it. Shields says flâneurs were poseurs, and accounts of the time recall a fashion for them to walk out in the busy city with conspicuously slow pets—turtles and lobsters—"displaying [their] nonchalance provocatively" (Benjamin 1985: 129).

If this is a pose or demeanor which became more widespread into the twentieth century it is easy to see how sunglasses might enable this performance. Sunglasses would not only offer a physical barrier against the urban chaos, visually diminishing those "sharp contrasts," but, being highly visible, they have the power to signify that blasé attitude—"I'm not bothered by all this stuff." To some extent modern fashions in general began to offer greater anonymity and protection, as suggested by Heyl (2001) and by Elizabeth Wilson (1985) when women began to use veils, bonnets, and dark hooded cloaks in the urban setting. Many streetwear aesthetics of the twentieth century have developed which echo this—caps and hats pulled down over the eyes, the denim or leather jacket, the "hoody," the "parka" coat, and so on.

Some further indication of the benefits of accessories and garments which might protect the eyes is also given by closer consideration of how urban dwellers were using their eyes.

Eye activity in urban spaces

The anonymous, alienated, and fast moving city crowd requires a lot of "reading." The intent of strangers is unknown, and there are a lot of them. Clothing becomes a means to attract or deflect attention, and a critical source of information about the self and others which, while being "all we have to go on," is also essentially "not to be trusted," creating an environment in which looking and being seen takes on a new level of importance and complexity and where something which legitimately obscures your eyes could be useful.

By the eighteenth century, Heyl says that "eye contact between strangers" had already become "a taboo," quoting from *The London Magazine* of 1734 (2001). The public were advised not to stare at the faces of passers-by and not to make eye contact with a stranger who enters a public room "for fear of shocking his modesty and dismounting his assurance" (2001: 128). Erving Goffman's mid-twentieth century work *Behaviour in Public Places* identifies some relevant social rules which emerged more recently to help make encounters with anonymous others more manageable. One is what Goffman calls "civil inattention," where two people crossing one another's path in the street would openly look at one another up to a certain distance, but then look away, "so as to express that [the other] does not constitute a target of special curiosity or design" (Goffman 1963: 83). Making eye contact with strangers can be a dangerous business in the urban setting, it can burst the bubble of anonymity; even trigger the sudden outbursts of hatred and violence Simmel spoke of in his essay on the metropolis (1964 [1908]). If avoiding eye contact in public places is polite, making it indicates that the stranger *is* a target of special curiosity, and, therefore, potentially threatening.

As the number of encounters increases, avoiding eye contact becomes harder to manage, requiring increasingly fine levels of self-monitoring, so much so that Goffman says we might expect people to want to evade these complex rules, and indeed he does cite dark glasses as portable "involvement shields" which might circumnavigate the requirement for civil inattention (1963: 39):

> By according civil inattention, the individual implies that he has no reason to suspect the intentions of the others present and no reason to fear the others, be hostile to them, or wish to avoid them…Dark glasses, for example, allow the wearer to stare at another person without the other being sure that he is being stared at. (1963: 84)

Walker Evans' famous documentary photographs of American urban scenes illustrate this—the hurried "inattentive" walk of passers-by, their suspicion of his

Figure 2.1   Shoppers, Chicago 1946. (Photograph by Walker Evans. © Walker Evans Archive, The Metropolitan Museum of Art.)

camera, and, by the 1940s, the widespread adoption of sunglasses as city wear in America. With your sunglasses on, you may both detach yourself from the complexity of the situation—and gain an advantage.

Bachelard identified similar power-play in how people used their lanterns after dark in cities pre-street lighting. To avoid being "exposed defenceless to the gaze of the other" (Schivelbusch 1986: 97) people would put out their own lantern. This placed them in the dark, but prevented them from being seen, enabling them to weigh up strangers at their leisure. Sunglasses do not, in these kinds of encounter (outdoors, in unfocused interactions), demonstrate unequivocal intent to disguise or mask the wearer, because their presence is rationalized by having the function of sun-protection. This gives them the additional power of ambiguity.

To become detached in some way is therefore both a form of protection and a consequence of transitory encounters with increasing numbers of people, but it can also be a *display* of superior adaptation to these conditions—of being self-possessed, at home in the modern world, and wise to its ways.

However, just as taboos against eye contact were increasing, opportunities for looking at others were expanding. Elizabeth Wilson, locating the development of modern fashion culture in the urban experience, refers to Simmel's point that in the city looking dominates; "Interpersonal relationships in big cities are distinguished by a marked preponderance of the activity of the eye over the activity of the ear" (Simmel in Wilson 1985: 35). The close physical proximity encouraged by economic imperatives to fit as many bodies as possible into railway carriages, elevators, and so on, puts random groups of people in the novel position of "having to look at one another for long minutes, or even hours, without speaking to one another" (Simmel in Wilson 1985: 35). This looking might be prolonged, but would also need to be surreptitious—to assess the level of threat this stranger poses initially perhaps, but also to satisfy a voyeuristic curiosity undetected. Sunglasses would enable uninhibited voyeurism in this setting. But in masking the direction of the wearer's gaze, they also give the false impression to others that it might be "OK" or "safe" to look directly at the person in sunglasses, to break Goffman's rule of civil inattention. Hence, in sunglasses you can check out whether others are looking at you, without giving anything away. This dramatizes the anonymous gaze and lends it the frisson of seductive power. Heyl discusses a similar dynamic in the early modern fashion for the "vizzard," in eighteenth century London parks (2001). Initially a winter accessory for well-to-do women, it covered the upper part of the face, but developed into a full face mask, sometimes semi-transparent (the "cob-web" vizzard). Marco Ricci's 1710 painting (*A View of the Mall from St. James's Park*) depicts a woman alone in a busy park, wearing a vizzard, seemingly staring directly at the viewer, daring a level of confrontation more in keeping with twentieth century images of women. Ostensibly an act of modesty, covering the female body in public, Heyl says:

> The mask assumed a dialectic function of repellent and invitation, its message was both "I can't be seen, I am – at least notionally – not here at all", and "look at me, I am wearing a mask, maybe I am about to abandon the role I normally play." (2001: 134)

The mask could "both endanger and protect one's respectability" (2001: 134). A seventeenth century poem by John Cleveland about vizzard wearers claimed *"they are veyl'd on purpose to be seene"* (Heyl 2001: 127), rejecting the notion of modest motivations for "covering the dish." Unlike universal veiling within a culture, covering part of the face that is *not normally* covered raises the question of individual motives for doing so, while simultaneously obscuring those facial expressions which might betray those motives. And there's little doubt that a delicate woman whose eyes are both framed and obscured by a dark mask, vizzard, or glasses is a striking sight, undercutting gender norms (creating a less "emotional" or "expressive" demeanor) and playing with the ambiguous—even immodest—mystique of the anonymous gaze.

This example highlights new and particular forms of eroticism noted by Wilson, who, mindful of the writings of Baudelaire, suggests that certain visually-focussed sexual desires and practices—fetishes even—"rejoice in the stealth and irresponsibility of the crowd" (1985: 36). The increasing and often unavoidable opportunities afforded for surreptitious and anonymous looking transformed the way in which desire could arise, be manifested, and acted upon, and not merely for the fetishist. Hence anyone seeking a new sexual partner in an anonymous space might find shades potentially advantageous; a fact underlined by the brand of sunglasses named "Boywatcher" in the 1960s (Banham 1967: 959).

Equally, for someone not wishing to be interacted with, sunglasses act as what Goffman called an "involvement shield" (this could also be a book, a cigarette, a mobile phone, or other device)—ll give a sense of the individual's preoccupation, perhaps in a much more general sense staving off the appearance of being a lonely or vulnerable "single atom" in the crowd; "I may be alone here, but I am not in need of company."

Self, identity, and appearance

This brings us on to the relationship between identity and appearance in the urban setting, where fashion and external appearances became increasingly important in the business of survival. To potential employers, or partners, your "first impression" would now be used to make judgments which may lead to success or failure in ordinary life (Williams in Ewen 1992). There were more strangers to deal with, but with that came a new sense of the self as a "stranger" to others, which led to greater objectivity when assessing the self, and a greater sense of the importance of outer appearance to self-image. Aware of being "just one" in a mass of many similar people, the tension between the individual and the group (which Simmel identified as being at the heart of fashion) was (and still is) keenly felt; not merely to "stand out" but also to deflect unwanted attention. In fact, Gundle (2008) says that the need to both attract and deflect motivated a specifically modern aesthetic in fashion—glamor.

The availability of cheaper, mass-produced clothing facilitated opportunities to play with identity through appearance, the anonymity of the city allowing transformations of identity that were perhaps impossible to pull off in traditional communities. (What simpler way to achieve this than with sunglasses, once they had developed? John Lennon, Lolita, Jackie O, a Reservoir Dog—all are possible.) Previously, complex rules (and in some contexts, legislation) of class, profession, and standing governed who was "allowed" to wear what (Entwistle 2000). But through expanding consumption and the attendant acceleration of fashion such rules became a basis for renegotiation of identity, as people used their "strangeness," their anonymity, to their advantage—dressing up, down, and sideways to change their apparent status. Mark Twain's short story *The Million Pound Bank Note* (1996 [1895]) highlighted this new reality, as a poor young man is given a million pound note by two wealthy men to transform his status. The million pound note has almost no effect on the way he is treated, but once he secures a (very) good suit, he doesn't even need the money, because all manner of goods and services come for free on the basis of his *apparent* status. He is taken at face value.

Ultimately the sense of the self as a potentially alluring and mysterious visual object, anonymous and subject to the speculations of others, casts new doubt on the links between appearance and identity, and in addition to offering us freedom to choose, *obliges* us to make "the right choices" about how to appear (both in the real world and, now, in our online personae).

Toward the end of the twentieth century, TV advice shows began to offer seemingly life-changing "makeovers," genuinely stressing the deeply felt impossibility of forming and maintaining relationships and self-esteem without the right appearance: for example *What Not to Wear* (BBC2 c. 2001); *10 Years Younger* (C4 2004–); *Snog, Marry, Avoid* (BBC3 2008–). All these shows provide "clueless" individuals with "feedback" from the anonymous crowd, whose judgment, by virtue of being "strangers," is perceived to be "objective," unfettered by knowledge of, or emotional attachment to, that person (Simmel 1971 [1908]). These shows dramatize the perils of getting it "wrong" in a postmodern culture of pluralistic fashion choices, and relate to further development in the conception of the self we will consider in Chapter 7. But they highlight the idea that the onslaught on the senses, discussed in the first part of this chapter, was also the start of an onslaught on the sense of *self*.

In fact, the dramatic proliferation of images in modernity, still and moving, surrounded urban dwellers with more "models" (and opportunities for self-critique) than ever before. Developments in glass manufacture and architecture enabled a similarly dramatic increase in mirrors and other reflective surfaces (Schivelbusch 1986). In Walter Benjamin's *Arcades Project* (c. 1927–40), he observed how the "reflective" qualities of the Parisian urban environment might affect the sense of self:

> women see themselves more here than elsewhere, thus arises the specific beauty of Parisian women. Before a man looks at them they have already seen themselves reflected ten times. But the man too sees himself flashing up physiognomically... Even the eyes of passers-by are hanging mirrors. (2002: 537)

Gazing into one of the new display windows, the self was reflected alongside the mannequins, offering a comparison between what already was and what could (or should) be, resulting in the sense of standing on a shiny, semi-transparent threshold between reality and fantasies of the self. In the 1920s, Atget's photographs of shop windows readily illustrated this, with the mannequins, the clothing, the street and its passers-by all reflected in one confusing plane. The city may produce a sense of self as "just another face in the crowd," but Buck-Morss concludes that the city also produces "extraordinary narcissism and self-absorption" (1986: 128), traits identified both in the behaviors of the dandy and the flâneur. As fashions began to change more rapidly, regular self-renewal was not only possible, it was expected.

The growth of still photography provides another dimension to the idea of being surrounded by "mirrors." To possess an image of yourself was a symbol of status; Giles identifies photography as a cultural form of reproduction offering illusions of immortality, mimicking the reproduction of our DNA (2000: 53). Hamilton and Hargreaves say that photographic portraiture "emphasis[ed] ... status in the radical new order of this capitalised, urbanised world" (2001: 32). The enthusiasm for photography during the nineteenth century and beyond, both of professionals and amateurs, helps to demonstrate further the growing importance of image, its role in driving aspiration, consumption, and adding to the glittering phantasmagoria; that "higher place" which was now so much more widely visible, if still unattainable for most. Braudy says that the explosion of interest in portraits was in fact the start of "a great wave still rolling" (1986: 493). The self-portrait offered a seductive and permanent revelation of "how you appear to others," "objective" evidence of yourself "as object," but it also confirmed participation in that glossy world of representation; ladies carried small portraits known as "cartes de visite" (Aperture: 1991), not unlike today's online "profile picture" in their self-promotional purpose as "calling cards".

New media, together with the architecture of retail display, were of course also crucial to the growth of mass fashion. Alongside the means to mass-produce products, information and persuasive media enabled fashions to travel faster geographically and through the classes than before. Women's magazines— carriers of information about appearance, adverts, images of society women and, later, celebrities—also exploded during this period, with *Vogue* first published in the United States in 1892, *Harper's Bazaar* in 1867, spreading to Britain by 1916 and 1929 respectively (White 1970: 325–7). Winship notes (1985) that in Britain the number of women's magazines had more than doubled by the twentieth century.

Sunglasses would go on to become a staple of fashion imagery and an economical means of glamorizing the self in the context of modern fashion. But in connoting "self-possession," being narcissistic in their creation of mystique, and their sense of lack of concern for others, they also developed the potential to be a "sign of the times," a signifier of this kind of "self-aware," "self-fashioned" existence.

The meaning of the eye

Meanwhile, other developments also gave new meaning and importance specifically to the face. The idea of "reading the face" was not new, but cinema, the primary twentieth century urban entertainment, encouraged new levels of facial scrutiny. Close-up shots invited audiences to gaze upon every detail of an actor's face at a wholly unnatural proximity and scale, the camera lingering over the emotion expressed in the eyes:

> Looming over the audience, magnified, far larger than life...these strangers were seen with erotic narrowness and nearness. We do not see our closest friends so intimately, or the people who share our homes, or our lives, except perhaps in the act of making love. (Schickel 2000: 35)

It seems likely that this intense scrutiny made cinemagoers aware of their own faces as objects of other's potentially similarly critical gazes in real life and in photographs (as well as intensifying the link between desire and physical appearance). Certainly, the market for make-up increased dramatically under the influence of the early years of Hollywood, moving from being something associated with deceit and loose morals, to an essential part of fashionable dress (Bruzzi 1997; Lussier 2003). The "flawless finish" seen in the Hollywood close-up created an illusion of perfection under what appeared to be great magnification but what was in fact a dazzling glow of reflected light. The influence of celebrity and Hollywood on the popularity and meaning of sunglasses will be explored in Chapter 5—the point here is the new critical emphasis on the face.

The other significant impact the close-up must surely have had is on the expression and representation of emotion. Schickel says Griffith (the director most associated with the exploitation of the close-up in early film) called his technique "photographing thought" (2000: 35). Live theatrical representations of emotion have to make use of the whole body, since, at the distance an audience is likely to be, expression must be exaggerated. As Schickel suggests, without the close-up, any silent expression of emotion is necessarily "panto-mimic" (2000: 35). Using the close-up caught a "subtler play of emotions on his actors' faces, in their eyes" (2000: 35). Given that Griffith's films were still silent at this stage, facial expression was especially important, and although the facial expressions may look overwrought to audiences today, it began a trajectory in Hollywood film for expression to become more muted, until tiny flexings of facial muscles are enough to indicate deep inner struggle, as in the performances of somebody like Marlon Brando.

Apart from what this might suggest about the value placed on subtler expression of emotions (cooling), it also demonstrates an increasing popular understanding of the location of the "inner life of emotions and personality" in the face and eyes, in a context where the "truth" of such things was increasingly ambiguous. This increases the potential allure of the image of the eye, and the shaded eye. Indeed around the time of early Hollywood, fashions for make-up reflected the filmic use of heavy emphasis of lids and lashes, which created contrast in black and white film.

This highlights a potential technical factor in the eventual widespread use of sunglasses as a signifier within modern representational media. In film stills, photographs, and drawings, even at quite a small scale, sunglasses are still visibly sunglasses. Human perception is oriented to seek out pairs of eyes from chaotic pattern and color (Deregowski 1984: 122). Bolder than unshaded eyes, they are a very flexible visual form, handy to the commercial artist hoping to make their image or product stand out on the printed page—or even, today, on a small mobile device. They can be shown without arms, filled with flat color, reduced to the symmetry of two approximately square or circular shapes—and still be recognized as sunglasses or "eyes."

Summary—urban cool

This chapter has shown how, in modernity, culture was moving toward conditions in which something to shade the eyes could become necessary, fashionable, evocative, and, ultimately, associated with cool. The urban experience neces-sitated new forms of etiquette as well as survival tactics; Simmel's "blasé detachment" and Goffman's concepts of "civil inattention" and the "involvement shield" offer a clear rationale for the use of sunglasses in urban spaces. In this context, shading the overstimulated eye could also come to signify composure when immersed in the most extreme conditions of modernity. This might then suggest a special kind of status within modernity or a superior level of adaptation to it; being the most modern, or being best suited to modern life. This is an urban form of cool. Idealized figures like the dandy and the flâneur exhibited behaviors which involved looking and being looked at in ways which suggest this and which would potentially be facilitated by sunglasses—providing models for "cool" eye activity.

At the same time, the growth and proliferation of visual media offer the beginnings of celebrity culture, new models for self-presentation, new awareness of the self as a viewable object in an anonymous crowd, with the film close–up intensifying focus on the face. Modern, print-based, visual culture also favored readily recognizable forms with strong appeal. On another level, because sunglasses have the ability to suggest vision, the façade, or the masquerade, and are themselves a product of fashion, they may also be able to stand for this condition of modern narcissism or the fashioned self.

This chapter has considered the city as a place of chaos and change, but there is much more to bring out about the experience of *speed* in modernity. Speed not only provided a key context for shaded eyes to become fashionable, but it also changed culture, perception, and consciousness in ways critical to both the idea of cool and to the potential meaning of sunglasses.

3

SEEING THE BLUR— PERCEPTION, COOL, AND MECHANIZED SPEED (1910–PRESENT)

Introduction—sunglasses and speed

Although the now-ubiquitous image of bikini, shades, and sun-lounger might suggest that the ideal wearer of sunglasses enjoys the luxury of being blissfully inert, the dynamic power, excess, and seductive glamor of men and women speeding along in shades is undeniable—from the tough sheen of Marlon Brando in *The Wild Ones* to twenty-first century pop acts like Britney Spears in "Toxic," where impenetrable diamond-studded lenses glint and luminous red hair blows in the obligatory wind-machine as her motorbike zooms purposefully into the night. The tense and nervy atmosphere of the 2012 Olympic velodrome is exacerbated by the sharp, mirrored wraparounds worn by the competitors as they spin ever faster and closer in pursuit of the win, visibly enhanced by hi-tech innovations offering tiny margins of advantage. Cyclists, pilots, drivers of cars, speedboats, and jet-skis: associations with speed have been critical to the development of sunglasses as a desirable accessory in Europe and the United States, and to their continued associations with cool.

In the earliest years of the twentieth century, optical journals for the American manufacturers promoted "protective goggles" for multiple purposes protecting the body from new dangers; dangers largely produced by mechanization. Industrial, military, and leisure applications of the machine prompted new protective needs and aesthetic possibilities. Like the urban environment, they also prompted new kinds of consciousness and strategies for survival and social distinction. Technical innovations increased the pace of production, communication, and change. Some enabled the human body to travel—and to perceive—at a *super*human speed.

Figure 3.1 Britney Spears zooms into the night in studded shades in the promotional video for single "Toxic" 2003, dir. Joseph Kahn.

This chapter looks at the types of goggle developed for protection at speed, considers their early connotations and entry into fashion imagery, and explores how the experience of modern speed could have helped to shape the meaning of sunglasses as they evolved, continuing to build on their connections with cool in modern culture. To understand how speed contributes to the broad appeal of sunglasses, we have to grasp the extent and the centrality of the value of speed in modern life.

Speed, modernity, and fashion

In modern life, speed is good. As Lista says "the new man was a man of speed, able to rebuild space and time around his own power… [in] the era of machines entirely submissive to human desire" (2001: 11). Awe for acceleration is evident in many twentieth century authors' work, from the futurists' celebration of mechanized speed in the early twentieth century, to Baudelaire's musing on the fleeting and the ephemeral, Walter Benjamin's recognition of change for change's sake, and even Paul Virilio's more recent (and provocative) theory of modernity in which speed plays a central role. Speed captures the modern imagination seductively in academic and popular discourse. Speed of warfare, speed of production (and consumption), travel, and communication accelerated dramatically in the period of high modernity, going way beyond human or animal capabilities to the exhilarating and alarmingly limitless potential of the machine, with the development of bicycles and railways, then the aeroplane and the car.

The competitive dynamic of capitalism has driven this acceleration, speed of delivery being a primary means to beat the competitors. But speed is also a tyrant—it demands we keep up, and potentially transforms our sense of ourselves and the nature of our relationships with people, objects, places, and ideas. Nietzsche made a strong connection between "the haste and hurry now universal," "the increasing velocity of life," and "the cessation of all contemplativeness and simplicity … almost … the symptoms of a total extermination and uprooting of culture" (1983: 148). Nietzsche was looking for a philosophy which could protect people against what he called "that haste, that breathless grasp of the moment, that excessive hurry which breaks all things too early from their branches, that running and hunting" (Frisby 1985: 31). Thus, speed poses another dimension of threat to the quality of human life in modernity, just as it provides opportunities to "rebuild space and time around [our] own power" (Lista 2001: 11), to forge ahead, to stay ahead of the pack.

Now speed is equated with winning, success, and status—"life in the fast lane." As Paul Virilio says; "Power and speed are inseparable, just as wealth and speed are inseparable" (Redhead 2004: 43). Tomlinson describes a contemporary culture of "immediacy" (Tomlinson 2007): "24/7" services, fast track, priority boarding—underpinned by the digital revolution and available to all those who can afford it. Virilio speaks of "speed classes," a loose term used to indicate the hierarchy of access to speed. But if speed is a tyrant, I would suggest status also comes from displaying the ability to cope with its tyranny; managing to keep up without breaking a sweat, assimilating new information easily, embracing rapid change and the future it leads to. As Lista says, modernists "called forth the future with all [their] might" (2001: 10).

Fashion culture as a whole embodies this idea brilliantly; personal status is achieved by having the latest look, commercial success comes from quick response to trends; "the principle of fashion is to create an ever-increasing velocity" (Svendsen 2007: 28). As such, fashion has been discussed by many modern philosophers and early sociologists, among them again Simmel and Benjamin, as an exemplar of modernity (Lehmann 2000). What to modern eyes appears to be a system based on a fairly gradual evolution in form was replaced at the end of the nineteenth century with rapid and radical changes of silhouette and style. Indicative of this is the dramatic change in the appearance of influential designer Gabriel Chanel, who went from the corseted, full-length, Edwardian clothing (which now looks like an incremental step from the Victorian sartorial norms for her class) to slacks and other modern separates in under a decade (Charles-Roux 2005). Interestingly the form of these garments celebrated movement, just as their rapid succession and development celebrated change.

The fashion system could also be said to shape the perception of time, with the industry presenting novelty on a seasonal basis. The so-called "fast fashion" of the new millennium has fragmented those seasons, offering three or more phases during both spring/summer and autumn/winter in mainstream high street stores. New styles now arrive weekly, or even daily (Brown 2005: 24–6). New fashions make the recent past irrelevant, "semiotic redundancy" stimulating new purchases far faster than wear and tear could. Replacing clothes costs money; hence Veblen's notion of fashion as a display of wealth (1994 [1899]). However, as highlighted by Blumer (1969), it also requires ever more frequent assimilations of the new. To "move with the times" requires certain cultural knowledge or capital, and mental flexibility. Those who can appear to be effortlessly on top of these changes, or—like the dandy—be able to influence changes or even be above them, may be perceived as "cool"; unperturbed by one of modernity's greatest challenges.

Modern fashion photography, illustration, and magazine design has also tended strongly toward dynamic imagery and graphic techniques. Brodovitch, artistic director of American *Harper's Bazaar* for many years before and after the Second World War, pioneered an influential dynamic style, employing avant-garde photographers like German expressionist Munkacsi—who focused less on illustration of clothing and more on the "essence" of fashion (Aperture 1991) with movement as a key principle. Under Brodovitch, layout design created pace and rhythm, encouraging readers to turn the page, and consume those dynamic images fleetingly. More literally, images of cars, bicycles, motorbikes, and buses pile up through the twentieth century as fashion photography moves out of the studio and into the street (Radner 2000). Inside or out, photographers increasingly directed models to move while being photographed; to jump, leap, "give us a twirl" (Squires 1980). Mastery of movement, speed, and "changing scenery" became a preoccupation of modern fashion imagery as the pace of change picked up. Associations with speed and travel were signs of modernity and the fashionable life.

Goggles for the "would-be speed king"

The associations between sunglasses and speed evolved over a fairly long period between the nineteenth and the early twentieth centuries. In the early days of rail travel, carriages were open, and tinted, "d-framed" spectacles were used as "railway glasses." Originating in about 1830 and in production until about the 1890s (Handley 2005: 8), these glasses resembled spectacles but also had lateral shades (side pieces), made of colored glass or sometimes gauze, protecting the eyes from airborne hazards like dust, soot, sparks, and wind as well as the uncomfortable levels of light in the open landscape.

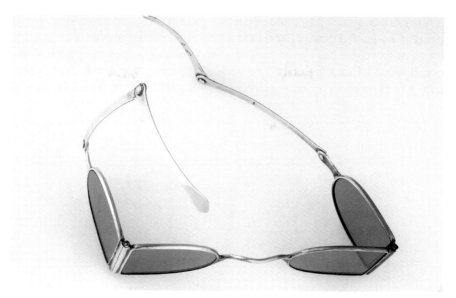

Figure 3.2   Silver d-framed "Railway Spectacles" with green-tinted lenses and folding side visors, 1829. (© The College of Optometrists, London.)

Some portraits of significant men of the era include the d-framed railway specs—for example, William Ball of the Coalbrookdale Iron Works, a figurehead of the industrial age in Britain (Handley 2005: 8). They may have been worn habitually due to eye injury, but they would surely have been a sign of speed and industrial progress, badge of honor or battle scar. Hence the dominant connotations of tinted lenses began to move away from "weak sight" as they picked up associations with some powerful aspects of modernity.

The British and American optical trade journals, *Amoptico* (from 1894, later became *The Wellsworth Merchandiser*), *Keystone Magazine* (all US), and *The Optician* (UK) demonstrate this evolution in their discussion of medical advice, marketing strategies, and product descriptions and illustrations for non-prescription tinted goggles. This market developed into a small but important trade between about 1910 and 1940, where a limited number of basic products morph into more diverse offerings marketed with a greater range of specific connotations and suggested uses, before settling into the more generic "sunglasses" for a variety of sporting and leisure pursuits in the mid-1920s and beyond. In these publications, protective glasses are called "eye protectors," "goggles," and "auto-glasses," and the earliest substantial reference to "sun" glasses (still two words at this point) is in May 1916 *The Wellsworth Merchandiser*, amidst reference to golf glasses, shooting glasses,and tennis glasses. Some manufacturers persisted with the term "sun goggles." A 1912 article in the *Keystone Magazine* about the use of tinted glass demonstrates that goggles were still a market niche (and a little-documented aspect of optometry) and that tinted glasses—even for those who ordinarily wore spectacles—were only advised for extreme conditions such as reflection from snow, water, chalk cliffs, or industrial applications (Harcombe-Cuff 1912: 637). In an application for

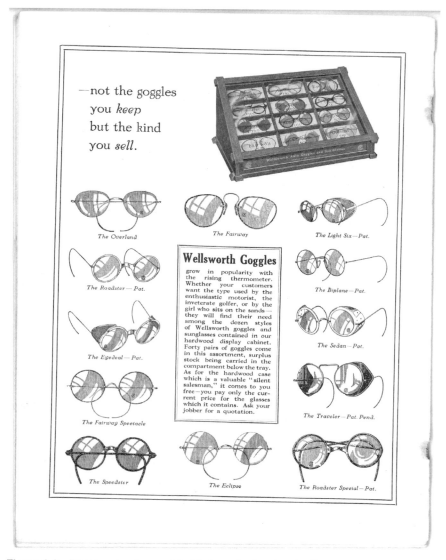

Figure 3.3 Display advertisement for Wellsworth Goggles detailing products named to suggest travel, speed, and adventure, July 1919. (*The Wellsworth Merchandiser* vol.VII no. 6, inside front cover © American Optical, Optical Heritage Museum, Southbridge, MA.)

patent in 1905, similar glasses were described as "Eye Protectors" from "dust and glare," A 1912 advertisement for the "Albex Eye Protector" from *Keystone Magazine* claims the product is "perfectly adapted to the needs of automobilists, locomotive engineers, drivers, motormen, grinders and stone cutters." This indicates the grouping of leisure, travel, and industrial purposes around one product at this time—as well as the strongly masculine context for the goggles.

Some early photographs of these kinds of protective goggles being worn are the snapshots by amateur French photographer Jacques-Henri Lartigue, who documented the life and hedonistic, high-speed leisure pursuits of his wealthy family and friends from about 1910 (Lartigue 1978). He captured the thrill of driving, speed cycling at the velodrome, and experimentation with flight.

The growing desire to be associated with speed—and its leisure-class associations—is evident from the designs displayed in *The Wellsworth Merchandiser* and the text used to anchor their interpretations. Although the designs were becoming less "industrial"-looking and lighter, model names from 1910 to 1919 show how important the connotations of speed and travel were to their promotion. "Auto goggles" make way for the "Overland," the "Roadster," the "Speedster," the "Traveler," and the "Biplane." The Biplane glasses are not flight goggles, yet the name appeals to a group of potential consumers the editorial refers to as "would-be speed kings" (*The Wellsworth Merchandiser* 1919: 212). In fact, these models hardly differ, suggesting that they are not solely designed for the purposes the model names imply, but that the model names are chosen simply to enhance the positive connotations for a wider audience aspiring to life in the fast lane.

Mechanized speed and panoramic perception

The new high-speed modes of travel didn't just create a context in which sunglasses would be worn however, they also had a profound influence on what was viewed through them and how, which arguably led to a "cooling" of perception which sunglasses could both enhance and signify. In Chapter 2 we saw how novel ways to perceive were a significant part of the experience of the modernity; as well as trying to depict the visual chaos of the jostling urban scene, artists also attempted to capture the distinctive experience of seeing at speed. Marinetti, in the first Futurist Manifesto of 1909, had explicitly stated, "We declare that the world's splendour has been enriched by a new beauty: the beauty of speed" (Futurismo 1972: 25). Some futurist art cemented the connection between mechanized speed and the modern: titles include Boccioni's "Dynamism of a Cyclist" (1913), Balla's "Abstract Speed, the Car

Has Passed" (1913), "Automobile Speed" (1913), and "Lights and Speed" (1913), and Pannaggi's "Speeding Train" (1922). One of the very first subjects filmed by the Lumière brothers (1895) was "the arrival of a train" (Mirzoeff 1999). These artworks tried to capture speed in still images, showing forms multiplying and disappearing in a flurry of impressions, of dazzling lights, reveling in the intoxicating pleasure of a confusing blur. Even where both viewer and viewed are static, in the case of a still-life or seated portrait, futurist art seems to indicate that this new mode of perception persisted beyond the specific moments of "seeing in motion," almost as if the increasing velocity of the modern world had somehow permanently affected their capacity to perceive the external world more generally.

This provocative idea is not limited to the futurists, nor to the period of high modernity. At the other end of the century, Paul Virilio claimed that "speed illuminates" (1999: 19); it allows us to see; and what it reveals is a modern form of sight he termed a "dromoscopy" (1978), an "aesthetic of disappearance," where nothing is solid. For him, art works no longer exist as material objects, but depend on *retinal* persistence between "frames" to make "sense'," to construct the work fleetingly in the viewer's mind. He also goes so far as to say that the "dromoscopy" framed by the car windshield or the train window is a new art, the "art of the engine" (Redhead 2004: 108). This transformation of the visual world was also considered by Schivelbusch, in his 1986 work *The Railway Journey,* using a concept similar to Virilio's "dromoscopy" called "panoramic perception" (1986: 61).

Some of Schivelbusch's ideas are worth pursuing, as they highlight some ideas which might have connected early sunglasses to cool, but which also resonate well beyond the experience of nineteenth century rail travel. Schivelbusch suggests that rail travel—which we know was one of the first major contexts for the wearing of protective glasses—heralded a new kind of relationship with the visual world which successive innovations in mechanized speed continued to develop and which was mirrored by certain other developments in modern culture.

Obviously traveling in a carriage with anonymous others for long periods heightened the value of "involvement shields" discussed in Chapter 2, and traveling faster increased the number of those "on-rushing impressions" Simmel had identified in the urban experience. But the train also afforded passengers a strange—and new—kind of *detachment* from the places it passed through, from physical sensation, and from emotion; an altogether "cooler" way to perceive the environment.

One important aspect of this detachment was seen to derive from a loss of perspective, or perhaps, focus. Schivelbusch quotes Sternberger:

> velocity blurs all foreground objects, which means there no longer is a foreground... the traveller was removed from that total space which combined proximity and distance: he became separated from the landscape. (1986: 63)

Visually, the hierarchy of focus, which situated the traveler, was radically altered to the point that Sternberger said that the range of potential encounters with a variety of places and people was reduced to a passive spectacle:

> The railroad transformed the world of land and seas into a panorama that could be experienced. Not only did it join previously distant localities by eliminating all resistance, difference, and adventure from the journey…it turned the travellers' eyes outward and offered them the opulent nourishment of ever changing images. (Sternberger in Schivelbusch 1986: 62)

Although the body moves through space, because the body itself exerts no effort, it is almost as if the world is moving past the body at speed, for its entertainment; reducing living, breathing places to a mere distraction. Gazing out of the window, a handy way of avoiding the other passengers, also requires a different kind of attention. As with Simmel's blasé attitude in the urban setting, Schivelbusch suggests that very few objects can be taken in with any degree of concentration. Instead of attempting to properly perceive the discrete, it is better to accept the pleasure of the blur. This requires a "novel ability," identified by a travel writer, Gastineau, as "the ability to perceive the discrete… indiscriminately" (Schivelbusch 1986: 60–1); to learn not to try to focus, to accept the detachment and revel in it. As well as toning down the contrasts, relaxing the eyes amidst this particular kind of onslaught, enabling this "novel ability," sunglasses also prevent others seeing any effort made by the eyes to assimilate the rush of information. To onlookers, the traveler in sunglasses is more likely to look "accustomed" to such experiences.

Subsequent developments in mechanized travel offered slightly different forms of detachment. The car provided ultimate physical detachment from other road users, and the motorway system inspired Augé's concept of the "non-place" (1995); places designed never to "stay" in. In this case the panoramic blur is made up not of villages and towns but merely of tarmac, signage, lighting, and the rest of the architecture of transit. Perhaps this is still a form of spectacle; Gastineau had in fact said that "it is the *velocity* that made the objects of the visible world attractive" (Schivelbusch 1986: 601, my emphasis). He even drew a correlation with the world of goods, and the experience of shopping in a department store, suggesting that the movement encouraged around the store increased the sense of novelty. Indeed, velocity is inherent in the fashion system, with its ever-faster flowing succession of trends deterring any long-term connection with any particular thing.

This more detached form of perception was perhaps also encouraged through developments in photography. Once the camera became portable enough to take outside, and to be used on a moving subject, the unnaturally still and expressionless studio shot with the air of a timeless vacuum gave way to the "decisive moment" of the snapshot. Although this might appear to restore the focus lost by our human eyes, Paul Virilio says that the snapshot photograph became a kind of marker for "the hidden but nevertheless imagined sequence" (Virilio 1998: 22). We cannot help but consider the possible other images surrounding the single shot. Furthermore, the democratization of photography has led to the increasing speed of production and consumption of these images—now surrounding us with a constant stream of representations—screens full of images we "scroll through." Which of these snaps are we actually looking at? As Sternberger said previously of the views from the windows of Europe: "[they] have entirely lost their dimension of depth and have become mere particles of one and the same panoramic world that stretches all around and is, at each and every point, merely a painted surface" (Schivelbusch 1986: 60–1).

Mechanized speed and industrialized consciousness

The detachment characteristic of "panoramic vision" is not only the product of the speed at which the viewer travels but also the comparative lack of physical sensation. Today passengers on "heritage" steam trains might feel the machine's weight, noise, and human effort in a nostalgic contrast with contemporary high speed travel, but, at the time, some passengers described the sensation of rail travel as being like *flight*, so immaterial seemed the connection with the ground in comparison with the living, breathing power of the horse (Schivelbusch 1986: 23). This smoothness was thought to cool the emotions and concerns of the passenger, who might previously have been aware of excitable and vulnerable horses on bumpy roads, or indeed have been afraid of the steam engine, or Schivelbusch cites an anonymous source from 1825, which extolled the benefits of this for the "sensitive man" who "may relax in the carriage without fear of nervous excitement" (1986: 14). For the passenger, the motion was effortless, and the uniformity of the engine's performance enabled passengers to become far less conscious of "how" they traveled. Thus to onlookers, rail travelers may have appeared unusually calm, further reinforcing those links between modernity and emotional control or cool.

However, this detachment from fears associated with travel does not mean that fear disappeared completely. As much as rail travel may have presented a way to appear less "excited," mechanized speed presented greater risks and anxieties than ever (air travel made another leap in this regard). We are not simply talking here about dust, wind, or sunlight in your eyes, but the potential disaster of the crash. Paul Virilio reminds us that "no technical object can be developed without in turn generating its specific accident … the accident is thus the hidden face of technical progress" (1999: 92). Schivelbusch says that the apparent unlikelihood of the accident (when the motion is so consistent, so seemingly effortless, and the supercool stewards are so able to pour tea without spilling in the dining car) made the accident—when it did occur—a shock of unprecedented severity.

Here Schivelbusch identifies something he calls "Industrialised consciousness," a psychological phenomenon similar to Simmel's blasé attitude, but which derives from experiences of speed and industrial technology. Schivelbusch says we become accustomed to the risks and shocks of modernity with repeated exposure—creating what Freud calls a "stimulus shield" (Schivelbusch1986:164). This is not an object (like Goffman's involvement shield as discussed in Chapter 2), but a psychological outer "crust" which gets "baked" through experience, protecting the soft inner core. To some extent perhaps sunglasses were—and still are in appropriate contexts—able to function as an outward sign of that inner "stimulus shield'," the tough, experienced detachment, because they not only show material equippedness for engagement with risky modern pursuits, but they also prevent the eyes "giving away" any hint of anxiety.

Schivelbusch also indicates that no matter how "cool about it" we might have become on the surface, having become "habituated" to the new risks, the fear cannot really have disappeared—"it has only been forgotten, repressed, one could even say, reified as a feeling of safety" (1986: 163). If there is a crash, no matter how much we have traveled we will not be more able to deal with a sudden and potentially catastrophic outcome. In fact, a condition initially diagnosed as "railway spine" (and subsequently understood as post-traumatic shock) quite quickly made it clear that catastrophes which occurred very suddenly, at speed, and with little or no warning gave rise to psychological injury which went far beyond the physical (1986: 138). Furthermore, this injury did not necessarily emerge immediately, giving the impression of bravery or calm in the immediate instance. Nerves baked hard, or worn down, buried, sensibilities blunted—these ideas characterize the response to increasing levels of stimulation and shock which is both necessary for survival and idealized as a sign of being thoroughly "modern." Schivelbusch's ideas support those of Simmel and Elias; a certain kind of detachment from emotion has, as a consequence of modernity, become a cultural condition. Mechanized speed exacerbates and exemplifies it, resulting in this "industrialised consciousness" which permanently alters the way we perceive (1986: 165). This consciousness is a cooler, more blasé, toughened exterior, but one which is nevertheless haunted—albeit in the background—by multiple layers of risk to both mind and body.

Aviator cool

For the First World War fighter pilot, the stakes were higher still, and the demands even greater. Goggles developed for fighter pilots (as discussed in Greer and Harold 1979) influenced one of the most iconic fashion styles of the later twentieth century—the "aviator." This style, defined by the 1930s American Ray-Ban, is a much lighter, thinner, and more elegantly proportioned version of flight goggles like the First World War Triplex Safety Goggle, which took the form of two chunky, tear-drop shapes hinged in the center, itself similar in form to the early twentieth century "Autoglas" of American Optical. The First World War prompted the rapid development of not only aviation but also the requisite protective clothing.

The War was a further revelation of the sheer might, scale, power, and horror of the modern world, and prompted further transformations of perception. Fashion theorist Gabriele Mentges (2000) suggests that the speed at which war was waged—and the risks of flying as a means to wage it—necessitated a new kind of military demeanor and gave rise to new definitions of the heroic stance which was to have a profound influence on modern fashion.

Where the railway enabled a sense of detachment from the immediate, especially for its passengers, Mentges notes the life-or-death necessity for the

Figure 3.4 Triplex Safety Goggles, First World War.

fighter pilot to be utterly aware of his immediate surroundings, yet detached from fear, acting with the "head not the heart." High-risk decisions had to be made quickly, requiring "a controlled mind and a controlled set of senses, which have to be available every minute" (2000: 37); no time to "dither." Pilots' memoirs place critical value on the ability to stay "cool," or, as Manfred von Richthofen put it, having "nerve" (2000: 37). Loss of control was spectacularized in many a war film as a kaleidoscopic rush of spinning forms and sensations as the plane hurtled toward the ground and almost certain death. Controlling the machine offers what Zechlin—a writer about motoring—called "a consciousness of strength, power and a confidence in one's own value and superiority" (Mentges 2000: 36).

Mentges states that German fighter pilots were in fact described as "cool" at the time, as well as *lassig*—indifferent, casual. They were distinctive in appearance and behavior, partly because they were not army men (many were mechanics, motorcyclists, drafted in for the specific job) and partly because they had no official uniform (Greer and Harold 1979; Mentges 2000). This gave their improvised clothing a highly irregular and conspicuous look. To withstand the physical extremes of high speeds, pilots (and indeed motorcyclists and drivers) literally required a "tougher skin," made of leather, rubber, even metal to withstand the "coldness" of high altitudes and speeds. Mentges is focused on clothes, but the goggles were undoubtedly part of this distinctive appearance.

Out of the air, pilots also attracted attention for their seemingly undisciplined demeanor—"relaxed manner" and "non-military carriage;" a deliberately slow, lazy way of walking which was indifferent to the severity of the situation and quite provocative to the German Army. Their display of ease, "contempt for death," and competence with the modern world even invited comparisons with the regency dandy, a "cool" figure discussed in Chapter 2, from German author Ernst Junger (Mentges 2000: 31). These pilots exhibited behaviors not unlike a subculture—a shared but exclusive knowledge of the world, disrespect for traditional authority, exemption from rules others follow, and visible style. They showed extreme self-possession and detachment in the face of great and unfamiliar risk. If the view from the window produced a detached rail passenger, the view from the plane, must have—at times—afforded an unprecedented sense of almost god-like detachment from others' petty concerns and physical limitations. The legacy of these powerful men in machines is noted by Mentges. She argues that in these extreme engagements with speed, cold, and modern machinery, the protective outer layers (such as the leather flight jacket, denim) became imbued with highly durable connotations of "cool" which continued to resonate in civilian fashion throughout the twentieth century (and beyond). But it is not simply because fighter pilots and other "speed kings" had elite status that their clothing was emulated. For Mentges, the wider experience of modernity requires us all to "toughen up." She says "clothes have the function of armour, not only to protect the physical body but also its sensory and nervous systems… dress [is] a social protection against 'the alien'" (2000: 36), something modernity increasingly forced us all into contact with, while delicate human skin was increasingly perceived as a vulnerable threshold. This would support the idea that the conditions of modernity have encouraged the adoption of a protective aesthetic which alludes positively to encounters with mechanized speed.

Indeed, unlike other protective clothing, both goggles and sunglasses have the curious ability to suggest danger (you need protection), therefore bravery (you are brave enough to face the danger), *and* the calm-faced, unflinching victory over that danger (you don't even look worried). Not looking worried also indicates the blasé competence of experience in high status, high-risk, highly modern pursuits.

Goggles and women's fashion

Although protective goggles and sunglasses were available to women and evidently being used—at least for sunbathing—during the 1920s (more so in the United States), influential women's fashion magazines like *Vogue, Marie Claire,* and *Harper's Bazaar*, did not tend to feature "sunglasses" in editorial fashion images until the late 1930s. However, protective "goggles" and visors began to appear in fashionable images of the 1920s alongside references to the speedy leisure pursuits of the period. In 1921, Jacques-Henri Lartigue photographed his wife "Bibi" in avant-garde dynamic stripes, complete with driving visor, casually bottle-feeding their baby in the back of the car. Similar images (without the baby, needless to say) appeared in *Vogue* around the mid-1920s. Women with androgynous silhouettes are depicted driving or by the side of their cars, with goggles or visors either on or in their possession (for example in an illustration by Georges Lepape for *Vogue*, 1925).

It is evident that the display of participation in these mechanized forms of travel was thought to be appealing by fashion editors of the time—suggesting the new youthful ideal of the active, mobile, androgynous woman (Harris 2003; Zdatny 1997). The goggles suggest the latest technology, risky, expensive pleasures, and the public, masculine sphere. The ideal female body of the 1920s did not emphasize childbirth, but movement and activity, in keeping with the development of sportswear, casual daywear, and the modernist "functional" aesthetic (Campbell Warner 2005). As Breward notes, Paul Poiret justified designing "more practical garments" with the remark "even princesses take the omnibus" (2003: 35); suggesting that the modern world might require certain forms, but also that in these contexts, looking functional could be desirable. Fashion illustration especially demonstrated the masculinized ideal body, taking liberties with flatter chests, narrower hips, and wide, square shoulders on

Figure 3.5 1925 cover illustration for *Vogue*, by Georges Lepape, depicts desirable driving paraphernalia, including goggles, although not obscuring the model's eyes (© Condé Nast.)

long, lean torsos. Some clothing "rationalized" the body into simpler, smoother geometric forms, as with the cloche hat which fitted close to the head and pared down the brim, drawing comparison with the war helmet. A character in Aldous Huxley's *Antic Hay* (first published 1923) remarks that an attractive woman's outer clothing made her look "tubular" and that her hat was so "small and sleek" that it "looked almost as though it were made of metal" (2004: 109).

These androgynous, mobile women of fashion embraced modernity in a manner which contradicted the female role as the static guardian of hearth, home, and tradition as well as the feminine association with emotional weakness and vulnerability. As Zdatny notes, this rebellion was as symbolic as it might have been real (1997), with the signs and symbols of a "new woman" forming a valuable currency.

Traditional forms of sunshade—large brimmed hats and parasols were not practical for the "mobile" modern woman, nor were the turn-of-the-century "maisettes" (hand-held sunshades). Maisettes were suitable for temporary use while motionless, and indoors. Hand-held, made of wood, and decorated with upholstery fabric, they suggested a waning notion of genteel and stationary womanliness.

So it seems that the idea of shading the eyes to suggest a blasé or detached attitude was first made fashionable in the context of speed. The future was coming so fast it made sense to put on a pair of goggles. Also—in this context—speed was a metaphor for female emancipation, making goggles and, later, sunglasses a metaphor for the modern, more androgynous woman (why sunglasses didn't quite make it into fashionable imagery at this point will be considered in the next chapter). Other intrusions on the eye area also prevailed—hats worn with brims set down across the eyes, intense black eye make-up (applied to the whole socket, as in a 1929 illustration for a *Vogue* special on bridal wear) and heavy eyelids in painting and illustration.

Avant-garde artist Tamara de Lempicka's 1929 "auto-portrait" depicts her at the wheel, with no goggles but flat, dull irises the same color and surface quality as her cloche hat. Heavy eyelids armored with kohl cut decisively across the pupils as she confronts the viewer; unworried, unimpressed, unconcerned. Where we might expect to find liquid life, depth, and vulnerability, we find instead an eye baked hard by the experience of modernity. Visors, goggles, heavy lids, and so on resonate within the fashion image not just because they assist the depiction of a new leisure pursuit, or a "liberated female" but because they illustrate a new—and in some complex way—desirable form of consciousness brought about by the conditions of modern existence, significantly shaped by awareness and experience of speed.

The cool streamlined body

In the 1930s, it became possible—and desirable—to make sunglasses for high-speed pursuits much lighter and thinner, they became less obviously "speedy" and more generalized leisure-wear as sports casuals began to define daywear. Stronger connotations of high-speed were reintroduced post-war in the form of the "wraparound" sunglass.

Around the 1930s, the "stream-form" or "streamlining" strongly associated with designer Norman Bel-Geddes celebrated the idea of the speeding object in product design, where an outer skin (usually metal) was used to smooth and simplify form (Maffei 2009). This was based on the principle of the aerodynamic design, where resistance to air was eradicated—leading to the bullet-shaped train, for example. Eventually, following wartime developments (Lipow 2011), streamlining could be seen in sunglass design, notably with "wraparound" frames given iconic expression in the 1980s and 1990s by sports brand Oakley. Wraparounds gave those who needed it better protection from on-rushing air and sometimes better vision, but, as with many "stream-formed" products, also gave the appealing impression that dynamic energy resided within the object. Or, in the case of sunglasses, that the speed was so great, and that the force encountered was so strong, as almost to cause the glasses to bend and melt into the human face behind them, dramatizing the riskiness of the wearer's high-speed pursuits. Curved lenses, and the mirrored lenses associated with this kind of design, also afford reflections of light and shade which create arcs; dynamic swooshes which echo those signs of speed much favored by futurist art and which remain visual codes for dynamism (as in the Nike brand "swoosh," designed in 1972). In hugging facial contours, the suggestion of impermeability is also increased.

Wraparounds now have strong associations with competitive sport, and in iconic images of sports heroes like runners, cyclists, and now even swimmers, whose goggles are frequently tinted and even mirrored. Sunglasses communicate a special sense of detachment and superiority which perhaps brings all of these ideas together. Given that control over emotion is also crucial to performance in sport, sunglasses might afford the wearer (and certainly suggest to others) the sense of "having the blinkers on." Competitors are met with the "anti-gaze," a seemingly limited gaze which implies that the external world is of no importance (Carter and Michael 2004: 275). However, in pointing more obviously "forward" wraparounds suggest the wearer's purposely limited vision does have an object—the finish line, the goal; a better performance. Derived from these contexts, sunglasses which suggest speed have the potential to imply escape from rules and limitations; a "pioneer-gaze," the gaze of someone looking to the future. The high-tech object, adapted to the face, yet decidedly inhuman, emphasizes the idea of the sporting body as machine, something we will explore in more depth in the next chapter.

Summary—dynamic cool

In terms of the chronological development of sunglasses as a fashion accessory, we can see that goggles designed for high-speed pursuits enabled the connotations of dark glasses to change from weakness or physical defect toward additional or even superhuman capability, and elite social status. This is visible in the morphing of goggle forms into the shapes we now recognize as sunglasses, and later, wraparound sunglasses—but the goggles, visors, and other eye shades of the 1920s also allude to emerging cultural conditions and values which would have a lasting impact on life in the twentieth century and which sunglasses could readily signify: new forms of perception and consciousness, new needs for protection, engagements with new technologies, new articulations of gender, and, indeed, the insistence on "the new," "progress," and the future, exemplified by fashion and by the image of the speeding body.

As with the context of modern visual culture and the urban environment, increasing speed enabled, encouraged, and required greater composure, effortlessness, and detachment. As well as being an "accessory" to speedy pursuits, sunglasses could help the wearer to achieve, and appear to have achieved, those qualities—all of which are consistent with behaviors identified as "cool." Hence sunglasses distinguished those most immersed in, and most equal to, the challenges of modern velocity, and in so doing, became a signifier of the "dynamic" form of "modern cool." In the next chapter we will look further into this idea by considering the role sunglasses played as a more general signifier of superior adaptation to modern technology.

4

SEEING THE CYBORG—
EYE-SHADING, COOL,
AND THE HI-TECH BODY
(1910–PRESENT)

Introduction—sunglasses and the hi-tech body

Exploring speed in the last chapter has already enabled us to consider some aspects of the relationship between sunglasses and modern technology. But this relationship goes further. Sunglasses became a more general sign of encounters with the wonders and perils of modern technology; in the early days of TV advertising, sunglasses were worn by immaculate, 1950s housewives shading their eyes from the terrifying brilliance of whites achieved with innovative washing powders.

In particular, by the mid-to-late twentieth century, certain super—and indeed *sub*—human qualities which arose from engagement with the new culture of technical rationality were being almost routinely visualized with shades, as questions of identity and the shifting boundaries of human/machine began to feature heavily in popular culture: unstoppable robots, cyborg tricksters and aliens; all wore sunglasses. This is perhaps because as "hands-free" additions to the body, spectacles, goggles, and sunglasses have the capacity to raise questions about the "nature" of the body it is worn on/with/by.

First, this chapter will consider sunglasses as a signifier of "modern technology," followed by connotations of the "alien" and the related idea of "ugliness." Then, we will examine the role played by sunglasses in suggesting new, hi-tech forms of consciousness, exploring connections between cool, the modern, and the hi-tech—"techno-cool."

Sunglasses as new technology

The idea that glasses might in some way themselves signify technology is borne out by Gafforio and Ceppi, who say that even the pince-nez demonstrated spectacles' modernity as "a place for experimentation with new materials and technologies" (1996: 32). Indeed spectacles had presented considerable challenges to engineers and product designers, even in terms of simply how to keep them on; (especially while the wearer was moving). Many early spectacles relied on being hand-held, like the lorgnette, or on muscles to grip the lens in the eye socket (like the monocle). A variety of techniques were tried to achieve what could only ever have been a fairly precarious pince-nez, or grip on the nose. Springiness, sturdiness, balance, and fit—all of these aspects were problematic. It took until the mid-eighteenth century for Edward Scarlett's "riding temple glasses" to emerge as the form which eventually displaced the pince-nez, monocle, and lorgnette. Even then, it was a while before the arms (which at first clung to the temples) were extended to rest on the ears (Gafforio and Ceppi 1996: 31; see also Drewry 1994). These were visibly "engineered;" one significant innovator of the nineteenth century, Richardson, even referred to his inventions as "machines" (Handley 2005: 3).

Scientific and medical understanding of light, vision, and lens technology continued to develop at a pace during the twentieth century, creating opportunities to innovate with sunglasses functionally (for example: UV filters, glare-reducing lens coatings, photochromic lenses which darken in the presence of UV light). The practical uses of sunglasses in combative and competitive situations also makes any technical advantage valuable; this alone would logically perpetuate continued technical experimentation with them (although, of course, the market for them extends well beyond those who will actually utilize these functions). In 2009, Oakley was boasting of models developed for the military with lenses which were bulletproof at 10 meters (Oakley 2009: online). Developments in materials (especially plastics) and engineering enabled aesthetic changes to telegraph—or simply allude to—such functional innovations.

Given that glasses are also a cliché of the "boffin" stereotype; to some extent glasses could also suggest scientific or technical knowledge by association. Although the scientist might be considered a "geek" (hinting at the "madness" of the scientist, intellectual, or "tech-head" with its possible derivation from the word "geck" meaning fool or freak), there is no denying the cool which can be derived from the power to know and control, and the prevailing ideal of modernist objectivity and rationality is neatly expressed by the unemotional eye. Hence, although many real scientists might not wear sunglasses, they have appeared in popular images of "boffins" advancing the "white heat of technology", resolutely pursuing progress. The eye with vision unclouded by emotion and superstition is one which would seem to be unshakeable in purpose, perhaps also suggesting a lack of concern for others (in the consequences of their discovery) or the kind of blinkered vision required to pursue scientific research with dogged determination (one striking image here might be Tim Burton's Willy Wonka from *Charlie and the Chocolate Factory*, who, at his most reckless, dons giant, white, 1960s style, round sunglasses before physically "televising" first a bar of chocolate, then a small boy).

A significant thread of design and promotion of sunglasses brings the connotations of new technology to the fore, hoping to appeal to consumers on this basis, as we have already seen in the case of the Wellsworth range aimed at the "would-be speed kings." After the wave of enthusiasm for protective goggles and sunglasses focused around the 1920s, another wave of expressly "hi-tech" glasses came through in 1960s fashion in the context of the innovations of space travel, op art, and mod culture. In the 1980s and 1990s, the advent of wraparound, high-performance sunglasses for sports again made sunglasses a means of announcing a superior and positive relationship with the latest technology.

Some of these significant historical forms will come up again later on in the chapter, but an Oakley advert published in *Blueprint* 2002 (notably, "*the leading magazine of architecture and design*") shows how the theme of modern technology has persisted. In it, the frames hover mid-air, literally defying gravity—another common visual metaphor for hi-tech modernity (Bukatman 2003)—and rewards the committed reader of its dense copy with reassurances of "23 precision-engineered components" constructed from "the lightweight titanium alloys of fighter jets and nuclear submarines," which have been subjected to "half a million watts of metal-vaporising electricity," "bombarded by x-rays," and so on. The smallness of glasses makes them a relatively cheap and risk-free way to associate with fighter jets and nuclear submarines, and their compact, sharp, sleek, and shiny forms speak of strength, lightness, precision, and control. The idea of technological progress remains central to the Oakley brand in form and content. Indeed, a quotation from a sponsored athlete used in their marketing equated their own pursuit of technological progress with the athlete's pursuit of better performance and the consumer pushing themselves to a higher level of consciousness; "Never stop exploring. If you are not constantly pushing yourself, you're leading a numb existence" (2009 online). This exhortation implies that "keeping up" with technology is an important way to "get ahead," competitively and, seemingly, spiritually.

Evidently, the base materials sunglasses are made from—plastics, steel, glass—have also all been heavily coded as signifiers of newness and modernity throughout the twentieth century (Fisher 2013; Maffei 2013); critically being hard, shiny materials which do not tend to show obvious signs of "wear and tear" or patina. Celluloid, an early plastic used to make frames, was unstable and could fail in certain conditions, but this was a dramatic failure; cracking, melting, etc., as opposed to gently gathering dust, grease, and passing time. Compared with those turn of the century wood and upholstery "maisette" sunshades, these little "machines" announce their "just-made" newness with smooth, impermeable power—paradoxically, perhaps even when they are old.

As well as being a *product of* modern technology, goggles and visors had been developed as a very necessary protection for some of the harshest activities of the industrial revolution. Welders wore, for example, small tinted goggles with mesh and velvet cushioning around the frame and eye socket (British Optical Association archives). Indeed, according to the *Manufacturing Optician*, Crookes, manufacturers of "the world's first mass-sale sunglasses" had developed their product specifically for "furnace men," only to find that their success came from selling these glasses to "vacationists" (1966: 67). Welders and furnace men were literally forging the modern world with the white heat of technology, and the work was high-risk, and intense.

Goggles, ugliness, and fear—early twentieth century

Crookes, however, did not choose to use this potentially heroic link to the industrial to promote the sunglasses. If anything, Crookes attempted to downplay the connection as they began to consciously attempt to expand the market around 1915 (prior to the 1920s fashions for driving visors and goggles discussed in Chapter 2). Goggles, with their heavy technical associations, were initially perceived as ugly, prompting manufacturers to periodically announce innovations which might counter "the usual objections… their weight and unattractive appearance" (*The Keystone Magazine* 1910: 489).

However, in the early years of the twentieth century, the uncanny appearance of goggles certainly seems to have added to their visual power, if not their popularity. Greer and Harold's discussion of British flying clothing used in the First World War refers to photographs of fighter pilots with make-shift, leather face protection which certainly dehumanizes the wearer; it gives them an air of the henchman, Frankenstein's monster, an effigy even. This might be a one-off, as these are improvised garments for extreme conditions, but Mentges confirms that an early guide for automobile drivers warns that their goggles and leathers had the potential to frighten pedestrians so much they would run away (2000: 34).

In a slightly different setting, goggles were shown to be strange and humorous. In 1911, Jacques-Henri Lartigue (who was later credited for his exceptional ability to shoot the off-guard, the informal, the "not to be photographed") took a shot of a family member in a river, in huge waders, hat, and tinted goggles. He titled it "Impeccably dressed as usual" (Lartigue 1978), typical of his warm and humorous commentary. This also highlights the perceived strangeness of goggles' appearance at the time, and their power to shock.

Manufacturers may have wished to do battle with this strangeness, but strangeness or ugliness is not necessarily to be avoided in modern fashion. Far from it; Elizabeth Wilson speaks of the modern "aesthetic of the ugly" (1985) where something considered to be strange or ugly is actively desired by the avant-garde as a means of rebelling against norms of fashionable appearance and temporarily satisfying their unquenchable thirst for the new. Barthes' idea that "every new fashion is a refusal to inherit, a subversion" (Barthes in Svendsen 2006: 24) supports the idea that modern fashion might be deliberately antagonistic to prevailing aesthetics, hence initially striking some people as "ugly." Often this ugliness connects with the socially unacceptable (coincidentally Wilson's example is the fashion for the tan, which in the 1920s contravened class-based ideals, suggesting taboo cross-race and class desires and identities.) But exactly what is unacceptable about the kind of ugliness presented by goggles and sunglasses? We are back to the issue of the prosthetic.

There certainly seems to have been some reluctance to accept goggles and sunglasses as fashion accessories—until the 1920s and the celebration of the machine in art and design more generally. Even after that it was a while before they were fully accepted as part of a fashionable look in editorial fashion photography. There may have been a variety of reasons for this delay, but it seems that the "heaviness and masculinity" of the designs already noted were compounded by the connotations of the prosthetic role of corrective spectacles (many of which were also tinted), or the kind of dark glasses worn to mask damaged eyes. Aldous Huxley later remarked on the transformation of dark glasses' connotations, commenting, "as a small boy, I would look at a be-goggled man or woman with that mixture of awed sympathy and rather macabre curiosity which children reserve for those afflicted with any… disfiguring physical handicap" (1974: 29). The optical journals of the first two decades of the twentieth century indicate that weakness, ageing, and ill-health were strong and unwelcome associations for potential consumers, and seemingly no less so in the 1920s; a time and place where fashion was so focused on youth and fitness.

Twentieth century western fashion has certainly had an uncomfortable relationship with prosthetics more generally. Surrealism and representational politics notwithstanding, on balance, very few glasses, hearing aids, or artificial limbs have found their way into popular aspirational images. At the time of writing, certain spectacle forms have recently been a desirable accessory and motif with connotations of cool—known as "geek glasses" or "hipster glasses;" however this has developed from a complex signification of deliberate irony and nostalgia, bearing some similarity to the early twentieth century use of the monocle. It is worth mentioning that such glasses are only perceived as cool when the corrective function of the lenses is not made evident to onlookers by thickness or obvious magnification, suggesting that the association between physical weakness and spectacles has not really dissipated. Clip-on, sunglass lenses, photochromic lenses which darken on exposure to light, struggle to be perceived as cool (except potentially in ironic ways) precisely because they announce the corrective function of the "spectacles within." Corrective spectacles are one of the most common and familiar prosthetics, and although definitions of the prosthetic have been contested, expanded, and debated in recent years, most authors seem to use spectacles as an obvious example of an object—a technical artefact—which constitutes an "addition" or "replacement" to the body (Smith and Morra 2006: 2), an "artificial" part making up for some kind of lack.

The integration of human and non-human components within the human body has long been taboo, a source of fear, used as a sign of evil in extreme cases—for example Captain Hook's hook. To those unfamiliar with prosthetics, a piece of wood, metal, or plastic standing in for something of the human body might seem to be what Mary Douglas termed "misplaced matter;" therefore an object for disgust, adding to the signification of ugliness and fear. Masahiro Mori's theory of the "uncanny valley" (1970: online) also draws attention to the fear of the prosthetic which looks life-like but does not move. As movement is a sign of life, the lack of animation of those features is a sign of death and therefore alarming. Mori suggests that the more life-like a prosthetic looks, the more shocking (or strange) it is when eventually it becomes apparent the prosthetic is not real. Mori's theory is also based on the idea that we feel most comfortable with the familiar. Although glasses are not the same level of uncanny as glass eyes (as to some extent they merely cover or augment rather than replace), dark tinted lenses "replace" the moving eye with a still lens, and the expression of the eyebrows is potentially replaced by the rigidity of frames. Hence, the early goggles associated with driving and flying may well have appeared startlingly *un*familiar, uncanny.

However, goggles and sunglasses are prosthetics of a different kind in that they extend, augment, and enhance already "healthy" bodies; enabling them to potentially achieve superhuman powers.

From prosthetic to cyborg

In fact, as discussed by Smith and Morra, the prosthetic has been used in academic and popular discourse as a metaphor for the generalized interactions between humans and technologies in modernity (2006: 2). Mentges points out that fighter pilots' protective clothing "assimilated the human to the machine" because the materials used were more like those making up the machine (and less like traditional clothing fabrics). Upholstering new civilian modes of mechanized travel domesticated the interiors, assimilating the machine to the human travelers. Fighter pilots' clothing did the opposite—it made the human more suitable for the machine.

Whether goggles or sunglasses, that little bit of modern technology, highly visible, and close to the face, perhaps emerges in popular culture as a sign of a more generalized condition—or at least, as a way of visualizing possible conditions; perhaps as a signifier of a "cyborg" identity. Clyne and Klines' original definition of the cyborg concept was a permanent fusion of organic and inorganic "live" matter in one body (Farren and Hutchison 2004: 463). However, Donna Haraway (1990) and others broadened the concept to acknowledge the vast array of dependencies and interrelationships modern people have with technology, whether or not they are physically or permanently embedded in the same body. (This broader concept could even include the transformations Schivelbusch described as the development of "industrialised consciousness.") Grey says our lives are "intimately shaped by machines" and that "some of them we merge with almost unconsciously" (Farren and Hutchison 2004: 463). Farren and Hutchison argue that in fact all clothing is technology which physically and expressively extends the function of the body, but that it is so familiar to us that it is easy not to think of it in this way. They therefore claim that "artefacts and devices with which we are in close contact.... hair extensions, wigs, spectacles, and sunglasses" should be understood as elements of technology which make humans cyborg (Farren and Hutchison 2004: 464). Whether or not this is a useful or justifiable conclusion, their comment demonstrates how familiarity changes our perception of technologies as "technology." We might therefore expect goggles and sunglasses to have strong connotations of technology when first invented and first available, or when new innovations make novel forms and finishes. However it does seem that unlike many clothes and accessories, sunglasses have had a particular power—perhaps because of their relatively recent invention, modern manufacture and materials, and position before the eyes—to continue to signify technology, and even this "cyborg status" in visual culture.

Certainly, the goggles, visors, and sunglasses of the 1920s and early 1930s in women's fashion indicated not only enthusiasm for mechanized speed, but by association, for modernity and a new technologized future more generally. This was a theme to which fashion and sunglasses return, significantly, in the 1960s. With renewed affluence and post-war optimism for a high tech future, the 1960s has been seen by some as a period in which some of the cultural themes of the 1920s were reprised—but this time with mass participation. Underpinned by new developments in plastic technologies, futuristic novelties in eyewear now defined the distinctive looks of collections from André Courrèges, Paco Rabanne, and Pierre Cardin. The British optical journal *The Optician* published

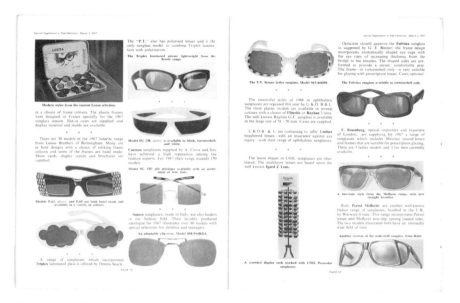

Figure 4.1 References to altered modes of perception in late 1960s sunglass design trends and model names featured in a U.K. optical trade journal. (Special Supplement to *The Optician* (on Sunglasses), pp. 34–5.)

a special edition about sunglasses in 1967, which featured many styles similar to these designer looks, demonstrating that these images had widespread appeal. Strongly geometric and emphasized by frames sometimes in op art black and white, the sunglasses return to and exaggerate the unavoidably odd appearance of early goggles, celebrating their inhumanity, looking like bugs or aliens, or bits of plastic engineered as squares or tubes for some other utilitarian or industrial purpose. The model names for some of these glasses are similarly alien, for example "the Seez" and "the Oy," or they refer to new media—"the TV screen." The poetic possibilities of sunglass lenses being analogous to screens provide a further justification for their use as signifiers of technology.

Many of the designs also seem suggestive of different kinds of eyes—*The Optician* bemoans the "unfortunate" influence of Courrèges' famous "Lunettes Eskimo" glasses which allow vision "only through a narrow slit in a solid opaque 'lens'" (1967: 13). Based on a traditional design for snow goggles made of whale bone, these glasses were completely white and seemingly designed for protection against the metaphorically blinding light levels of the future, or possibly the moon (with a little play on the term "lunettes").These glasses, and others like them, are not designed to *frame* human eyes, their forms are so bold that they *replace* them, a fact which is remarked upon in another *Optician* article about advising customers on choice of sunglasses generally—"sunwear

… cannot be fitted to enhance nature's own props of attractiveness in the upper facial area; they must be introduced as a substitute" (Dowalisky 1961: 61). The look of something unnatural is desired, something which declares its newness; its alien-ness to human eyes and skin announcing enthusiasm for new "ways of being."

Mid-century developments in popular science fiction would no doubt have been playful reference points for some of these designs. Illustrators for sci-fi comics and costume designers for films had been busy since the 1950s envisaging what "other life forms" might look like. Many mid-century representations of aliens showcased the fearful power of more advanced technologies, ray guns, x-ray vision, and so on. Images of twentieth century robots and aliens repeatedly emphasized expressionless eyes—sometimes by shading with dark lenses to create fly eyes, or a single visor strip, or by making them empty holes like skeletal eye sockets. Lid-less, brow-less bug eyes or fish eyes abound (numerous examples can be seen in di Fate 1997). This apparent emotional deadness or blankness often anchored the superior rationality of these other life forms and their potential ability to conquer us earthlings; compounding the idea of the superior being as hi-tech, and the hi-tech being as emotionally cooler.

Before we go on to look at some of the most iconic images of cyborgs in popular culture, we will return once more to those who wield modern technology where the stakes are highest—warriors. We have already considered the fighter pilot's relationship to mechanized speed but there other important ways in which sunglasses have meaning, and articulate notions of cool in the context of warfare.

In general, throughout modernity, warfare has become increasingly reliant on emotional and physical detachment. Stearns describes how, by the twentieth century, as war was rationalized and mechanized, the impassioned rage of the pre-modern warrior was no longer necessarily an asset (1994). For, in a carefully organized unit of command, strategy might require soldiers to carry out actions which run counter to their emotions. Weapons of mechanized (and, since the Gulf war, even digitized) war also detached the warrior from the physical act of killing. The most powerful soldiers are perceived to be the least emotional ones, those most like a machine. Masking the combatant's gaze does some particular things. Edwards says that an image of anyone wearing sunglasses won't let the viewer's gaze rest, that "their eyes shift, disconcerted" (1989: 57–9). This "disconcertion" derives from an inability to read the other's intent. In the urban environment Goffman (1963) suggested that sunglasses could help to avoid possible conflicts, partly through facilitating the convention of "civil inattention," politely avoiding the other's gaze. In the military context, there is however no doubt that the other is a target—the military figure is already positioned in a combative relationship with the other, and is marked out as such by their uniform. The twentieth century fighter pilot or airborne gunner can sometimes

Figure 4.2 Dark glasses increase the warrior's perceived power and control—gunner in dark goggles, U.S. Air Force, 1940s. (Photograph by Keystone-France. © Getty Images.)

be seen by his opponent but the direction of his gaze cannot be read. Therefore he could be aiming right at you (enhanced by the technologies of the gun, the bomb, the plane, it is dangerous to assume anything else). The sunglassed warrior (or policeman or even security guard) enacts what Carter and Michael call an "unhidden hidden gaze" (2004: 275); "I am letting you know that I am not letting you know where I am looking." This might also be expressed as a "'panoptic' gaze—because I can potentially see you, you had better behave as if I can," hence the sunglasses magnify the power of surveillance. The warrior is aligned closer to his technology by masking his humanity, indicating a fearsome and unmerciful lack of emotion not just in relation to the risks they may be taking, but also in relation to his opponent. Nothing about the eyes allows an appeal to shared humanity, and the glasses themselves might even communicate the advanced technology supporting the campaign.

There are many examples of sunglasses in popular images of military power; for example, General Macarthur and Colonel Qadaffi both of whom tended to be sunglassed (in Qadaffi's case, even when addressing the United Nations). Another example is "the man with no eyes," an iconic military figure from the 1967 film *Cool Hand Luke*, who habitually wears mirrored shades to enhance his seemingly sadistic power. The film works with the mirrored lenses to reflect the fearful gazes of those in his presence, magnifying his power to instil fear.

This capacity for sunglasses to suggest a lack of humanity and potential aggression (or, rather, cold-blooded intent) is compounded by the gesture of *removing* sunglasses for an encounter with another, which now means something analogous to the handshake of long ago, where the open hand revealed "no weapons." For example, in a TV recruitment ad for the British Army (c. 2005), sensitivity and diplomacy was suggested by the military officer's "wise" decision to remove his sunglasses in the midst of an escalating argument with a Middle Eastern local. The glasses are used to enact a variety of military gazes in these images.

For modern warfare, the power to see without being seen also became critical—indicative of this is the dramatic change in military clothing from highly visible and aggressive regalia ("war paint") and weapons, to camouflage and the use of stealth and shock (Schivelbusch 1986). Virilio says that the modern battlefield "is first a field of perception. Seeing them coming and knowing they are going to attack are determining elements of survival" (Redhead 2004: 63).

The idea of the gaze as a weapon in its own right also gained momentum in the twentieth century. From the deadly hi-tech laser-eyes of invading robots from outer space in 1950s fiction to the disembodied "eyes" of unpiloted drones in the late twentieth century, the unemotional and targeted gaze has inspired awe. Although it is not literally the case that military sunglasses constitute a "deadly weapon," it is perhaps this link between military power and technologically enhanced vision that sunglasses have an allusive ability to signify. Toward the end of the First Gulf War, some Iraqi soldiers isolated in the desert actually surrendered to an unmanned drone, an event seen by Virilio as a poetic example of the terror of the inhuman eye (Redhead 2004: 69). This kind of eye is armored and almost always stripped of its function as a gauge of emotional response. It sees—but it cannot care. In a way, this is precisely what sunglasses have the potential to suggest.

The cyborg and sunglasses

The fear and delight in the potential of a merging between human and machine was exemplified—fleshed out, if you like—in the compelling visions of a cyborgian future in late twentieth century films like *Bladerunner*, *Terminator*, and *The Matrix trilogy*. Sunglasses and other eye-shading techniques are consistently used in the sci-fi genre to signify the cyborg. (In fact, a late 1980s anthology of cyberpunk fiction was named after them: *Mirrorshades* (Sterling 1988)). All of these films contain elements of combat, presenting a conflict between human and non-human, and explore the leaky boundaries between those two categories; they also all feature interesting uses of sunglasses and shaded eyes which are worth some closer analysis.

Indeed Arnold Schwarzenegger as the *Terminator* (1984) is one of the most enduring cinematic images of sunglasses. In the promotional poster, sunglasses are used in conjunction with leather jacket and gun—all three represented as hard, shiny, and reflective. Facial expression is set hard, and laser beams emanate from behind him in rays, also suggestive of new technology and dynamic power. Balsamo says *Terminator* represents "the extreme of techno-logical rationality" (2000: 150), and that this is aligned with specifically masculine cultural associations.

Exaggerating the value of emotional control in modern warfare, nothing deflects the Terminator from his purpose and this is clearly shown in the film to his advantage. Untroubled by fear of killing the wrong target (he has been sent to "terminate" one particular woman)—he methodically tracks down and kills *all* the women with that name in her town. Fatigue, fear for his own safety, and frustration are also meaningless to him; when he cannot succeed in a specific scenario he is not angry, or embarrassed, or fearful, he simply utters the iconic deadpan line "I'll be back" and goes off to retool. He is *exaggeratedly* casual since he has no human *fear* of death, no need of esteem from others, and he *objectively* knows he has superior strength. His dispassionate relationship with his own mechanical body is part of this; demonstrated in a scene where his fleshy "eye" becomes badly damaged. Looking in the mirror, he takes a knife and cuts out his own eye ball, revealing the evil, red electrical glow which powers it. He literally "does not bat an eye lid" at this necessity. But he does cover up the "wound" with a pair of sunglasses, which thereafter become the film's trademark, and a signifier of readiness for battle, as putting them on is frequently shown as the final stage of preparation.

Balsamo says that the cyborg

is a hybrid, but the specific traits which mark its human-ness and machine-ness vary widely... [functioning] not only as markers of the 'essences' of the dual natures of the hybrid but also as signs of the inviolable opposition between human and machine. (2000: 149)

Sunglasses ambiguously suggest the cyborg status of the Terminator. Covering the wound with sunglasses "humanizes" the robot within the interior world of the film, by disguising robot eyes with what, by the 1980s, is a familiar part of human dress. On the other hand, for the viewers, the sunglasses confirm his status as cyborg, as well as his superior "technical rationality."

Equally, the aspirational qualities of the Terminator's cool demeanor cannot be ignored. In the sequel, the Terminator is presented as being an ally to the human race, a savior. These apparently inhuman, emotionless, cyborgian traits were easily recast as heroic, desirable, powerful, something to aspire to. The Terminator constitutes a popular marker of the new traits of the hero in the modern world—cool and tooled, neatly and efficiently signified by those shiny 1980s Ray-Bans.

More recently *The Matrix* (1999) employed sunglasses very literally as a code signifying a special kind of technical knowledge. The central conflict in this film is between artificially intelligent agents and human rebels. In a post-Holocaust world, a computer system simulates a preferred reality in exchange for human energy—leaving most humans unaware that their life is a simulation. The film uses sunglasses to distinguish between the "real world" and the simulated "matrix;" and between "rebels" and "agents" when inside the matrix. In the real world, the rebels' eyes are naked, but inside the matrix, they wear small, black, oval sunglasses with wire frames. The agents of the matrix hunting the rebels are identified by sunglasses with smoked lenses, drawing on connotations of FBI uniform for the agents and on military/subcultural cool for the rebels (and functioning just like the black and white cowboy hats of the western genre). Sunglasses of any kind in this film signify knowledge of the matrix, something most ordinary humans do not possess.

However, this knowledge has to be acquired in a specific way—by learning to *ignore* the apparent threats of the simulated world. Since these are illusory, they can be controlled if you can resist their power to frighten or delight. Once you have mastered the art of ignoring the threats of your simulated environment you can progress to learning to control the matrix yourself. Only when Neo, the

Figure 4.3 Neo (Keanu Reeves) dodging bullets—sunglasses in *The Matrix* (1999) imply oneness with hi-technology.

central character, has been successfully trained, is he seen in shades. At this point he is deemed ready for combat and enters the matrix, displaying apparently super-human ability to defy both gravity and time. The sunglasses are coterminous with a superior sight, the ability to see through and beyond circumstances, enabling superior control of any situation. When an agent's sunglasses get broken, we know he has "lost it."

The film was produced using innovative techniques which allow the action to be paused, while our point of view tracks 360 degrees around the center of the action. This allows us, the audience, to see "more" than naturally (humanly) possible and slows the action right down in so doing, giving us "more" of the spectacular fight scenes. In *The Matrix* this 360 degree slow motion is an exaggerated demonstration of the heroic quality of control over both technology and speed. At the film's epic climax Neo has learned to control the matrix and move so fast within it he is able to catch the agent's bullets in his hand effortlessly. For us to be able to perceive this, the action is of course shown slowed right down, as graceful and balletic, which further dramatizes the lack of effort Neo needs to thwart any attack.

Finally, an earlier film, but perhaps one which indicates a more complex, *post*modern take on the fusion of human and machine, and hints at a more complex vision of "cool," is *Bladerunner* (1982). In this film, robots have become so like humans that the only way to distinguish them as robots is to perform the "Voigt-Kampff empathy test," which monitors emotional reaction to questions by focusing on, and enlarging, the image of the respondent's eye (reminiscent of the magnifying lenses used in seventeenth century courts (Heyl 2001: 131) to help discern the guilt or innocence of the accused). This test is needed because these "replicants" are now rebelling, attempting to force their inventor to extend their artificially shortened lives. To squash this rebellion, they are being tracked down and "retired" by a hired "killer" (the "bladerunner"), who we assume to be human, but who has to exhibit unflinching control of emotion in order to kill beings so very like humans in every other respect. The distinction between human and replicant is therefore not straightforward. In fact, the reason for the replicant rebellion is that they have begun to develop emotions; two of them are in love. Ironically, Deckard, the bladerunner, himself becomes attracted to an experimental replicant who has been invested with fake memories and believes herself to be human.

Emotion, expressed through the eyes, is the primary index of humanity in this film. But can we believe what we see? The film is peppered with visual devices which draw attention to the eye and reveal the unreliability of the image as an index of reality or truth. *Bladerunner*'s cityscape is shrouded in hazy confusion as light flickers from screen to screen: "veils, mirrors, rain, smog, smoke, and neon lights" which "cloud human vision and distort sight" suggesting paranoia, unstable identity, or soullessness (Rushing 1995: 152). Deckard, the *human* "bladerunner" (played by Harrison Ford), is described by Rushing as "burned out" (like Simmel's blasé metropolitan), a "cold fish," and an exemplar of "human mechanisation" (1995: 151). Indeed, all the humans in the film represent "mechanised somnambulism" (Rushing 1995: 150); none of them appear to care about each other, unlike the replicants. *Bladerunner* plays with the idea that perhaps the replicants *are* "more human than human" as the Tyrell corporation slogan goes, suggesting that perhaps the old human race has become *too* cool, and that these fresh beings, who seem to value life, deserve it more than we do.

But what interests me is how the appeal of *all* these characters is achieved through their detachment. Rachel, the experiment so like a human Deckard falls in love with, embodies the cool demeanor of a 1940s film noir femme fatale. Heavy lids, a heavy fringe, veils, expressionless face, often shaded. Pris, a rebel replicant, has an androgynous appearance defined by the scene where she blacks out her eyes with make-up, creating the illusion of a mask or wraparounds. Although she has "fallen in love," she is depicted as unsmiling and combative, and this *image* functions as desirable. This future cyborg creature with such impressive power and self-control became a cult heroine. This is also the film that made Harrison Ford famous. Whatever the apparent meaning of his character within the narrative, his blasé competence, knowledge of the technology, his suitedness to the postmodern dystopia made him desirable to the audience. The cool of being "burned out" (or perhaps "beat") is something I will explore in more detail later, for now, suffice it to say that just being immersed in modern technology and blasé about it, continued, and continues, to be

Figure 4.4   Replicant "Pris" with shaded eyes in *Bladerunner (*1982).

aspirational, and dulled or shaded eyes continued to be a key signifier of this state.

Terminator and *The Matrix* also ostensibly offer *dys*topian visions of the future and their narratives demonstrate the challenge of cyborg power to human identity (perhaps the folly of our technological progress). However, the appeal of their central characters is also constructed around their superior control over emotion and their competence with these threatening technologies, again defining the late modern hero as one with a close relationship to new technology.

The visualizations of cyborgs become more subtle, with less obvious "joins" throughout the twentieth century—no sign of Frankenstein's bolt or stitches in *Bladerunner's* replicants or the agents of *The Matrix*. In the previous chapter I mentioned how the form of sunglasses got closer to the human face with the aerodynamic wraparound style, and, in the 1990s, hi-tech glasses (again, typified by Oakley) took on a new, organic aesthetic reminiscent of Geiger's *Alien* (1989), with skeletal and sinewy qualities, closing the aesthetic gaps between human and machine.

In fact, as technology merges with the organic increasingly seamlessly and invisibly, we might actually expect the need for glasses and sunglasses to recede, and their poetic currency as a signifier of technology to become decidedly twentieth century. The shaded/technologized eye motif certainly continued into the third millennium, with *Minority Report* (2002) advertised with an image of the hero with one visibly pixelated eye, just perceptible through a bandage.

Sunglasses may well persist in such imagery in spite of perhaps now being a cliché, partly because truly integrated technology is too *invisible* to signify itself—as is needed in representation where "technology" is to be celebrated or discussed. Technology is also still "re-newing" the currency of sunglasses. Because they are now a familiar prosthetic, they have been a site of experimentation in wearable digital technologies: incorporating tiny cameras, solar energy panels to fuel mp3 players, phones, and Steve Mann's wearable computers which have utilized sunglasses as conduits for a "heads up" display (which projects information from the internet directly onto the retina, popularized in 2013 as Google's "Project Glass"). These new innovations have often seemed clumsy, strange, and ugly—just as those early goggles did. Indeed, as this goes to press, it is reported that Ray-Ban and Oakley have been charged with the task of making the Google Glass more aesthetically pleasing.

Another reason for the continued use of sunglasses as a signifier of technology in visual culture is that they now have a hundred years of popular history, meaning that in a late or postmodern culture a variety of positions toward technology could be suggested by selection of period styles. Similar to the dandy taking a turtle for a walk, the "granny specs" worn by the likes of John Lennon in the 1960s, for example, signified a nonchalant lack of concern for "progress."

Summary—techno-cool

There are many other interesting articulations of sunglasses as technology; their role in cyber- and steampunk, for example. But the main points can be seen in the examples we have covered. The first is that most if not all sunglasses, even in otherwise historical, traditional, or natural settings, strike a general note of modernity, because they are a product of the twentieth century, because they are worn in modern, industrial settings, but also because of their construction, their materials, and—sometimes—forms designed to express that. And perhaps even more so, because they are worn against the human face, contrasting with and reinterpreting such sacred natural organs.

The second is that this has made them a ready signifier of desire for new, modern forms of consciousness characterized by the invulnerability and rationality of the machine. This further explains the strongly masculine set of associations for sunglasses identified in the previous chapter. It also helps to explain why they have had such enduring appeal, as technology is central to the experience of modernity. Technology cools—it enables us to make less physical effort, tends to detach us from others and our surroundings, and allows us to break ahead of dominant ideas.

It also requires that we discipline our emotions (getting angry with your computer does not help) and acquire new knowledge. This is not necessarily easy; as with modernity more generally, speed and fashion too, technology is a discourse of perpetual change—it is a tyrant. Therefore the person who is immersed in technology, and emotionally controlled with it, is better adapted to modern life, and becomes a model for others.

Thus, there is a specific cool which derives from aligning ourselves more closely with the culture of technical rationality which authors like Mentges and Schivelbusch, with their ideas of protection against the alien in modernity and industrialized consciousness, have helped to identify over the last two chapters. Also important is the capacity of technology to suggest rebellion against prevailing norms and escape from limitation—a notion of the avant-garde. As with fashion, embracing change or even innovating it involves breaking rules and somehow standing outside of society. This is "techno-cool"—emerging in the twentieth century as a form of social distinction of which sunglasses became a powerful symbol.

But what modernity—and its new technologies—has also brought with it is a proliferation of light—the white heat of technology, the illumination of artificial lighting, reflective surfaces and architecture designed to maximize all kinds of light, not to mention the flashbulbs of paparazzi, studio lights of Hollywood, the blaze of the sun on tanned fit bodies. This where the sun really starts to shine on sunglasses—when they become a signifier of modern life "in the light."

5

SEEING IN THE LIGHT— "SUN"GLASSES, MODERN GLAMOR, COOL, AND CELEBRITY (1920s–PRESENT)

Introduction—sunglasses for life in the light

Today, a more general sense that sunglasses protect our eyes from *sunlight* dominates. After all, the name finally settled on for all kinds of motor goggles, protective spectacles, autoglasses, and so on was (and is) *sun*glasses, conjuring up countless images of those bikini-clad women and casual, white linen-clad men basking in the glow of their own attractiveness, their sunglasses bouncing back that gold-colored light of happiness and success. Smiling or not, these men and women are embodiments of the stuff to aspire to—warmth, sex, leisure, confidence, status, wealth, and the admiration of others. In fact, this chapter will explore the idea of sunglasses as a sign of "life in the light;" as a sign of being in an environment where there is an abundance or *excess* of light.

Here we will take a look at the context for the development of sunglasses as a widely available fashion accessory, looking at sunbathing in 1920s and 1930s Europe and the United States, the appearance of *sunny* sunglasses in fashion imagery, and the growth of their associations with celebrity, glamor, and aspiration through the mid-twentieth century. A "life in the light" suggests status and success in the modern world, from the glittering cafes of nineteenth century Paris and beyond to the arena of international sun-seeking, media repre-sentation, luxury, and indulgence enjoyed by modern elites like the avant-garde Riviera set of the 1920s and the stars of Hollywood, who were the first "victims" of the paparazzi on the Via Veneto in Rome in the 1950s. Of course, we also need to think about how notions of "cool" might have been articulated in these contexts. I have already suggested that cool could be seen as an idealized adaptation to modernity; what might be the relationships between modernity, cool, and light? We will explore the meanings of sunglasses in light-filled contexts, but first, we will look at some of the ideas surrounding the meaning of light in the modern world.

Light and modernity

The possibilities for the "meaning" of light are multi-dimensional and contradictory. They are also closely connected to conceptions of sight and knowledge in modern thinking—when we think of light, we often also think of seeing and knowing. It will be useful to go into a little more detail here. Martin Jay, in his work *Downcast Eyes* (1993) says the foundation of modern thinking about sight and knowledge is actually derived from two different (originally Greek) conceptualizations of light: *lux* and *lumen*. *Lumen* was characterized by "the straight lines of reflection and refraction where the essence of illumination was perfect linear form" (1993: 30). *Lux* was more about the *experience* of human sight, emphasizing color, shadow, and movement.

Jay also describes two ways of conceiving of knowledge in visual terms— speculation (the eye of the mind) and observation (real experience of sight). These, he says, are perceived differently depending on which model of light was being employed. Hence, speculation (the eye of the mind) could either derive from lux, giving rise to "irrational, ecstatic bedazzlement by the blinding light of God" like a religious visionary, or from lumen, which would enable unclouded purity of perception like that of a rational scientist who refuses to be fooled by appearances. Similarly, observation could be pure sensation and emotion activated by lux or, if considered in the sense of lumen, it could be given primacy as the Cartesian perception of "that which actually exists" (1993: 30).

In the modern city, lumen-like light was used in a variety of ways to reveal, control, and survey, while sparkly mirages of lux seduced and distracted in commercial displays. Ideologies of modern progress, as well as modern glamor, were frequently communicated through the medium of light. In Chapter 2, we considered Walter Benjamin's idea of nineteenth century Paris as the "city of mirrors" as key to the visual chaos and self-awareness produced in the modern city. The modern city has been characterized by many writers and artists as a place of concentrated light, both natural and artificial. Practically speaking, modern cities radically increased the amount of light its inhabitants and visitors were exposed to through architectural design, plate glass, mirror and lighting technology; "bright lights, big city." Highly significant was the creation (or "clearance") of the boulevards in mid- to late-nineteenth century Paris. Clearing slums and building wide, straight roads and parks offered city dwellers and visitors spectacle, an impressive view. Marshall Berman's landmark book on modernity *All That is Solid Melts into Air* (1982) describes how Haussman, then mayor, "blasted" a "vast network of boulevards through the dense, dark heart of Paris" (Berman 1982: 150).

Creating additional light in the industrial city was perceived as a solution to some difficult urban problems—it would conquer the city's dirt, relieve chaos, ill-health, and squalor. Haussmann's project "wrecked hundreds of buildings, displaced uncounted thousands of people… but it opened up the whole of the city, for the first time in history, to all its inhabitants," where "great sweeping vistas were designed with monuments at the boulevards' ends, so that each walk led to a dramatic climax" (1982: 151). Berman describes the resulting cityscape as a "uniquely enticing spectacle, a visual and sensual feast" (1982: 151). A cat may look at a king, and, here, spectacle was free for the first time, democratically offering everyone the kind of illumination, symmetry, and classical perspective once available only to the inhabitants of a grand residence. More sunlight and more air made the city lighter, brighter, and clearer. This eventually became a global blueprint for modern urban space.

Light, vista, and clearance were also highly valued in the modernist archi-tecture of the early twentieth century. Le Corbusier, for example, recommended that a person "demand a bathroom looking south, one wall to be entirely glazed, opening if possible to a balcony for sun baths" (Sparke 1995: 116). Much modernist architecture seemed to celebrate lumen's objective clarity—there was also a passion for white, light-maximizing paint; le Corbusier declared that "every citizen is required to replace his hangings… with a plain coat of white ripolin. His home is made clean. There are no more dirty, dark corners. Everything is shown as it is" (Sparke 1995: 117). To see is to know, and similarly to Haussmann's boulevards, le Corbusier and others like him attempted to blast the walls and dark (or cosy) corners from home and city. Modern "belief" was that light promoted health, morality, scientific knowledge, and objectivity (Jay 1993: 30). Proliferations of more lux-like light were also evident in the blurring and refraction of modern expressionist architecture (for example Bruno Taut's Glashaus 1914). The motivations of Haussmann, Taut and le Corbusier may have been different, but the solutions bear striking resemblance; more light.

Developments in artificial lighting also changed the scopic experience of the urban scene. Schivelbusch, who explored the cultural impact of mechanized rail travel, gave similar attention to changes in lighting technologies in his book *Disenchanted Night* (1995 [1983]). Street lighting in cities underwent a series of developments during the nineteenth century, further advancing the scope, scale, and quality of what may be seen (Schivelbusch 1983), culminating in ambitions to obliterate night altogether with "artificial suns" like the "tour du soleil" (sun tower), an unsuccessful bid for what became the Eiffel Tower. It was a recurring modernist, utopian notion to eradicate night, with all its inefficiency and unknown quantities, a desire to marry the idea of "enlightenment" with the literal illumination of space.

Urban night life was also made possible and more accessible through the ability to "mass produce" lighting. With cheaper and more effective lighting, activities of all kinds could go on longer into the night, and the magical scenes once the preserve of the aristocracy were increasingly visible to the lower classes (Schivelbusch 1995: 138). Schivelbusch says that this romantic form of twinkling light (lux) which obscures and dramatizes promises transformation from the mundane world to a "second symbolic life," where cosmic relations and fantasy are set free, but also where simply being up late offers a taste of the glamor and freedom of the aristocracy or the leisure class. With artificial lighting, the full modernity of the "city that never sleeps" emerges. Schivelbusch confirms that artificial light was a *metaphor* for modernity, "gaslight, like the railway, reigned supreme as a symbol of human and industrial progress" (1983: 152).

Light and glamor

Illumination was also a major tactic in the creation of another "symbolic" life — the one on offer in the cathedrals of consumption. Galleried department stores based on the "panoptican" design created a sense of immense and glittering spectacle, inspired by the structures and interiors of the "world's fairs," the Crystal Palace of 1851, for example, in Britain (Hvattum and Hermansen 2004). The capacity to mass produce glass and other reflective substances, real or fake, enhanced the explosion of light and glitter. Around 1850 saw the first floor-to-ceiling glass store-fronts; shop windows became "display" windows, providing the streets with a theatrical sense of fantasy, encouraging browsing (Schivelbusch 1983). The power of light-reflecting mirror and glass inside the shop had been gaining recognition since the early-to-mid eighteenth century. Schivelbusch notes how the "uninterrupted transparent, sparkling surface acted rather like glass on a framed painting" (1983: 146) and quotes Hirth, saying at the turn of the century, "glass makes [paintings] appear better than they really are… confers on good copies an element of deception. The plate glass of shop windows, too, has an improving effect on some goods" (Schivelbusch 1983: 147). Gundle discusses the later use of cellophane to give goods an allure he describes as "almost cinematic" (2008: 250). Beyond cellophane, it is worth noting the tendency toward shiny coatings in modern culture (occasionally interrupted by a retrospective fashion for matt). The shine keeps getting shinier. Gleaming blonde hair, nail varnish, glossy paper, chrome, screens, filters in Photoshop designed to add the "bling" of glow and sparkle… the list goes on.

In the 1920s, Kracauer noted the power of glitter in the department store, speaking of the

> comforting influence that the flood of light exercises not merely on the desire to purchase but also on the personnel… sufficiently bewitched by it that it can drive away the pain of the small, unlit apartment. The light deceives more than it enlightens. (Frisby 1985: 169)

Most significantly he speaks of shop workers' "aspiration to higher strata" which, as Frisby says, is "not for its content *but for the glamour*" (Frisby 1985: 169, my emphasis).

Connections between light, sparkle, and concepts of glamor abound in discussions of modernity. Berman says that in Baudelaire's influential and evocative writing from the late nineteenth century "modern life appears as a great fashion show, a system of *dazzling* appearances, *brilliant* facades, *glittering* triumphs of decoration and design" (1982: 136, my emphasis). He focuses on a passage where Baudelaire describes a café on one of the new boulevards, whose "most splendid quality was a flood of new light" (1982: 136); "The café was dazzling. Even the gas burned with the ardour of a debut; with all its power it lit the blinding whiteness of the walls, the expanse of mirrors, the gold cornices and mouldings" (Berman 1982: 149). Like Kracauer, Berman sees access to light as a driver for aspiration, referring to the description of the collision of rich and poor in Baudelaire's tale "The Eyes of the Poor" (1964a [1869]), where a poor family unable to enter the glittering café, stand outside, noses pressed up against the glass in wonder and desire, he says "they too want *a place in the light*" (1982: 153, my emphasis).

Similarly, Stephen Gundle's book on *Glamour* (2008) contains numerous metaphors relating to light—"glow," "dazzle," "display," "theatre," "flashy," "glitz," "burning bright"—in an attempt to describe the elusive quality which Gundle states is a profoundly modern phenomenon. Gundle also highlights glamor's transformative potential; while seemingly magical and almost otherworldly, it "contained the promise of a mobile and commercial society that almost anyone could be transformed" (2008: 7).

This is not to suggest that people habitually began to wear sunglasses in all these brightly lit contexts, but to indicate the far-reaching connections between light and modernity's ambitions and promises for a "better life," giving sunglasses another layer of wide appeal. Sunglass lenses promise the human face the same "improving effect" as the cellophane packaging, the glass of a display case, having the same smooth, attractive, reflective quality as the mirror, the shop window, and the modern connotations of a windscreen or skyscraper. Here I am, they say, *immersed in modern light*.

However, in the same way that other aspects of modernity could be seen as placing new levels of pressure on human life, this abundance of light has also been seen to be—in some way—"too much." For example, Schivelbusch makes a distinction between the pleasure and persuasion of commercial lighting and the lighting of the state, which suggests surveillance and the keeping of order (1983: 134; see also Boyd-White in Hvattum and Hermansen 2004: 49). Perpetual light from such structures as the "tour du soleil" could also warn of modernity's attempts to know and control, adding to the *threats* of modernity to the individual. Schivelbusch quotes Michelet in 1845, describing large, gas-lit factory buildings, with "no shadowy corners in which imagination can indulge its dreams… . Incessantly and mercilessly, it brings us back to reality" (1983: 134), and refers to the "glaring and shadowless light" permeating the dystopian visions of H. G. Wells. Even the pleasurable commercial spectacles would contribute to Simmel's idea of overstimulated senses; here again sunglasses possess that dual ability to signify both a desirable level of immersion in light and protection against its excesses.

Sunglasses and modern leisure

Equally important to the expansion of light in modernity was, of course, the growth of leisure and travel. Possibly the first fashion photograph to feature sunglasses is an image of the model Mary Sykes basking in the sun in Puerto Rico, writing postcards in a cotton dress, headscarf, and white-framed shades (Edwards 1989). Taken by Louise Dahl-Wolfe in 1938 for American fashion magazine *Harper's Bazaar*, this rich and arresting image has been discussed by other authors as significant in the histories of fashion and photography (Arnold 2002; Edwards 1989). A tanned woman, a cotton frock, and exotic accessories implied travel (she's writing a postcard), big shades—this image contains all the typical ingredients of the glamorous and leisurely life in the light, making it a useful case study which also highlights how sunglasses may have related to notions of "cool" when they entered fashion imagery. Can it really have taken until 1938 for sunglasses to appear in fashion imagery of this kind? Before discussing this in more detail, I will consider how sunglasses developed as an accessory for sun-drenched leisure.

The leisured elite who wore goggles/sunglasses for modern, high-speed sports also engaged in other outdoor pursuits supported by the modern belief in the health benefits of light and fresh air. As mentioned in the previous chapter, in July 1915, a front cover of the optical journal *Amoptico* had offered "Crookes lenses for the vacationist", alongside an illustration of people sitting in the sun, under a parasol, skin mostly covered. The lenses are described as tinted in the text, but the tint is not depicted in the drawing; in fact the glasses are kept very slight, minimized, unlike the impacting chunky white frames and black lenses at the center of Dahl-Wolfe's fashionable image 23 years later. An early mention of sun*bathing* in the U.S. optical journals appears in an advert from *The Wellsworth*

Figure 5.1 Fashion editorial image by Louise Dahl-Wolfe for *Harper's Bazaar 1938*. (Photograph by Louise Dahl-Wolfe © 1989 Center for Creative Photography, Arizona Board of Regents.)

Merchandiser which lists potential customers for "goggles" (further defined as "autogoggles" and "sun glasses"—still two words at this point); "the girl who sits on the sands" is referenced among more confident appeals to drivers and sportsmen (July 1919: 6). But the notion of the emancipated female considered in the section on speed helped to draw outdoor leisure activities like golf, swimming, and skiing into the fashion arena in the 1920s and 1930s, with the attendant development of "resort" wear and more casual, more active fashions.

Sunbathing and tanning is generally said to have become fashionable during the 1920s among the European avant-garde who visited the French Riviera

Figure 5.2 Front cover of the *Amoptico* trade magazine (July 1915) announces a novel use for tinted lenses: "… for the Vacationist." (© American Optical, Optical Heritage Museum, Southbridge, MA.)

including Picasso, Chanel, and some notable Americans, for example the Scott-Fitzgeralds (Turner and Ash 1975). Chanel had been photographed sunbathing hatless as early as 1918, but was still wearing gloves to protect the genteel connotations of her hands; Charles-Roux says she did this until about 1923 (2005: 144). In a 1925 article from American journal *The New Republic* about the young, trendy "flapper," the desirable complexion for the face is still white, described as "pallor mortis," but the legs are described as shockingly brown and stocking-free, a trend attributed to chorus girls of 1923 (Bliven 1925: 65). This seems to indicate a turning point for skin tone, a celebration of both natural and/ or artificial light, before the tan really took off.

Connections between notable flappers (like actress Louise Brooks) and the Riviera set (and ultimately, Chanel's influence) made the tan part of an elite fashionable look for the very first time, which eventually became the dominant sign of modern glamor. Indeed, the desire to get a tan is later argued to have fueled the rise of mass tourism (Turner and Ash 1975); it undoubtedly fueled the market for sunglasses. A 1928 application for patent stated that "large quantities" of sunglasses were being sold and that they are "available at ten cent stores" (Spill 1929: online), indicating that they had reached a mass market. By 1929, Foster Grant were selling them "in number" in a Woolworths on the boardwalk at Atlantic City (Foster Grant 2009: 1). However, although sales of sunglasses were up, they certainly were not common in late 1920s/early 1930s fashion imagery—promoting beachwear or anything else. In images of sunbathers on cruise ships in women's magazines, and photographs of Riviera beach life in biographies of people like Chanel, they are also notably absent. Given that driving goggles were featured on the cover of *Vogue* in 1925, perhaps in the context of sunbathing, connotations of weak sight, the "prosthetic," masculinity, and technical "ugliness" were still too strong (hats were still fulfilling the shading function). Jacques-Henri Lartigue photographed his wife Bibi (she who had been snapped in driving goggles in 1921) sunbathing in sunglasses in 1924, which indicates they were worn by at least some of the fashionable set by then, but this could easily have been another of Lartigue's playful "off guard" shots, which we know tended to undermine notions of propriety and dignity. Sunglasses were being used to aid tanning, but they weren't necessarily a desirable or acceptable sign of life in the light yet.

The appeal of the tan and the cultural context in which it emerged is important. It can be tempting to polarize the desire to tan as a "return to nature;" an opposition to modernity, an "escape" from the urban environment. For example, Graves and Hodges (1961) trace tanning back to the Weimar Republic of 1920s Germany, where sunbathing was a wholesome, outdoor, mostly prole-tarian leisure practice. This may be true, but the tan certainly became a sign of highly sophisticated modern leisure. Nigel Clark says the tan "enabled privileged bodies to inscribe the characteristics of the iconic cinematic body onto their own superficies" (1995: 117), highlighting the modernity of something seemingly so "natural" (the influences of Hollywood cinema and celebrity on sunglasses will be considered in much more depth later in this chapter). As well as being a semi-permanent sign of having been in the light, the resulting darkened skin provided an ideal background for modern light-reflecting fashion aesthetics.

Figure 5.3 Jacques-Henri Lartigue's wife Bibi in sunglasses on the beach at Royan, 1924. (Photograph by Jacques-Henri Lartigue © Ministère de la Culture—France/ AAJHL.)

Wilson says the tan enhanced the brilliance of pearls, satin shoes and oiled hair (1985: 131) and it gave a deeper contrast against the youthful sparkle of eyes and white teeth.

Seeking the light costs money. In the industrial age this can be done through artificial lighting, technology or through traveling, using that technology to transport the body to open spaces and sunnier climes. Industrial speed provides humans with another superhuman power—to control the shining of the sun, and the twentieth century tan is the visible sign of that power. The young, avant-garde, cultural elite who made tanning fashionable centered around Sara and Gerald Murphy, American heirs with the means and the confidence to visit the French Riviera during the summer when it was very hot, as opposed to the winter, as was the convention for people of their class (Turner and Ash 1975: 73). This made their tans both a signifier of their enviable capacity to choose their climate, and of their desire to rebel against the ingrained conventions of their class.

The avant-garde modern tan was initially a seemingly "democratic" provocation to the status quo, in keeping with numerous aspects of Chanel's "casual" style (such as the using of lowly fabrics like knitwear, previously only used for underwear) (Charles-Roux 2005: 108). Symbolic allegiances were made by this young "left wing intelligentsia" with the perceived freedom, simplicity, and honesty of the peasant, as Turner and Ash state "when [the] aristocracies and their empires began to collapse, [the] hierarchic attitude to skin-tone also began to collapse" (1975: 79). The only aristocrats admitted to the Murphys' circle were "those who had rejected to some extent the moral values and ritualised social habits of the ancient regime in favour of more unorthodox, Bohemian models" (1975: 77). Turner and Ash state that "Americans who joined the Riviera set, did so in flight from … philistinism and Puritanism" (1975: 73). Here there is a connection between the agenda of the European artistic avant-garde and the emerging challenge to Europe's historical cultural dominance posed by American fashion, and culture more generally—indeed the casualization of fashion was also encouraged by American designers and by Hollywood; in 1932, Hollywood stars Joan Crawford and Douglas Fairbanks were photographed by Edward Steichen for *Vanity Fair*, "off duty" on the beach, in a very early example of sunglasses as part of an aspirational image.

Like Graves and Hodges, Wilson claims that in the late 1920s the tan signified proletarian pleasure (perhaps evidenced by the modest reference to the mere "girl who sits on the sands," in the early ad for sunglasses), but also racial impurity and a *lack of concern for the prevailing ideal* of pure white skin (1985: 130), and that it was perceived by some as "ugly." The tan struck at the conventions of class and race distinction in middle class society, while also being a magnificent and literal badge of "life in the light" as the working classes of the west grew newly pale from factory work and unhealthy, smog-ridden cities (Turner and Ash 1975: 80). Baring flesh in public in order to tan, as well as indulging in the sensual pleasures of exposing skin to the sun, air, and the application of tanning oil, continues to give tanning connotations of liberation from sexual limits. Ultimately the tan was taboo and rebellious as well as a sign of modern travel, wealth, and success, as well as health and youth. We might now think of "working on" a tan; but given the efforts expected to maintain the genteel white skin, the tan had an element of cheeky casual nonchalance about it—as if avoiding it were simply too much effort. The tan was new and shockingly modern, a cool rejection of the prevailing rules, and sunglasses were perhaps initially an especially jarring element. But, of course, they would go on to become an essential and desirable aspect of the look and a sign of tanning.

Sunglasses shed some of their unappealing connotations during the 1930s, when, as we saw in the last chapter, there were developments in plastics which prompted more variety in shapes, form, and color, enabling them to become more "feminine" while selling the clean, bright, modernity of plastic. This change

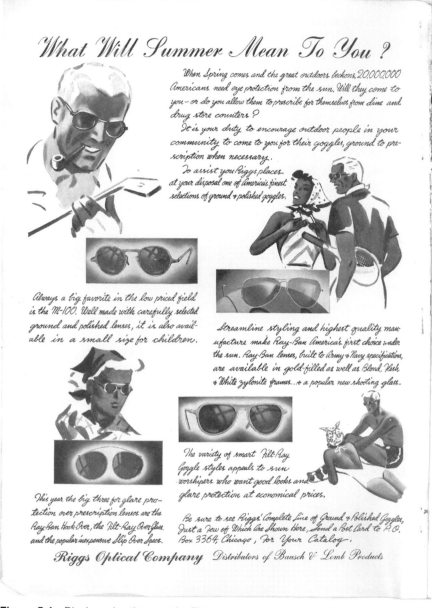

Figure 5.4 Display advertisement for Riggs lenses depicts sunlight on dark tints and tanned skin, late 1930s. (Reproduced with permission from *The American Journal of Optometry* March 1939, inside front cover © The American Academy of Optometry.)

was introduced as a potential selling point for frames in the optical journals, especially in the *American Journal of Optometry* (c. 1935). Many of them were white, as they are in Dahl-Wolfe's photograph—contrasting with the dark lenses and emphasizing the darker skin tone of the new, tanned body. By the late 1930s sunglasses were "gaily coloured" (Corson 1967: 225), and in 1939, the U.S. journal *Popular Science Monthly* reported a "craze" in the United States which saw sales rise from "tens of thousands" to "millions" (Corson 1967: 225). By the late 1930s, illustrations in the optical journals depicted tanned bodies in very obvious glasses with evidently black lenses.

This brings us back to Dahl-Wolfe's photograph. If this is the first, or one of the first, fashion editorial image to use sunglasses, what kind of image is it? Can it tell us anything about how sunglasses might have been regarded? And what kind of meanings might sunglasses have picked up by virtue of being included in it? Were they cool? Arnold's view is that Dahl-Wolfe's work "provided scenes of warmth and light that welcomed the viewer in" (2002: 59) and that they were "never intimidating" in terms of form or content (2002: 46). These interpretations do not initially appear to support the idea that sunglasses had connotations of cool at this point. Terms like "warmth" and "welcome" are not usually associated with cool; although relaxation is a more complex matter, as being relaxed when everyone else is hurrying, might be a sign of that nonchalance we've already seen in the demeanor of several cool types.

For sure, the model's pose is relaxed, spontaneous, and casual, her skirt ruffled by crossed legs; this is not an image of someone on edge. In an important literal sense, "relaxation" is afforded by the sunglasses, and the protection they offer from heat and glare. The sensual experience of "cooling" offered by sunglasses, was reported in the same year by a reviewer of what was then the new "Ray-Ban" "sunglass" (Dickinson 1938: 417–18). Dickinson is initially skeptical about the need for sunglasses, but concludes that behind Ray-Ban sunglasses "one experiences a coolness only to be described as delicious" (Dickinson 1938: 417–18); no squinting or frowning in spite of the obvious exposure to the midday sun.

In another sense, the sunglasses might suggest the relaxation of informality. Edwards suggests that Dahl-Wolfe used them to give her models a more "informal" or human air (1989: 57), similar to Lartigue's 1924 image of his wife in sunglasses, and the off duty snaps of the occasional Hollywood star. In the context of fashion photography (and, indeed, formal portraiture) of the time, sunglasses seem to have been a "rogue element" which might previously have been tidied away from the composition. Sunglasses had been featured in *Harper's Bazaar* one year previously, in society reportage showing two princesses on the beach in "goggles" (Morel 1937: 62–3), but this was presented as a "snap," as opposed to a fashion editorial. Allowing sunglasses into Dahl-Wolfe's shot may well have seemed more "authentic," less "staged," less bothered by convention—fitting in with the mood of avant-garde photography and *Harper's Bazaar's* "radical and controversial" style (Grundberg 1989: 119), which set it ahead of *Vogue*. At *Harper's Bazaar* Dahl-Wolfe worked alongside possibly the most radically modernist fashion photographer of the period, Munkacsi. Although their styles were different, some similar techniques associated with a more "natural" or "authentic" aesthetic were employed by Dahl-Wolfe; for example, using only the available light, and elements of the snapshot technique (Grundberg 1989; Squires 1980). This means that being "informal" or even "democratic" has to be contextualized within the challenge to the existing aesthetic order presented by the avant-garde. If Arnold's interpretation of these images as "welcoming" is right, it is a welcome which also presents a challenge. If it is relaxed, we should not simply assume that it is also without complication.

Critically, Dahl-Wolfe's work exemplified the American challenge to European high culture and class, and Parisian dominance of fashion specifically, in its representation of women and clothing expressive of an idealized, modern, American female identity whose appeal lay in democratized style (Arnold 2002; Globus 2000). This challenge came from Hollywood, American fashion design, and from the boldness of Carmel Snow's editorship at *Harper's Bazaar.* Part of this challenge was that very "informality," something signified in the image also by the clothes.

The dress is a simple, minimal cotton; signifier of democracy, utility, and authenticity. As such it connects with the status of expensive simplicity, "dressing down;" something like Chanel's approach to fashion, but very much against the dominant traditions of Parisian haute couture. The classical symmetry of the composition of the figure against the terrazzo also evokes the statuesque. In place of a Venus, centered in her own universe, we have beautiful, tanned Mary, nonchalantly crumpling her minimal cotton frock. Perhaps, thinking of Arnold's points, this represents a triumph of the American dream over European high culture and class.

The model herself, not a member of the aristocracy, is displayed as a woman of status for admiration by others. This "ordinary" woman has been elevated *by virtue of this image*. The impertinent, but stylish tendencies of the regency dandies spring to mind here; ignoring the fashion rules of the prevailing class, they wore country clothes in town, and made new clothes look old. They equally employed a (carefully composed) appearance of effortlessness—don't be fooled, this is *not* a snap. Dahl-Wolfe's images were elaborately staged and then crafted after the event to *appear* to have been superbly spontaneous. (Just like the dandy's cravat tied and retied repeatedly until the "perfect accident" occurs.) The power of this illusion is in the implication that perfection came naturally, from within, from an "inherently noble self" (Campbell in Entwistle 2000: 170). And this is what makes modern fashion photographs like this potentially intimidating;

almost regardless of the specifics of their content, but perhaps especially where the prevailing rules are being subverted. It is therefore mistaken to assume that these images were simply "relaxed" and "welcoming."

Dahl-Wolfe's outdoor work in general does look strikingly contemporary; Goldberg calls it "blasé," and "ahead of its time" (2000: 4). Nochlin describes it as "effortless" and "modernist" (Globus 2000: 1). Squires suggests that Dahl-Wolfe's photographs can be read as progressive in gender terms, representing women with new levels of autonomy (1980:48). Dahl-Wolfe also created an unconventional aesthetic by using twins. Visually twins are unsettling, a little uncanny, and twinning has also been known as a lesbian tactic for dressing (Ash and Wilson 1992). Some of the connotations of "sportswear" would possibly still have been quite noticeably edgy; Campbell Warner describes how sportswear was still subject to quite rigid ideas of when and where it should be seen in 1930s American culture (2005: 91). The almost empty spaces the models often inhabit have a sense of the wilderness about them; locations are associated with "strength, independence and freedom" (Wright in Rojek 1993: 198). Being outdoors at all was relatively progressive; being confident and alone in these locations, in newly skimpy bathing suits, blasé (and even naked in one 1939 issue of *Harper's Bazaar),* suggested new levels of self-possession. Combined, these elements support the idea that sunglasses came into fashion imagery in a context of strong connections with modernity, and the power to challenge some dominant aspects of traditional society.

This leads us to thinking more specifically about the sunglasses in the Puerto Rico image. Dickinson, who reviewed Ray Ban sunglasses in 1938, concluded his article by saying they were "cool as an income tax demand note" (1938: 417–18), suggesting that there was already more to sunglasses' coolness than merely the physical affordance of lowering the temperature of the eyes.

In this, as in many of Dahl-Wolfe's other photographs, sunglasses draw our attention to the eyes but render them unreadable, thus raising the question of what the model might be thinking; as Marshal McLuhan notes, they are a "cool medium" creating "the inscrutable and inaccessible image that invites a great deal of participation and completion" (1964: 44). This woman does not offer the open expression and gentle smile of conventional femininity. This destabilizes the conventional power relationship between viewer and viewed in images of women, similarly to the images of eighteenth century women in vizzards, and some of the women in driving goggles. However, if we think of this as a fashion photograph, we know there is a purposeful withholding of information and access, there is no functional ambiguity. If we think of it as a snapshot, which it partly pretends to be, the model's lack of attentiveness to the viewer is simply rude. The photographer is close (perhaps intimidatingly close) enough to require the respectfully returned gaze of Goffman's face-to-face encounters (1963), but Mary fails to register. But as we seek some connection with this woman, searching her expression, all we keep getting is a metaphorical smack in the face from the blunt weapon of her dark lenses. She is utterly unphased by both her solitude and the presence of the camera, again calling to mind the independence, status, and composure of the dandy, as well as his "look of glacial indifference." Edwards calls it "the implied *insolence* of the direct sunglassed confrontation" (1989: 59). This sends a message to the old world as well as the immediate viewer—those of us in this league are at home in the modern world, equipped and self-possessed. *We* now set the pace and make the rules.

On the subject of pace and privilege, sunglasses' connotations of modern speed are also more relevant here than might at first be assumed, given that this is ostensibly an image of repose. As with the tan, powerful connotations of the glamor of modern speed remain (after all these are the pleasures of the "jet-set") and there are a number of ways in which this image alludes to it: first, the composition works to make this a dynamic image with an intense impact. Contrasting chequered tiles recede sharply, making the central figure rush forward toward the viewer, almost filling the frame, the viewer's notional field of vision. The high-contrast geometry of the setting relays with the black circular lenses edged with bright white (an "unnatural" tonal reversal of the eyes) and the tanned skin on the face, with an aesthetic that foretells 1960s op art with its illusions of movement and intent to overstimulate the eye. This woman may be sitting down, but that sense of a snapshot, a moment in time, cannot help but suggest "the dynamism of a hidden but nevertheless imagined sequence" (Virilio 1998: 22).

In addition to this, here she plays the role of the tourist—who has evidently traveled at high speed, detached from all places through which she passed—and is now afforded leisure. This "non" place in Puerto Rico—this old, tiled garden or square (actually the Escambron Beach Club)—has been colonized by model and crew. We see no locals, no fellow travelers, no partner, no children, no staff. This space has been cleared for her, to act as her "backdrop" for the few hours it may take to stage and shoot this apparently casual photograph.

Indeed this image seems brilliantly suggestive of the concept of "polar inertia" put forward by Virilio (1997: 69) which highlights the paradoxical coexistence of speed and inertia in privileged modern life. The moment of "doing nothing" is utterly dependent on the energetic technologies of speed. Gundle also notes the fusion of speed and leisure in modern glamor; "a world perennially in motion, leisured, stylish and beautiful… seemingly on a permanent vacation" (2008: 4).

Virilio's prime example of someone who "lived" polar inertia is Howard Hughes, film producer and aviator of the 1920s and 1930s. His career and status depended on speed; he had apartments all over the world, but his existence was ironically characterized by an acute lack of interaction with place, and an acute lack of human physical effort (Redhead 2004: 42–3). Sunglasses, with their connotations of modern technology and protection in travel (which remain, in spite of being impacted under later layers of meaning), combined with sunbathing's suggestions of leisurely lazing, would seem to signify polar inertia brilliantly, perhaps especially in this image, which also makes obvious connections with the dynamic. The status and speed required to construct this photograph, and all the others like it produced through the twentieth century, was not lost on the viewers of fashion magazines, who began to aspire to the lifestyle of the fashion model as well as that of those wealthy enough to buy not only the magazines but also the clothes, to renew their appearance on an increasingly frequent and seasonal basis, or even to play with differently nuanced versions of themselves through different clothing and accessories.

Playing with identity—"holiday" clothing

The idea of "playing" with identity connects with sunglasses' special ability to reinterpret the face. Holiday clothing more generally was changing between the wars—the Riviera set's approach set a new tone for twentieth century holiday wear in which sunglasses could play a highly accessible and effective part. Instead of wearing the "Sunday Best" for days of leisure, a pleasingly altered self was achieved, often playfully suggestive of escape from the "culture" and sophistication of the modern city to the "nature" and "simplicity" of "elsewhere." Turner and Ash comment that holidays in general increasingly offered escape from adult responsibility to an idealized child-like state of uninhibited play (1975).

There is a definite hint of this in the image of Mary Sykes, the fresh flower in her pocket, the peasant headscarf, and the utilitarian cut and fabric of her dress. Typically, the Riviera set had picked up on the clothes of the local peasants and workers. But the resulting garments do not look like attempts to become a local, to live like a peasant. They *play* with the idea of poverty, authenticity, boundary-crossing, and so on, in the context of a lifestyle which was glamorous, frivolous, and hedonistic, punctuated with what the Murphys called "bad" parties on the beach, costume balls, and masquerades (Turner and Ash 1975).

On a broader scale, from about the 1930s, holiday wear showed more color and novelty in less formal, more revealing garments, as well as idealized versions of destination cultures' "native" dress. Sunglasses became more colorful, and by the 1940s to 1950s, similarly to other plastic products of the post-war boom (Ward 1997), designs were cheap, highly expressive, playful, and frivolous. Be a mermaid in shells or starfish frames, a nymph in flower petals, or a "native" in mask-like glasses decorated with raffia, or moulded to look like bamboo or wood. Lipow suggests that shorter hairstyles following the fashion for the "bob" haircut (which had been popularized by Irene Castle, Louise Brooks, and Chanel) had prompted plastics manufacturers who had previously traded in

Figure 5.5 Miami Beach, 1940s. "Playful" holiday wear—Turkish trousers, shell frames, and a dried fruit necklace. (Photograph by Alfred Eisenstaedt © Getty Images.)

fancy hair combs to transfer their skills to the production of sunglasses (2011: 129); resulting in protean frame designs referencing swans, butterflies, cats' eyes, feather-forms, and all kinds of swirling and surreal forms.

These were predominantly for women, perhaps reflecting a certain kind of femininity which emphasized being light hearted, decorative, and more child-like. These glasses are so far from the dark and masculine "cool shades" that they might appear to offer a significant challenge to the notions of sunglasses as cool. But in spite of such "happy" and "cute" connotations, these glasses with their dark lenses still cannot help but have the potential to suggest refusal and cool detachment in the context of women's wear. Blanking the eyes with frivolity declares a resolute lack of concern for anything serious, sensible, or adult. In being playful and short-lived in their appeal, novelty glasses refuse

Figure 5.6 Paris Hilton, California 2010. (Photograph by Jean-Baptiste Lacroix © Getty Images.)

to engage with parental or traditional ideas of thrift, the protestant work ethic, or the feminist call for women to assert their adult intelligence; these glasses represent a heightened state of feminine narcissism which had traditionally been associated with elite women and their role of display. Today, popular films like *Legally Bl*onde (2001) and *Marie Antoinette* (2006) celebrate a heroically resolute "girliness" which can perhaps also be seen as "postfeminist." This can also be seen in contemporary "cute/cool" subcultural styles, for example, Japanese "kawail" culture (McVeigh 2000). These representations suggest cool by means of various combinations of the "fluffy" and the "tough"—think of Paris Hilton in shades, accompanied by a tea-cup Chihuahua, possibly sporting shades of its own.

For those on stricter budgets, holiday fashion represented a particular opportunity to renew and improve. Until the 1930s, dressing "up" in Sunday best (smart clothing which emulated that of the class above) was normal for the beach; certainly in Britain, where only in the 1920s did "going off clubs," and eventually paid holidays, enable workers to save for holidays and the annual wardrobe renewal (Hudson 1992). As a small, portable, affordable, and visually impacting sign of "difference" which does not lose its shiny sparkle, it is unsurprising that sunglasses became a signifier of a "better, newer" identity. Design historian and cultural critic Reyner Banham even noted in the 1960s (1967: 959) that sunglasses impose a new external "bone structure" which could make anyone look like a "horse-faced aristo." Whether cheap or expensive, sunglasses became a token of lifestyle, a means to play with identity.

The fashion industry continues to reproduce the "need" for different clothes and accessories for holidays, and the fashion media have been offering advice to women about what sort of self to present and how since the earliest days of mass tourism. Numerous features about holiday clothes in spring/summer editions of *Vogue* (and a range of other contemporary women's magazines) throughout the twentieth century emphasized the idea of the tourist herself becoming part of the visual spectacle, or enjoying a new or different sense of self made possible through holiday clothing, diets, tanning, and sunglasses.

Since sunglasses affect both how you *see* and how you *appear* to others, they have a strong connection with the idea of an altered state of identity as well as perception. In his book *The Tourist Gaze* (1990), Urry explains that tourists are invited to look in specific ways. As with the modern city, destinations are transformed to satisfy these spectacular anticipations, with holiday beaches and promenades being prime examples. Urry states that the tourist experiences "a much greater sensitivity to visual elements of landscape or townscape than is found in everyday life" (1990: 3). Culler (Urry 1990) says that tourists see everything as "a sign of itself." These remarks about "visual sensitivity" could reasonably include the person's own presentation of self and belongings, evidenced by the tendency to want photos of yourself taken in holiday destinations. Indeed, Urry indicates that the development of modern tourism and popular photography were mutually dependent.

This emphasis on looking at the self, the other, and the other place also points toward the suitability of sunglasses as a signifier of the holiday, not just for sunbathing but for tourism and this "tourist gaze" in general. These factors, together with the contrasts between "home" and "away," place the tourist in an especially self-conscious relationship with his/her own personal style, belongings, and appearance. Furthermore, the small number of objects required for use over a relatively short period of time creates an exciting potential for exercising enough control to create a temporarily quite different or more idealized self-image. The tininess of the sunglasses and the large impact they can have on appearance make them ideal for the smallest capsule wardrobe, in the most compact of flight cases (it's cool to travel light, after all).

Indeed, sunglasses and camera are the tell-tale elements of the enduring stereotypical tourist image—so much so that in a recent British children's programme, a small girl states that you cannot pass through customs without "a passport… and sunglasses." At this point, an objection could be raised that tourists are sometimes perceived as anything but cool, but this is largely dependent on the subtleties of how the tourist behaves in this "other" place. We will return to this subject later, but next we will think a little bit more about these "other places"—the golden spaces in which sunglasses are worn.

The beach is, of course, a prime context in which sunglasses are worn, as this is where sunbathing largely takes place. Beach resorts (the location of those "bad" parties held by the Murphys), like urban spaces, were products of a modernity which facilitated a heady cocktail of play, exhibitionism, voyeurism, rule-breaking, and pleasure seeking. The modern pleasure beach is a place of abundant natural light during the day and, at night, artificial illuminations and glittering distractions (even a glow stick or luminous body paint surely counts as such).

At the beach, self-conscious urban dwellers (who know they are observed by thousands of anonymous others) abandoned the dark cloaks of Victorian respectability described by Wilson, and lay themselves increasingly bare to scrutiny. They also scrutinized others. This space was like a giant railway carriage or lift, with hundreds of relatively motionless, anonymous bodies racked up against one another with little to do but look, and be seen. "At the beach, the body becomes a spectacle, put on display according to elaborate unwritten codes" (Lencek and Boskev 1998: xix) The promenade is a stage for organized flânerie, "aimless" strolling, displaying, and looking, desire for "love at last sight." Similarly to the seductions performed by the wearers of vizzards in early London parks, legitimized at the beach, sunglasses finally came into their own as an attraction of and protection from the gaze, enablers of voyeurism and exhibitionism. To be more sexually active, promiscuous, and to take greater risks has been identified as part of the tourist experience (Turner and Ash 1975) typified in late twentieth century Britain by the popular image of the "Club 18–30" holiday, and seemingly boosted by the anonymity and freedom from habitual identities and roles. As a highly portable tool of both seduction and at least partial disguise, sunglasses were well placed to become indispensable in such contexts, functioning as disguise, point of attraction, or involvement shield in the context of the crowd. Botz-Bornstein suggests that sunglasses are not erotic, because in covering the eyes, they refuse the viewer intimate engagement (2013: online). However, a real human being may enact a certain kind of invitation to cross the self-imposed threshold of sunglasses in what Carter and Michael call a "fleeting partial gaze" (2004: 275) somewhat similar to previous uses of the fan; they can be looked over, taken off, or replaced, to dramatize the giving and taking away of access. In a focus group conducted by Glenn Wilson for Dolland and Aitchison in 1999, one of the young males in the group commented that he felt women in sunglasses on the beach were more attractive and more likely to be viewed by him as a "sexual object" since the lack of access to the woman's eyes encouraged him to think less about her personality and to focus on her as "body" (he said he felt this effect was "almost pornographic"). However, this contrasted with the women in the group, who had already agreed that they only felt able to expose their bodies on the beach because of the (evidently illusory) sense of protection and privacy afforded by sunglasses (Wilson 1999: 5–6). Edwards noted something similar in his article about sunglasses in photographs—that there might be a correlation between the increasing display of women's bodies and the covering of their eyes, as an inverted form of veiling (Edwards 1989: 58).[1] Furthermore, a type of sunglasses described by Reyner Banham (1967) called "Boywatchers," which was on sale in the United States in the 1960s, highlighted the potential voyeuristic pleasure for women in covering their eyes at the beach. Ultimately the ambiguities of identity and the gaze in this context heighten sunglasses' capacity to encourage the pushing of the usual social boundaries while appearing to afford some protection from the same. A number of authors also discuss the beach as a "liminal" zone where "since deepest antiquity" the beach has been understood as "a site of transformation, releasing us from the straightjackets of routine and repression" (Lencek and Boskev 1998: 30). Rojek says this is a place where it is believed you can "be yourself" because it appears to be "beyond the control of civilised order" (1995: 88).

In fact, Zygmunt Bauman's essay "Desert Spectacular" finds a contemporary form of flâneur at the beach, who is

> out on vacation—from reality. In reality, he is overdetermined; he wears his determination as the beast of burden wears its yoke. Out there in the desert or the city, he plays the game of underdetermination… for a moment deem[ing] himself free from the reality [he] detest[s]. (1994: 141)

Bauman also calls this flâneur a "travelling player" (1994: 142). Whether performed at home, at the beach, in the city, or even in the desert, to be a flâneur is "to rehearse the contingency of meaning; life as a bagful of episodes none of which is definite, unequivocal, irreversible; life as a play." Although Bauman insists this could happen anywhere, he calls holiday beaches "the high temples and cults of the creed" (1994: 142); the spaces where identity play through consumption becomes a seductive illusion of mastery and freedom in the service of which sunglasses continue to be sold.

Sunglasses, cool, and the global traveler

Thinking of the flâneur's detached and incognito sovereign spectatorship brings us back to the privileged leisure of Mary Sykes as depicted at the Escambron Beach Club in 1938, and the relationship between the international or global tourist and the spaces they temporarily inhabit. In spite of theories about how the technologies of travel may engender a cooler demeanor, in fact to be cool as a tourist or traveler in a new place is very demanding. Encounters with the unknown and the unrehearsed constitute numerous little (and large) threats to composure.

Like Dahl-Wolfe's images, many fashion spreads which depict resort clothing make a deliberate display of easy competence with the "otherness" of the foreign setting which, while jaunty, feels quite colonial. In a similar way to Chanel's beach clothing, the traditional wear of locals around the world has been appropriated and adapted in one feature from 1950s U.K. *Vogue,* where the models pose, carefully and in focus, before a curiously flat scene of locals going about their business. They could almost be a studio backdrop, bringing to life Bauman's idea of tourist destinations as "stages on which to play" (1994: 141).

As tourist/traveller clothing has developed, the adoption of styles from locals has been globalized and homogenized—with Bermuda shorts, sarongs, and Hawaiian shirts, for example, now a staple of western holiday fashion almost irrespective of the destination. But sunglasses (and camera) simultaneously became a tell-tale sign of western progress in the global setting, and of a particular detached way of viewing the world, protected by relative wealth and the modern conveniences that travel with most westerners (Craik in Rojek and Urry 1997: 115). Craik refers to this as the "tourist bubble"—of which, what better sign than sunglasses? Whether or not the sunglassed inhabitant of the tourist bubble can be perceived as cool depends on how well they can also carry off the necessary ease of the dandy and the incognito of the flâneur, but shaded eyes certainly help.

Sunglasses and celebrity

Moving away now from the themes of "life in the light" raised in Louise Dahl-Wolfe's photograph, the next part of this chapter adds another highly significant layer to the appeal of sunglasses as it developed through the 1930s and to the present-day celebrity. The Riviera set were a well-known and influential elite, but they had nothing like the mass exposure and power to define desirability and success that celebrities were gradually gaining. Hollywood created a highly visible gap between the lives of the "atoms" and the "stars," a gap which could be filled with imitative desires. Hollywood celebrities were absolutely drenched in the lights of modernity—studio light, photographers' flashbulbs, the sun of L.A., and the lights and glamor of the high-octane leisure spaces they frequented. Not only did sunglasses connote modernity, wealth, leisure, status, and identity play—since about the 1940s they connoted *celebrity*.

As much as the modern self might be offered the possibility of being—or becoming—the center of the universe, sovereign spectator; the evidence was simultaneously everywhere that the self might merely be just another "particle" in someone else's panorama. The sense of the "self under scrutiny" encouraged by the film close-up discussed in Chapter 2, also created the sense that personal *significance* was defined by having a camera pointed at you. You could say that in the modern world, everyone is part of the panorama, but only some deserve a close-up... . Schickel (2000: 10) claims that the close-up created the phenomenon of celebrity. Separating the individual features from the other players and from the role, and cues of setting, the mystique of the actor's identity could be elaborated on by viewers attempting to read the nuances of the face and facial expression. Viewers knew the actor was acting, but as the same face appeared in film after film, playing different characters, the question of the actor's private self was raised. Initially Hollywood actors remained anonymous and were paid little, but it was not long before salaries began to increase dramatically and out of all proportion to the work (Schickel 2000: 46–7) and an international "fellowship of the accomplished" (Schickel 2000: 48), a glitterati, was possible—a group of rich and influential people whose international community relied on emerging technologies of communication and travel and whose lifestyles (real or imagined) were to become the commodity purchased in an ever growing number of celebrity magazines.

Douglas Fairbanks cultivated such a group in the late 1920s and early 1930s, with an annual trip to Europe to collect society connections from the English peerage and the elites of culture and industry. As Gundle points out, "those … who had once sought to secure the presence of the most noble and distinguished of guests now also pursued athletes, entertainers, speed kings, aviators, fashion designers as well as film stars" (Gundle 2008: 150). The status and power of those involved in the modern forms of distinction was growing, raising them into a new "class" (Gundle 2008: 230), and in the modern world, to be seen, to be "in the limelight" became a defining feature of status.

The earliest associations of sunglasses with celebrities in images are not from within the movies but from the "off duty," "behind the scenes" snaps produced to help promote the studios in the 1920s and 1930s; perhaps the occasional early morning shot of someone like Joan Crawford arriving on set without her eye make-up. In this setting the "off duty" and "off stage" took on a glamor of its own—a glimpse into the "real" lives of the stars. Another early example is a shot of Marlene Dietrich eating backstage at Paramount studios, which appeared in *Life* magazine in 1938. None of these images show the subjects looking directly at the camera, suggestive of the idea that they are being "caught." (This would support the idea that Dahl-Wolfe's use of sunglasses suggested "informality" and "casualness.") However, these images were still carefully controlled. Once the grip of the studios loosened and stars began to demand more independence in the industry, their private lives could begin to be commodified to promote their celebrity beyond the films they appeared in, bolstering their desirability to film producers.

At the same time, developments in photographic technology enabled shots to be taken in a range of atmospheres and at speed, creating the conditions for the emergence of the paparazzi in the Via Veneto in Rome during the 1950s and 1960s, where erstwhile tourist photographers would snap Hollywood stars among the Italian elite who went there to eat, drink, and parade (Howe 2007: 57). The Via Veneto was favored because it was close to the Italian studios used by American companies, but apparently also because it was a wide, open avenue which easily accommodated celebrity cars (Howe 2007: 57). This was clearly a locus of modernity, velocity, light, and privilege. Barillari, one of those very early paparazzi, recollects in interview with Howe that the best month for this was September, "because all these famous people were just coming back from vacation, so they were tanned, looking smart, and they went there to show off—you know, just to look beautiful" (Howe 2005: 59). Outdoor shots of "off duty" stars there and elsewhere were available, giving more frequent insights into their leisure wardrobes, more glimpses of "actresses in their beach bikinis," in other words access to images of "that sacred space" or parallel universe, inhabited by celebrities' (Giles 2000: 99); as Schickel describes it, that "place of beauty and freedom from life's ordinary ills that [press] pieces about famous people seem to imply that the favoured enjoy" (2000: 15); a truly modern Mount Olympia. The casual clothing and the "unaware" poses featured in these images will of course have been fetishized in the process. Oh, to step off a plane, looking effortlessly amazing in sunglasses and headscarf, in a warm, sunny resort, smiling and excited, possibly to a small crowd of press photographers; mythologized of course in Fellini's classic *La Dolce Vita* (1960).

Violent light—sunglasses and the paparazzi

But for the celebrity, the potential of being "papped" will also have blurred the distinction between being on and off stage. Even before this, some insightful stars realized they were trapped by their celebrity role—as Myrna Loy said to a journalist:

> I daren't take any chances with Myrna Loy, for she isn't my property... I couldn't even go to the drugstore you see without looking 'right' you see... I've got to be, on all public occasions, the personality they sell at the box office. (Giles 2000: 22)

And from the very earliest days of the paparazzi, there was a sense of "attack" about the paparazzo's "shots." They worked together to set up little incidents to create drama, or show a celebrity in a surprising light. At the end of relatively drab evening's work in 1958, Secchiaroli spotted Ava Gardner waiting by herself as her date Walter Chiari parked his car—he got a couple of other paparazzi to hide while he "went up to Gardner and exploded his flash right in her face" (Howe 2007: 30). Shocked, she screamed, and Chiari, who was just returning, attacked Secchiaroli while another photographer got the pictures. These were widely published, and crystallized the realization that by creating confrontations paparazzi could get more valuable pictures.

The habitual wearing of sunglasses by off-duty celebrities while in public places seems very likely to have stemmed from this kind of incident. The shades provided necessary protection against the sudden and violent glare of a Rolleiflex flashbulb, which had to be used at very close range (Howe 2007). Hollywood celebrities used sunglasses for privacy—as a portable "back stage;" to avoid being recognized and to make the shots less valuable. However, by doing this they visually communicated their extraordinary status; being a particle so significant as to be focused on to excess. Here is a person who is so immersed in the light they now crave shade from it. This may be experienced as a negative thing by the individual celebrity—but importantly such images are still read by the wider public as highly evocative signs of success and status. Giles says Greta Garbo was among the first to revolt openly against the pressures of dealing with the general public, so much so that she spent many periods of her career "in hiding," and even took to donning disguises to avoid recognition: "The story of my life is about back entrances, side doors and secret elevators" (Giles 2000: 90).

Chaplin too struggled with attention in public—"I had always thought I would like [it], and here it was—paradoxically isolating me with a depressing sense of loneliness" (Giles 2000: 91). Giles has noted the problems of fame in his book *Illusions of Immortality* like Simmel speaking of the metropolis, picking upon the stress of innumerable encounters with others:

Figure 5.7   Greta Garbo caught by paparazzi, Athens, 1966. (© Bettman/Corbis.)

probably the single most important cause of unhappiness reported by celebrities is the effect of having to deal with so many people all the time. The
loss of privacy is one aspect of this… But fame forces us into so many new
relationships that the sheer numbers of these can be stressful in itself… It
is estimated that in the middle ages the average person only ever saw 100
different individuals in the course of a lifetime… (Giles 2000: 92)

Sunglasses gave the off-duty celebrity a degree of protection for the "real" self
but simultaneously projected the effortlessly desirable self through their other
associations of lifestyle and glamor, making them indispensable. The sunglasses
also withheld access to that intimacy promised by the cinematic close-up,
increasing desire. The role of sunglasses in the cycle of seduction and rejection
celebrities enter into with paparazzi for mutual financial benefit is now so well-
rehearsed that minor celebrities (and "wannabes") sometimes pastiche the look
of these early Hollywood stars in hiding as part of their performance of celebrity
identity. The connection between sunglasses and celebrity became so strong
that Jackie Onassis allegedly took to going out without sunglasses because she
was *less* likely to be recognized without them.

Pressure on celebrities' own sense of access to off duty or backstage regions was exacerbated during the 1960s when long-focus lenses enabled the paparazzi to use stealth and to snap without being seen (Howe 2005). The feeling of being potentially photographable even when no photographers appear to be present has increased the background sense of risk, not only the risk of being photographed, but also the possibility *no* photographers will come. Maybe no photographers will want your picture—a constant measure of the flux of your fame.

Figure 5.8   Jackie Kennedy Onassis, with her trademark sunglasses *off*, 1970. (Photograph by Ron Galella © Getty Images.)

Jackie Onassis, widow of President Kennedy, was a "bread and butter" star for American paparazzi in the 1960s, indeed her name now describes a style of sunglasses she favored. The internet is full of huge, round, black glasses described as "Jackie Os," and references in blogs to "looking like Jackie O" in such glasses. Ron Galella, who pursued Jackie for many years and was eventually outlawed from doing so, said that Jackie's mystique was enhanced by the fact she "wasn't co-operative and didn't pose or stop" (Galella in Howe 2005: 114). He added, "her glamor was a mystery. Most stars expose every-thing… celebrities sort of pull out their souls, leaving little to the imagination. Jackie was soft spoken, but she was very alive. She created an aura, a mystery" (Galella in Howe 2005: 114).

His most famous photograph of Jackie was taken "without the ever present sunglasses that she used to hide behind" (Galella in Howe 2005: 116), though the contact sheet shows that she was wearing them moments before in takes five and six, as she came down the street. Apparently, she removed her sunglasses, turned toward his camera, "not away from it as was her want" (Howe 2005: 116), and smiled—at the man she had been followed by for three years, and who, the following year, she would take to court. Galella insists in the book that Jackie "liked being pursued" and that she "protested too much" (Galella in Howe 2005: 119), but in the documentary about Galella *Smash His Camera* (2010), he admits, "I don't think she recognised me, that's why she smiled." On other occasions Galella used disguises of his own to pre-empt negative responses from celebrities he had annoyed. Whether Jackie recognized him or not, this incident still highlights the immediate power relations between paparazzo and celebrity, who can "give" an open face, a smile, and with it, respect and financial prosperity to the paparazzo. Recollections of the paparazzi show that some resented the status gap between them (often from deprived backgrounds) and the celebrities. The paparazzi soon realized their power—they could make Salvador Dali tip the doorman at Maxim's in Paris, just by being there to notice, they could also "help" or "hinder" a celebrity's career. Accounts in Howe's book point to a teasing element of the game of showing and hiding, especially when discussing the "relationships" between male photographers and female celeb-rities like Jackie and Liz Taylor.

Hollywood and cool

A number of themes have emerged here which connect celebrities with the blasé modern lifestyles we have been thinking of as cool so far. But there are elements of their roles as screen actors, which perhaps also contributed to the development of sunglasses as a signifier of Hollywood cool and of Hollywood in general. I spoke earlier of sunglasses as a portable "backstage" region; techni-cally this is inaccurate because, of course, Hollywood stars did not primarily appear on a live stage. This detachment from the audience behind a shiny screen, and the medium of film itself, was key.

There is a dandyish quality to the conditions of the film star's work—rehearsal. Like Dahl-Wolfe's staged "snaps", the opportunity to painstakingly rehearse "behind the scenes" increases the appearance of effortlessness. In cinema, even after rehearsal, scenes can be re-shot and edited to give the actor the literally superhuman power to demonstrate ease with the environment, to "know what to say," to appear unperturbed by all situations (comedically telegraphed by James Bond, for example). The labor, and the failure, is concealed—just like the secret notebooks and rehearsed gestures of the regency dandy's chambers. Often this appearance of ease was (and still is) made possible by sunglasses masking fear or anxiety, and often in situations involving new or dangerous technology, or any number of potentially disconcerting situations; think of Steve McQueen in shades on his motorbike in *The Great Escape* (1963) (or Daniel Craig in *Skyfall* (2012) if you like). Think of Humphrey Bogart and Lauren Bacall, James Dean, Cary Grant, Greta Garbo, Marlene Dietrich—the heavy eyelids, the calm demeanor, the lack of concern for authority, the impressive control of emotions, circumstances, and even clothing and accessories. Stars don't get flustered by an overstuffed handbag, they don't drop or lose their shades. Stacey's 1994 study of women's para-social relationships with stars revealed that "respondents had deliberately modelled their … behaviour on their idols… even pretended to be the star in certain social situations…" (Stacey in Giles 2000: 61). This would be difficult to achieve, further marking out the star and their qualities as desirable but out of reach.

Alienated communities and mass culture both require personalities "everyone knows" as hooks on which the sale of cultural images and artefacts may be hung, models of success which can function as a form of guidance through an increasingly bewildering and fast-changing sea of choices for identity. Emulation of celebrity fashion is surely now at an all-time high, with most fashion magazines now devoting a substantial portion of their content to the coverage of celebrity style (Pringle 2004: 29), but it began in the early days of Hollywood when styles worn by American actresses would sell out, like the puffed sleeve dress worn by Joan Crawford in *Letty Lynton* (1932), or fall out of favor as did the vest when Clark Gable appeared without one in the 1934 film *It Happened One Night* (Bruzzi 1997: 5). Costume in film continues to influence fashion, but nowhere near as effffectively as the paparazzi's glimpses into the privileged worlds privately inhabited by stars. By the end of the century this had become the stock-in-trade of much fashion trend reporting in women's magazines.

The earliest connections made with celebrity in the optical journals studied appeared around the same time as the "craze" for sunglasses and the Dahl-Wolfe fashion image—1938. In the *American Journal of Optometry*, an ad for Autoform Spurlock frames announced new decorative options with the slogan "a star is born." By the early-to-mid-1940s the same journal contains references to "fame and fortune" and "important people" listed as "a sheik, senators, Hollywood actors and actresses" (advert for Continental brand, May 1944). By 1952, *Vision* (the popular supplement to the British optical journal *The Optician*) was able to feature an article inviting readers to guess the star from the spectacle frames. By c.1960, a catalogue for the Rodenstock brand "Clear Vision" featured Sophia Loren on the cover, as well as Marianne Koch and Brigitte Bardot on the inside. In 1967, a celebrated campaign for the manufacturer Foster Grant (De Silva 2007) employed images of a range of popular celebrities with different kinds of appeal in off-guard snaps to suggest "they really wear them." Each ad bore the strap line "Who's that behind the Foster Grants?"

In 2007, a similar campaign by Duffy and Shanley relaunched the brand with "Who could you be?" trading on the idea of sunglasses offering instant trans-formation to a different and better self. In a report on the marketing company's promotional website, the creative director explained:

> This isn't about models or celebrities or rock stars…It's about regular people and how, with a couple of pairs of stylish, affordable sunglasses, I can be a model or a celebrity or a rock star or a hundred different versions of myself, without spending a couple hundred bucks. (De Silva 2007: online)

The apparent contradiction here could be viewed as desperation to dress an old marketing idea up as a new one. But perhaps it reveals the difference between idealizing celebrities and the increasingly widespread contemporary belief (heavily traded on by "reality" television) that somehow star quality is not particular to those well-known individuals, but something pre-existing inside all anonymous individuals that is waiting to be revealed—in this case by a pair of shades. The power of the appeal of celebrity as an endorsement of modern selfhood shows no sign of diminishing—even if the means of achieving it might be changing—and the connection between celebrity and sunglasses remains strong.

Sunglasses and advertising

After the Second World War, sunglasses become ubiquitous in advertising for other products. They foreground in Pan Am adverts showing glamorous women in business class, they feature in adverts for tires, canned soup, Coca Cola, to name a few.

One British advert which expressed this idea with almost kitsch blatancy was for the 1967 Potterton Boiler in which a large, plain, white cuboid form loomed out of the empty darkness on top of which sat a giant pair of black-framed

Figure 5.9   A bit of glamor for the Potterton boiler, advertisement from U.K. women's magazine *Good Housekeeping,* 1967.

sunglasses, almost filling its surface. In one lens, a game of cricket was reflected. In the other, there were some active figures, outdoors. The strapline insisted—"Pick a Potterton—you only need look at it once or twice a year." The proposition is that the hi-tech efficiency of the Potterton would afford you (or your husband, as this advert appeared in *Woman and Home*) a life of leisure, relaxation, and fun. Goods which in any tenuous way could be hoped to bring you closer to leisure and the good life could call on sunglasses to give their campaigns the sparkle of glamor and the idea of a "bettered identity" through "modern living" in an economical and attention-grabbing way. Literally changing your "view"—even if not all lenses were "rose-tinted"—sunglasses made an excellent metaphor for seeing into this new world of possibility, with many ads using the lenses of sunglasses as screens on which to project scenes of that more perfect life.

The other development of mass culture which made sunglasses a passport to glamor was branding. Between the late 1960s and the 2000s, sunglasses have become, like perfume, a mass market money-spinner for luxury fashion brands and couturiers to offset against the losses of their more genuinely exclusive offerings. In the 1950s, designer Schiaparelli created a collection for American Optical (Lipow 2011); in the late 1960s Christian Dior licensed their brand for sunglasses (Handley 2010: 109), and Elvis commissioned frames to his own design heavily featuring his TCB (Taking Care of Business) flash in three dimensional gold. The TCB style presages the big, glitzy frames by Chanel, Dior, Gucci, and others which announce to all viewers the brand allegiances of the wearer.

These sunglasses evoke the brash culture of powerful, cash-rich elites, with their supersized frames and logos which bluntly challenge ordinary mortals. As such, these sunglasses are routinely advertised with the disdainful anti-gaze of detached hauteur. Underhill (2011) makes a comparison between brand allegiance and religious faith; McMahon and Morley confirm that luxury brands now "provide the consumer with a sense of enhanced status or identity through invoked feelings of exclusivity, authenticity, quality, uniqueness" (2011: 69). Sunglasses are a vehicle by which this can be stamped across your temples—"branding" the windows to the soul with the mark of its "owner," and leaving us in no doubt of the continued function of sunglasses as a mass token of desirable lifestyle.

Figure 5.10   The Dolce and Gabanna logo boldly integrated into sunglass arms, 2008.
— *This summer at the pool, sport these Dolce and Gabanna sunglasses from Macy's*
(Photograph by Lexington Herald-Leader © Getty Images.)

Some of these images of branded sunglasses are especially "cold" emotionally, not a hint of a smile, a fascistic level of "grooming," highlighting the connection between glamor and cool. In fact a number of authors who have explored the idea of glamor have described a decidedly chilly element to its power. Like glass, it is not only shiny; it is cold to the touch. Gundle calls glamor "a weapon and a protective coating, a screen" (2008: 4). Wilson refers to "the sheen, the mask of perfection… untouchability" speaking of Garbo's iconic "icy indifference" (2007: 106). Gundle also insists on distance as a "necessary factor in the maintenance of glamour" (2008: 14), but one which also offers a lure of accessibility; like the steely charms of the courtesan who traded in simultaneous attraction and deflection.

Summary—glam cool

This chapter has shown how sunglasses entered fashion and became a popular sign of "life in the light," light functioning as a sign of everything modern; better, newer, and more significant, with a strong connection with the idea of glamor—democratized, mass produced—but which nevertheless promised elevation to celestial heights and liberation from the old determinants of class (and to some extent gender).

Sunglasses are evidently a tool for the emulation of the leisure classes in this context, but to leave it there would be to miss the strong elements of cool which also pervade these images. Sunglasses emerged as a fashion accessory via a European avant-garde which connected with certain American values, in a provocative detachment from the old order, making images like Louise Dahl-Wolfe's readable as a symbolic affront to history. Just as the dandy was a self-creator who achieved a new kind of status through manipulations of style and surface, unconquerable self-assurance, and the crafting of an appearance of effortlessness, so did access to mass-produced glamor of the twentieth century make potential dandies of us all, while Hollywood applied very similar principles to the creation of its stars, carefully staging effortless images of glamorous, cool self-possession. Having conquered the anonymity of the masses and detached themselves from normal constraints, celebrities showed superior adaptation to modernity's opportunities and threats to overwhelm, and sunglasses were a key part of their armor. By mid-century, sunglasses were the popular signifier of being totally blasé and in tune with modernity, more than willing to throw off the old rules.

As much as sunglasses might signify that the wearer is immersed in light, it ought to be acknowledged that when you put your sunglasses on, everything goes dark. Next we will consider sunglasses as an accessory to darkness, the modernity of those on the margins, "outside" the light.

6

SEEING IN THE DARK—SUNGLASSES AND "OUTSIDER" COOL (1940s–PRESENT)

Introduction—sunglasses and darkness

Many of the most evocative images show sunglasses worn in the dark, indoors, possibly because in these images we are forced to acknowledge their more oblique functions. Layers of darkness and blackness are compounded by dark frames with dark lenses in many of these images; think of Miles Davis in a murky club, in a dark suit, what light there is just highlighting the sheen of his skin against the intense glossy blackness of his shades.

To darken your vision in conditions where light is already scarce, minimal, or deliberately obscuring seems to go against all the modernist purposes of optometry—to illuminate, to free, and to uphold the singular value of clear sight. In Chapter 7 I explored how sunglasses signified modernity by suggesting immersion in light, but in this chapter we will consider modernity's darker side, where the emphasis is not on those basking in the glow, but on those in the shadows.

The examples given raise further questions about how the wearer of sunglasses perceives and is perceived, some of which demonstrate quite complex articulations—and evasions—of power. Wearing sunglasses when there is no obvious functional need to do so implies alternative kinds of sight—characterized by a deliberately muted, detached perception of the world beyond the lenses.

First, some theory of "deviance," "subculture," and "outsiderhood" more generally will help to crystallize how and why these examples might be considered "cool."

Then we will explore the wider and broadly shared cultural associations of darkness (night, blindness, shadows, and the color black), as these are powerful

Figure 6.1   Miles Davis, 1955. (Photograph by Marvin Koner © Koner/Corbis.)

ideas which resonate in many images, moving on to consider more specifically the growth of modern urban nightlife as the context for many iconic instances of sunglasses' use by subordinate, "deviant," or marginalized groups who have been identified as "cool." To some extent, this could include the avant-garde artist, as a type on the edge of society, often willing to deviate from the respectable rules of the day. Outlaws and gangsters, black jazz musicians of the 1940s and 1950s, the Black Panthers in the 1960s, femmes fatales in 1940s film noir, *Lolita* in the 1960s all deploy sunglasses. What especially links notions of "coolness" and "darkness" together is the issue of visibility and invisibility and its political significance for individuals and groups in the struggle for liberation, and the tendency for constructions of black and female identity to imply "natural" associations with the dark.

"Deviance" and cool

So far, the kinds of cool we have seen articulated by sunglasses have been those which demonstrate a superior adaptation to the challenges of modernity—an ability to stay in tune with, or ahead of, changes in technology and fashion, and to achieve significance in mass society. These inherently involve some breaking of old rules and, in various ways, encourage a special kind of detachment from others or from emotion. But by and large, these exist within the law and demonstrate the fulfillment of the promise of modern capitalism. For the most part, they are "insider" forms of cool. (I will discuss this potentially controversial idea in more detail in Chapter 9.) But by the mid-twentieth century, theories of "deviance" (as it was called by sociologists) were describing "adaptations" to life which appeared to refuse to play the game as it had been set. Whether a case of "refusal" or having been "excluded," some of these ideas resonate strongly with uses of sunglasses in these "outsider" images.

In particular, Robert K. Merton's 1949 essay offers an explanation of deviance deriving from Durkheim's concept of "anomie," a psychological condition not dissimilar to Simmel's blasé or neurasthenic attitude discussed initially in Chapter 2—Durkheim's idea is that modernity creates conditions in which some people are likely to become "detached" from wider society. Merton says anomie results from a lack of social and psychological support, the perceived indifference of leaders, a lack of clear goals and means to achieve them, and a general sense of pointlessness, which is contrasted with an "infinity of wanting;" generalized and insatiable lusting for that "bettered life." In modern society, perhaps *anyone* can become famous or glamorous—but the reality is that not *everyone* can.

Merton says that if a society's goals do not match up with the means to achieve them, various types of anomie will result (1967: 219). Although Merton did not set out to describe cool, he describes attitudes and behaviors associated with a number of iconic cool figures who have announced their detachment with shades.

Merton's first "cool" type is the "Innovator," who believes in the goals, but does not have access to the means. Typically, in the context Merton was writing about, the innovator will resort to crime (a means unsanctioned by society) to achieve wealth (a legitimate goal). In naming this type the "innovator" we are led to see this criminal as ingenious—having the wherewithal to find alternative means to achieve the goals he/she has been given. Another "cool" type is the "retreatist" who lacks both the goals and the means. This kind of character is typically an outcast, alcoholic, or drug addict, "hobo" or "bum;" Merton says they are "*in* but not *of* society" (1967: 209), a phrase also used by Macadams and Pountain and Robins about coolness. "Defeatism, quietism and resignation" are the means by which he/she absents him/herself from society. But in spite of this apparent (and seemingly very uncool) "failure," Merton's retreatist turns out to be an unlikely hero: "if this deviant is condemned in real life, he may become a source of gratification in fantasy life…" (1967: 209). Kardiner speculates that in pop cultures these figures create

> morale and self-esteem by the spectacle of man rejecting current ideals and expressing contempt for them… he is a great comfort in that he gloats in his ability to outwit the pernicious forces aligned against him if he chooses to

do so and affords every man the satisfaction of feeling that the ultimate flight from social goals to loneliness is an act of choice and not a symptom of his defeat. (Merton 1967: 209)

This helps to account for the cool appeal of the "slacker" or, for example, the heroin addicts depicted in Danny Boyle's cult film *Trainspotting* (1996).

Merton's final outsider is the "rebel." The rebel is in the same boat as the retreatist, but instead of giving up on both the goals and the means, he/she substitutes both of them with completely new ones. The inference is that this is someone who truly does reject the entire system. It is important that Merton does not fix these categories rigidly, indeed the example Merton gives is artists and intellectuals, "potential deviants" who can at least conform to a "somewhat stabilised" system which seeks prestige within an "auxiliary" set of values rather than financial reward (Merton 1967: 211).

His last type—the "ritualist"—is not cool, so much so that it seems to fit beautifully with the idea of the "square." The ritualist has given up on the goals, but sticks doggedly to the means. He/she does what they are supposed to do, goes along with the rules, in spite of getting nothing back.

These types will be useful in my analysis in this chapter and the next. But it is worth noting, too, how Merton's theory seems to reveal his own admiration for the innovators, the retreatists, and the rebels. There is no objective reason to believe that all criminals are ingenious, nor that all those who try to be "good" without hope of reward are necessarily to be pitied as unimaginative creatures of futile obedience, yet his support for those who go against what is prescribed for them is hard to ignore. A comparison with the bohemian type can be made here where the bohemian stands anywhere between the "bum" and the artist. Gold subtitled his book about bohemia "Digging the roots of cool" (Gold 1994). In fact, admiration for the qualities of those underneath or outside is a thread running through existing studies of cool, bohemia, subculture, even in writing about the dandy (who forces his way all the way in and creates "a rival aristocracy"). Academics are not immune to the allure of cool types, especially those who exist somewhere on the edges.

The sense of rejection, standing apart—alternative ways of seeing the world if you like—contained in these modern "types" is something which has been expressed sartorially in a variety of ways, but sunglasses seem ideally placed to function as a self-imposed barrier as well as a signifier of that "different perspective"—a "darker" perspective perhaps.

Sunglasses—a portable night

In the same way that light was expressive of modernity, so was black. Understood as an absence of color, because it absorbs all light, black has been associated with the "renunciation" of expressiveness in men's clothing which dominated the twentieth century. Black is intense, the most visible tone against white, hard and uncompromising. Black is the color of interiority—it implies depth, seriousness, and has long-held associations with thinkers—the "habit noir" of the clergy, academics, formal legal attire—and became the signature of the modern man (Lehmann 2000). Black embodied the new, rational world, the machine age. Futurists wore black, so did Stalinists. Henry Ford painted all model T's black, Chanel did the same to her tubular dresses. The sense of detachment or withdrawal from emotion and the association with rational, industrial masculinity make black an ideal color to connote "cool," but there are also other associations worth exploring.

In putting on dark glasses, we willingly engulf ourselves in night. At least, to onlookers it could appear so. The expressive potential for this is great, since the "meanings" of night are ancient in origin and many are widely shared, as Schivelbusch says, "In... most cultures, night is chaos, the realm of dreams, teeming with ghosts and demons… the night is feminine, it holds both repose and terror" (1995: 81). Associations with status, glamor, and even technology may push themselves forward, but these other meanings are old and deep. In some circumstances nature's night is not night enough—wearing sunglasses in the dark invokes a further layer of night. Darkness has been seen as modernity's enemy—the past, the unknown, nature to our culture, death to our life, and disease to our health, motivating architects and town planners to eradicate dark streets, dusty corners, and so on. Night is the home of the irrational, the unproductive; as Palmer says, the home of "moments excluded from the histories of the day, a counterpoint within time, space, and place governed and regulated by the logic and commerce of economic rationality and the structures of political rule" (Peretti 2007: 8). In discussions of the connotations of night, themes of absence, death, blindness, evil, rebellion, sex, and magic (or enchantment) reoccur. Night equals *absence* because of the great cosmic nothing "from which our world was extracted" (Mauri 2007: 64). Mauri also identifies night as "the natural habitat of evil," in the ancient Greek concept of gloomy Hades, in contrast with the white light of goodness from above, with Jesus as "the light of the world" (2007: 64). Night can also be an absence of life; death. As Fer says, "[the] entwining of night and death is so culturally and psychically embedded that it appears nothing short of primordial" (2007: 74) Blackened eyes are themselves a sign of this. Fer describes an artwork, "Night" by Jeff Wall (2001), in which she misreads the representation of a very small figure as either blind or dead. The fact the eyes are open is only discernible from very close up—as she steps back and forth in front of the image, the figure's life and sight is given and taken away. Black sockets can be skull-like, two black holes connoting an *absence of sight*.

Blind sight

At this point it is worth considering the earliest wearer of dark glasses. How the negative connotations of weak sight or blindness could be transformed into connotations of the "highest modern value" (Poschart in Mentges 2000) has partly been addressed already. But the potential "cool" values of being sightless or of diminished sight merit further exploration.

The relationship between vision, perception, and knowledge is not a straightforward one. The long established western idea that "to see is to know" has been the dominant way of understanding vision in the modern era, described by Jay as "Cartesian perspectivalism" (1993: 70)—the belief in the solid objectivity of a sight whose characteristics owe more to the functionality of the camera obscura than the actual workings of the human eye. Sight is "the noblest of the senses," and to be excluded from the world of the visual in the modern world means exclusion from an ever-increasing quantity of information and culture.

But considering the distinction between different kinds of light in the forms of *lux* and *lumen* discussed in Chapter 5, the way we think of the knowledge afforded by sight is also contradictory. The blind person may be perceived as at a physical disadvantage, but the potential spiritual advantage is in the immunity from the distractions and visual chaos of "worldly" existence. This has value in religious discourse as well as in modern philosophy which Jay says has increasingly come to denigrate vision (1993). As he says "often the third eye of the soul is invoked to compensate for the imperfection of the two physical eyes. Often physical blindness is given sacred significance" (1993: 12). Paulsen (1987) traces this back to Brueghel's 1568 painting *The Blind Leading the Blind*, and to an 1856 literary reference to the idea that a superior second sight is signified by the blank gaze and upturned face (1987: 205). He appears to see, but he does not focus. The logical conclusion is therefore that he sees something we do not. The blank, upturned gaze can be seen in images of transcendence, from the musician's performance of being "lost in music" (like Stevie Wonder) to the raver's ecstasy-induced "trance"; "blindness" can go beyond the superior detachment also implied in the aristocratic ethic, into a realm of knowledge accessible only to the few—possibly only to those denied conventional vision. The poet, intellectual, or artist can be viewed in this way as well as the guru; Paulsen cites Balzac's description of one of his characters (Lambert): "in the dark chamber of his interior sight, the textual order of signs replaces the spatial order of sight, only to produce the impression of a clearer and more intense sight than that of the eyes" (1987: 143).

The definition of "hip," a word sometimes used in close conjunction with cool from the mid-twentieth century—is "wise or knowing," about things unknown to "the square" (Macadams 2002); to those inside straight (often white) society. This, along with Sarah Thornton's conclusion that hip or cool is status through "subcultural capital" (1995: 207), confirms the relationship between cool and exclusive knowledges. This was seen in Chapter 4's discussion of *The Matrix*, where the dark glasses signify "raised consciousness." Hence, the tradition of the blind visionary may be mobilized through dark glasses to suggest a modern form of "second sight" which, through the associations with elite leisure and technology, could break free from the connotations of physical disability and dependence. This was clearly manifested in a fashion shoot "You can see clearly now" featuring desirable sports brands like Oakley and Porsche in *Line* (a men's magazine) in 1999, where Shiva Sadu males were used as models, linking hi-tech sports with the mystique of uncommon knowledge.

Night in the city

This idea of exclusive knowledge will be important later, but first we will consider the power play of light and vision in the city at night, for the control over light has long been an instrument of between its inhabitants and its governors. Night's blanket of blindness gives anyone with a light an obvious advantage, but in fact, *not* carrying a light—choosing to limit your vision—has sometimes been seen as the more powerful position. Schivelbusch states that in medieval times, "anyone who did not carry a light after dark was considered suspect and could immediately be arrested" (1995: 82). The light which lights your way, also lights *you* for the purposes of surveillance. Hence, reveling in darkness suggests delighting in subterfuge, disguise, and undisclosed intent. In medieval cities, at night the gates were locked, lanterns lit, and all good citizens expected to remain indoors until morning. Schivelbusch explains that the lights of the city were as much an instrument of rule and order as anything else, and were viewed as such by city inhabitants, causing them to be smashed in moments of uprising. Hence in Victor Hugo's novel *Les Misérables* "darkness is the counter-order of rebellion" (1995: 109).

In the vast and impersonal city, away from the "bright lights," darkness merges with tall, empty buildings to create loneliness, claustrophobia, and alienation. As Schivelbusch says, "social connections cease to exist in the dark" (1995: 221); and as Fer says "being lost in the night is an index of the modern subject's alienation." Night reveals "some unknown danger… beneath the veneer of modernity" (2007: 79). These ideas were explored in visual culture from Nadar and Brassai's photographic documentation of nocturnal Paris, its underground spaces, and the "demi-monde" (Fer 2007: 76), to the sad yet seductive paintings of Edward Hopper and 1940s film noir which aestheticized the antithesis of the "All American" dream.

Like the beach, night is a place for confusions and transformations of identity. In fairy-tales, for example Cinderella, night heralds magical transformation, a scene of that "second symbolic life" (Schivelbusch 1995: 138). The enchanting effect of light in the dark, whether by flames, candles, fireworks, or fairy lights, enables illusion. Peter Greenaway says that as soon as candles were available to the many "You could see the shadows and the glooms; you could in fact create them, engineering the lights and the half lights… reveal and obscure, emphasise and shade away and dramatise life like never before" (2007: 71). Schivelbusch claims "the power of artificial light to create its own reality is only revealed in the dark" (1995: 221). Brassai said that night-time Paris was "at its most alive, its most authentic" (1976). In the modern era, night (just like too much light) can be viewed as a confrontation with the least forgiving, harshest experience of urban life; or it can be viewed as a relief from modernity's pressures. As Peretti says: "The bright lights are a 'tonic light bath' for Poe's 'man of the crowd.' Everyday life is 'almost intolerable' so a great deal of New York nightlife is purely escape from New York" (2007: 19); an escape from the weight and relentless demands of industrialized life.

This allows the night-time wearing of sunglasses to suggest both a heroic relationship with the forces of modernity *and* an escape from a predetermined "role" to the freedoms to play with identity in a way that "feels" more "real." As with holiday clothing, night provides freedom from work (and work clothes), but perhaps the forgiving cover of night makes for more convincing illusions. The putting on of budget glamor, passing, or even cross-dressing, helped by the anonymity of night, is enhanced by the enchanting shadows which soften the distinctions between one thing and another, or the real and the fake.

Night is also strongly associated with sex, especially illicit sex. Brassai's 1930s Parisian demi-monde is packed with what he calls "night people," who belong to the world of "pleasure, of love, vice and drugs" … "pimps, whores… and inverts" [sic] (Brassai 1976). The abandonment of ordinary personal and sexual boundaries was easier in the dark, as Proust remarked in reference to the homosexual practice of meeting at night in Parisian "tearooms" (urinals) for anonymous sex (Brassai 1976). In New York, Peretti states that the presence of homosexuals and prostitutes was the most blatant indication that the night was a culturally alternate, liminal or inverted time (2007: 8). The strength of these associations can be seen in interpretations of night-time images. For example, the connotations of a lone female, photographed by Brassai in an unforgiving urban space, contrast sharply with those of a lone woman in a sunny, wholesome landscape (such as those photographed in the same decade by Louise Dahl-Wolfe). Day creates that sense of independence, strength, and freedom discussed previously. But a woman standing alone in a dark, urban street is more likely to be read as a victim, or as a "lady of the night."

According to Peretti, these associations were key to the growing notoriety and popularity of the urban New York club scene as it emerged in the 1920s. And for twentieth and twenty-first century urbanites, the notion of "nightlife" has added a different nuance to the connotations of the dark in general, which is significant to the concept of sunglasses as a "portable night." But the nightclub has of course also provided the specific context for many iconic images of cool shades.

Peretti says the nightclub became "an encapsulation of Americans' strongly ambivalent feelings about modern life" (2007: 6); not only in relation to changing sexual attitudes and leisure behaviors, but also to fear of crime. The ancient and superstitious idea of night as a time of evil, demons, and witches was mapped in the modern era on to the idea of the excluded, the criminal, or the feared "other."

At night, potential victims are off-guard, sleeping, or relaxing, and darkness facilitates stealth. Shading the eyes with a hat brim, or, later on, with dark glasses, was a barrier to recognition, which had the additional benefit of detaching the criminal from the victim. Brassai recalled the "extra flat cap worn down over the eyes" by members of the underworld, "as necessary for them as the gentleman's top-hat" (1976). He recounts a moment where he was attacked at knifepoint by a known mobster he had photographed, who, just before pulling the switchblade, pulled his cap down further over his forehead. Pearson (1983) describes the use of the peak as common to certain British turn-of-the-century, violent street gangs; "Hooligans," "Scuttlers," and "Peaky Blinders" were all identified with different cities, but all known for "a cap set rakishly forward, well over the eyes" (*Daily Graphic* 1900 in Pearson 1983: 288). As with the warrior, lack of concern for the victim is suggested by the shading of the eyes, exaggerating the power of the wearer.

The nightclub is identified as a locus of criminal glamor with gangsters, pimps, and drug dealers making an overt display of the "innovative" achievement of the goal of wealth; as did a well-known wearer of shades "Lucky Luciano." Criminal activity also took place in the clubs, making them spaces full of "risks for [the] gullible: (Peretti 2007: 9). Before the 1920s, dark glasses were used by some American poker players to prevent others reading their facial expression and gaining information about their response to their hand during the game (Harcombe-Cuff 1912: 637). The still facial expression, as I have already discussed, is a sign of inner resources or power, but the decision to *cover* a facial expression is slightly different, it always "reveals" the fact that the truth is being concealed. When worn out of the legitimate "functional" context (that is, outdoors in bright light), or combined with other cues, sunglasses therefore signify deceit; *the lie.*

In popular film, removing sunglasses has been used to signpost a moment of "sincere communication" (as in *Double Indemnity* (1944)), but it has also been used as a "double bluff" where the cue of removing the sunglasses "for sincerity" is used to manipulate and disarm (for example, in *The Matrix* 1999). This capacity to invoke the discourse of sincerity is central to the continued connection between sunglasses and dubious moral values hinted at in Chapter 1.

Peretti describes a kind of urban superiority which came from being wise to the trickery and risks of this attractive but dangerous nightlife (2007: 9), exaggerating the sense of risk abounding in the modern city. In the nightclub, where you rub shoulders with the underworld, these encounters are more fraught than usual, perhaps making the need for "protection" more acutely felt. As Peretti states, "almost every kind of club customer harboured some fear of losing face and lucre to con artists in a treacherous corner of nightlife" (2007: 9). Not attracting attention, looking unworried—maybe even trying to look like a smart poker player or gangster is in itself a form of protection and a display of nonchalance.

The visual and material qualities of the nightclub itself employed similar tactics. In the same way that dark glasses detach the wearer from their environment, the club carved out a secluded space within the urban night, with either no windows at all, or blacked-out windows, and overall they were "dark,

Figure 6.2   Barbara Stanwyck in *Double Indemnity* (1944).

closeted, and different." They aspired "to cut patrons off from the outside world" (Peretti 2007: 10).

Rituals of entry like code words and door staff highlighted the transgression of a boundary into a "different" space, especially during Prohibition. Together, these factors of detachment and self-exclusion seem to have enhanced their popularity and it continued to influence the design of clubs subsequently. That the nightclub itself was a protective barrier against dominant forces is apparent in Peretti's statement that a suitable place for a speakeasy was "any *enclosed area that might evade the gaze of law enforcement*" (2007: 10).

Another significant aspect of the nightclub was its role in the development of a scene that allowed white society to mix with the black urban population and begin the process of what Mercer has called "modern relations of interculturation" (Mercer in Gelder and Thornton 1997: 430). The clubs of Harlem and the likes of the Bal Negres and the Cabaine Cubaine in Paris (Brassai 1976) became very fashionable in the 1920s and 1930s, in fact Harlem became the center of New York's club scene, adding to the transgressive sensation.

Many clubs, certainly in New York, catered only for white people, but in black-run clubs white audiences were common, even more so once curious celebrities like Charlie Chaplin started to attend. In Paris, Brassai recalls elegant automobiles spilling out high society women desperate to dance with black men (1976). The Riviera set abandoned the elegance of parties and restaurants for the vibrancy and apparent authenticity of the new nightclub culture. Scott Fitzgerald explained, "we go because we prefer to rub shoulders with all sorts and kinds of people" (Peretti 2007: 12). Many members of the underworld and the elite and artistic/bohemian groupings became virtually nocturnal in this period; Brassai himself being one example, the Mayor of New York another. The status of participating in nightlife was contained in access to leisure time, expendable income, and in lack of concern for the bourgeois, protestant values of hard work, thrift, and sobriety. This blasé attitude could be afforded both by those who have much more than enough, but importantly, also by those who have little to lose.

The whole nightclub scene is "outside" of something, outside of "respectable" society (and therefore a fitting context in which to find dark glasses); but perhaps some are more outside than others. Peretti describes 1920s club interiors which traded in "racist representations" of African cultures and "jungle stereotypes." He says that this gave a "new face to the traditional identification of black people with private, covert, and illicit urges and behaviour" (2007: 19). The power relations in these clubs are complex and are important to my analysis because they exemplify some ideological associations between "people of color" and the idea of blackness, darkness, night, and nightlife, in a physical and historical space where cool became significantly linked with sunglasses, among jazz musicians.

Outsider cool; shades and jazz

According to Macadams (2002) and Pountain and Robins (2000), the origins of contemporary meanings of "cool" are located in the culture of the American jazz scene in the first half of the twentieth century. This coincides with the earliest examples of sunglasses being worn as part of a distinctive "look" in the nightclub setting. Jazz musicians were the first of many musical "subcultures" to use sunglasses as an expression of oppositional, outsider cool. Macadams describes a strong trajectory of connections in "cool" attitudes and values within bebop, beat, and the American avant-garde. The frequent use of the word "cool" as a term of approval in America is first seen within jazz, so it seems highly significant that jazz musicians should have been the innovators of the wearing of dark glasses when performing at night, and indoors. Jazz is also the location of an iconic connection between dark glasses and cool in the form of Miles' Davis 1957 album, "Birth of the Cool," the cover of which features an extremely dark photographic image of Davis playing in shades, although Macadams states that they were worn by Charlie Parker on stage in Hines' band in 1943 (and Dinerstein suggests this was a style borrowed from Lester Young (1999)). Macadams compares Charlie Parker to Dizzy Gillespie (also featured in the image), saying that they are at "opposite ends of the life-style spectrum. Gillespie is on Hines' extreme right, and looks earnest and clean cut. Parker, on the extreme left, is the only guy in the ensemble wearing dark glasses" (2002: 41). Gillespie is described by Macadams as having a stable family background and marriage, Parker as a heroin user (the "supreme junkie" of jazz) and sexually promiscuous, if not deviant (2002: 41).

Macadams makes a clear connection between the cool demeanor and illegal drug use. A significant number of jazz musicians on heroin described its effect as "cooling," but also adopted cool behavior while trying to score: "Junkies have to be cool, because junkies can't afford to attract attention. Everything has to be understated, circuitous, metaphorical, communicated in code. Loud voices are uncool. Hurried, overstated behaviour is "too frantic, Jim," as the junkies used to say" (Macadams 2002: 56). A connection between sunglasses and drug use begins here, through association with Parker and Davis. Sunglasses conceal the drug use by obscuring the visible evidence (the glazed expression, dilated pupils), but in doing so, ironically this *evidence* is replaced with a *legitimate* representation of a similar "glazed" expression, blankness. This has the potential to both conceal and suggest the engagement in illegal activity.

If to be cool is to be detached (from potentially threatening conditions, from the vulnerability of emotion, from the dominant culture) nothing expresses this as effectively as both the knowledge and pursuit of illegal drugs, and the transcendent state of being "high" when having scored. In fact Macadams cites

Clarence Major's tracing of the root of "cool" in the Mandingo word for high, "gone out." This connects with those ideas of spiritual transcendence, the blind seer, and sacred, exclusive knowledge discussed previously. In this context, and in a slippery way, dark glasses invoke a wealth of potential meanings pointing to superior detachment from the "ordinary world" and its rules.

While drug-use is quite often given as a reason for dark glasses being worn by jazzmen in anecdotal accounts, there is obvious potential here for sunglasses to have played a role in the negotiations of the unequal power relations between jazzmen, the club owners, and white audiences. However, before we explore some of these ideas I would like to think about jazz musicians as avant-garde artists, outsiders; rebels in Merton's terms.

A 1963 study by Howard S. Becker (1997) entitled "The culture of a deviant group: the 'jazz' musician" describes how musicians may become "isolated" or even "self-segregated" (1997: 62) from the rest of society—the hip (or even just "musician") versus the square. Becker downplays the issues of race and drugs, emphasizing instead the value of "the artistic individual" to the jazz musician (1997: 58). Becker's essay is obviously insufficient to fully explain cool and the wearing of dark glasses among black jazz musicians, but, based on interviews with jazzmen of the period, it provides some different historical reference points and makes connections with some aspects of dandyism as well as the avant-garde. For Becker (Gelder and Thornton 1997: 55) "unconventional" cultural values mark the jazzmen out as deviant (which perhaps aligns them most closely in Merton's terms with the rebel/retreatist artist) but importantly he situates their practice as artists within a "service occupation" (Gelder and Thornton 1997: 57). In service occupations, the worker "comes into more or less direct and personal contact with the ultimate consumer... of his work" (Gelder and Thornton 1997: 57). This means that often "the client is able to direct or attempt to direct the worker at his task and to apply sanctions of various kinds, ranging from informal pressure to the withdrawal of his patronage" (Gelder and Thornton 1997: 57). Becker says that people in service occupations tend to believe the clients incapable of judging the quality of their work, therefore they "bitterly resent" the clients' power, hence "defence against outside interference becomes a preoccupation ... and a subculture grows around this set of problems" (1997:5 7).

Becker interviewed both what he calls "jazzmen" and "commercial musicians." Although the commercial musicians are more prepared to bend to client demand, he demonstrates how both share a commitment to the ideal of the artist within jazz. Musical ability is seen as a "mysterious gift" which sets the artist apart from the other; this "sacred" gift should therefore render him "free from control by outsiders who lack it" (1997: 58). Even among jazz "colleagues" the strongest code prohibits interfering with another musician's work "on the job" (1997: 58). The aesthetics of jazz are individualistic, emphasizing improvised but skilful diversions which put the individual musician in control. However in the live performance within the club environment, "squares" in the audience ultimately have the power to pull the plug; as one musician said "Sure, they're a bunch of fucking squares, but who the fuck pays the bills?" (1997: 61). This tension seems to have been very real for Becker's interviewees. One of them defended his willingness to play commercial music by saying "at least… when you get off the stand, everybody in the place doesn't hate you" (1997: 61). This indicates the audience's resistance to the avant-garde, or at least the common differences in aesthetic values between musicians and audiences which have the potential to create antagonism.

Although Becker does not mention the wearing of dark glasses as a potential "involvement shield," he does describe some other attempts to isolate and "self-segregate:" "Musicians lacking the usually provided physical barriers [the platform or stand] often improvise their own and effectively segregate themselves from the audience" (1997: 63). One of his interviewees, Jerry, recalled shifting a piano at a wedding reception gig so it would cut him off from the audience. Asked by his colleague to move it, he refused, saying "No, man. I have to have some protection from the squares" (1997: 63).

Furthermore Becker found that:

> Many musicians almost reflexively avoid establishing contact with members of the audience. When walking among them, they habitually avoid meeting the eyes of the squares for fear this will establish some relationship on the basis of which the square will then request songs or in some other way attempt to influence the musical performance. (1997: 63)

Evidently the artistic independence of the performer is preserved by avoiding communication with the audience. Becker says "patterns of isolation and self-segregation" are expressed not only in the act of playing, but also in "the larger community" which "intensifies the musician's status as an outsider, through the operation of a cycle of increasing deviance" (1997: 63). The wearing of an accessory which enables detachment makes the "barrier" mobile—the portable barricade. At the same time (in a similar way as for the celebrity), it expresses the artistic "difference" or "specialness" of the musician which "deserves" protection.

The disdain for others of more "blunted sensibilities" inherent in aristocratic and dandy forms of cool is evident here, as is the detached spectatorship of the flâneur, a casual acceptance or blasé attitude toward anonymous others of all kinds in the audiences. Becker's respondents expressed wonder at the perspective they gained: "When you sit on that stand up there, you feel so different from others… you learn too much being a musician… you see so many things and get such a broad outlook on life…" (1997: 65). Expressions of tolerance *and* disgust were often concluded with a statement such as, "It don't mean a fucking thing to me. Every person's entitled to believe his own way, that's how I feel about it" (1997: 65). Just like the flâneur, the detachment of "the poet" can be seen as unshakeable superiority to, or acceptance of, the chaos of modern life. Thus, elements of jazzmen's cool derive from their status as artists in the modern world, courageously exploring the outer reaches of culture. As Baudelaire said of the dandy, they were marked by a special ability "to be away from home and yet to feel at home anywhere, to be at the very centre of the world and yet to be the unseen of the world" (1972: 400).

Black visibility and masculinity

When applied to the black male, the idea of the flâneur as "the unseen of the world" takes on an additional resonance, raising the signifying potential in both real acts of wearing dark glasses, and in representations of jazz. As already mentioned, black men and women were subjected to the white gaze in club spaces, and reproduced as spectacle, which fetishized the black body or demonized it, potentially reproducing gazes of ownership, dominance, fear, and desire. (This would be especially significant to black masculinity, since to be the object of the gaze is traditionally a feminine position.) Yet at the same time a common theme in writing about black experience is that of "invisibility." A novel of the period, Ralph Ellison's *Invisible Man* (1947) dramatizes this idea with the figure of a black man who lives underground, amid dazzling illuminations he has installed, hundreds of light bulbs powered by energy illegally tapped from "the corporation." This allegorical illustration of black experience suggests a rebellious retreat into a space where the world can be remade according to different rules, where visibility can be achieved. As Macadams puts it,

> like Shakespeare's Coriolanus telling those who would send him into exile, "I'll banish *you*. There is a world elsewhere", they traded their invisibility in the known world for the enhanced power of vision and exploration in an as yet undiscovered but more compelling world of their own invention. (2007: 46)

That sunglasses suggest a different kind of vision, as well as a "hidden" but "attractive" identity, connects here readily with the confounding of the gaze in a "refusal" to be seen and known. Although the political power of cool is contested by many—among them Frank, and Pountain and Robins—Mercer says that in the 1940s context "where blacks were excluded from… "democratic" representation," subversive style enabled a "sense of collectivity among a subaltern social block," and "encoded a refusal of passivity" (1987: 431).

Miles Davis, perhaps the jazzman most famous for wearing shades, is described by Gray as a "modern innovator in the aesthetics of music and in personal style" who "challenged dominant cultural assumptions about masculinity and whiteness" (1995: 401). Gray, who writes from a personal perspective, says that "for many of us, [he] articulated … a different way of knowing ourselves and seeing the world." He "explicitly rejected the reigning codes of propriety and place" (1995: 401). This would seem to be made explicit by the image of him in sunglasses; but the possible "cool" connotations of sunglasses on the black jazz musician are ambiguous and multi-layered.

The glasses favored by jazz musicians are all black—dense, black frames and lenses. When worn by the "dark-skinned," the signification of gleaming blackness is doubled, by layering more black on top of black. This has the potential to invoke the complexity of all I have explored about the meanings of night, blindness, blackness, and the nightclub. This intensifies the mystique of the "exotic body." Unlike the half-hearted grayness of photochromatic lenses worn indoors, which cast an unhealthy-looking shadow over poorly functioning eyes, black lenses are intense, uncompromising, and resolute. Pountain and Robins indicate that behind looks associated with cool there is often a tactic of exaggerating and highly stylizing the very things which are used to marginalize; "I make a virtue of what might exclude me" (1999: 8). Dark glasses make blackness gloriously and noticeably blacker. They make the "unseen" gloriously and noticeably invisible, and in the face of denied access to knowledge, they make the wearer gloriously and noticeably blind.

They also enable the black musician before a white audience to be both displayed and hidden, present and absent, which may offer a sense of protection from, or circumnavigation of, the problematics of being a black performer paid to entertain not just philistines or squares but in fact the people who oppress him. In Goffman's terms this could be seen as a form of "avoidance"—which he says is "the surest way for a person to prevent threats to his face" (2005: 64). He cannot avoid the context, but he can circumnavigate it. The resulting "absent presence" has a self-possessed mystique.

For in cutting yourself off from the other, you deny your need for them. By excluding yourself from the possibility of communication, there is an implication of self-sufficiency which it seems is ideally suited to the musical genre of jazz, allowing the dark glasses to function as a sign of a "jazz" sensibility which has a political, as well as an aesthetic, dimension. Jafa states:

> Classically, jazz improvisation is first and foremost signified self-determination... For the black artist to stand before an audience, often white, and to publicly demonstrate her (sic) decision-making capacity, her agency, rather than the replication of another's agency i.e. the composers, was a profoundly radical and dissonant gesture... There is no 'self-determination' without 'self-possession'. And 'self-possession' is the existential issue for black Americans. (Jafa in Tate 2003: 249)

We have already seen how wearing dark glasses could constitute an affront (for example in the analysis of the image of Mary Sykes) but this is given a more urgent expression in the live jazz context. Even between men of the same rank it is an affront, because it fails to offer the "open hand," to declare you have no "ill intent" toward them. It radically alters the balance of power in the exchange. As Goethe had said in 1830, a hundred years before the jazz musicians, to be the wearer of glasses in an exchange with another is to "penetrate my most sacred thoughts" and, with his "armed glances … destroy all fair equality between us" (Flick 1949: 29).

Dark glasses also impede your view—especially when worn in the dark—which gives an additional sense that what lies beyond the wearer may be of little interest to them. But it is the subordinate's role to care what the superior is doing and thinking, which of course the dark glasses disrupt, saying, "I am not really paying attention to you." So if there is already an assumption of hierarchy, this will be reversed. In his notes on deference and demeanor, Goffman points out that—"between superordinate and subordinate we may expect to find … the superordinate having the right to exercise certain familiarities which the subordinate is not allowed to reciprocate" (2005 [1967]: 64). The anti-gaze of the dark glasses, to an extent, blocks this right, enabling the musician to appear to comply while "insinuat[ing] all kinds of disregard" (2005 [1967]: 58). The refusal to follow the rules here is not dissimilar to the "frustration of the colonial gaze" presented by the veiled woman who Franz Fanon said "does not yield herself, does not give herself, does not offer herself" (Botz-Borstein 2013: online). For a black musician of the 1940s and 1950s to wear dark glasses was to refuse the interrogation of the white gaze, while simultaneously trading on and displaying the fetishized body, and inviting the taboo question of what the black man (or woman) behind the glasses might be thinking.

This again raises the connections between jazz and the intellectual avant-garde, where berets and glasses "signalled not only the musicians' personal rejection of their own all-too-recent rural roots, but an affinity with the European cultural avant-garde" (Macadams 2002: 45). The love affair between Miles Davis and Juliette Greco and meetings between Charlie Parker and Jean-Paul Sartre created a milieu in which both spectacles and dark glasses could also function as a signifier of the outsiderhood of the intellectual. In many ways, black musicians were responding to the conditions of modernity, which, for them, were frequently experienced in an exaggerated way, what Jafa calls "the unprecedented existential drama and complexity of the circumstance" requiring "new forms with which to embody new experiences" (Tate 2003: 249). The residual imagery of slavery in the popular imagination may connect black Americans with those "all too recent rural roots" but in fact, Coleman reminds us that "Slavery had been a preview to what it's like to be a machine" (Tate 2003: 74). Jazz has also been seen as a sophisticated, aesthetic response to modernity and technology (Dinerstein 2003).

Hence in images of black jazzmen, it is also important to acknowledge the wider meanings of sunglasses already discussed; the sign of status and achievement within modern capitalism. Associations with modernity, technology, speed, and glamor could function as evidence of distance from the "rural past," from the ideological association between blackness and "nature" and as evidence of having transcended the conditions of being "shut out of access to illusions of 'making it'" (Mercer 1997 [1987]: 431). The possibility of achieving significance in the modern world according to the *new* rules, to move from the position of atom to star, was all the more elusive for some and all the more significant.

Sunglasses and the Black Panther movement—the "counter-hegemonic gaze"

The use of dark glasses in imagery of the radical Black Nationalist group the Black Panthers suggests a more conscious strategy at work. In 1969, Black Panther Education Minister George Murray was photographed delivering a speech in dark glasses to university students by Stephen Shames.

Documentary images frequently show numerous members of the group wearing the same shades, including Kathleen Cleaver, along with black beret and military jacket. The Black Panthers were very aware of the power of the media and the need for strong, visual messages to promote their ideas and enhance their political presence. The graphic impact of dark glasses in print and their wealth of connotations meant that dark glasses in a newspaper or broadcast could instantly create curiosity. As an organized but unofficial political group, operating with violence outside the law, the shades (though very similar in design) take on a different significance from those of the jazz musician.

In Black Panther images the warrior/military significance of the glasses is mobilized by the presence of the gun, anchored by contextual knowledge of the group's willingness to use violence. The wearing of dark glasses also goes against the conventional necessity for political leaders to communicate sincerity or trustworthiness with an apparently open face. It seems the Black Panthers sacrifice the ability to communicate "openly" with the live audience in front of them, for a statement which is in fact aimed at the American audience at large, in a use of sunglasses which suggests Carter and Michael's "unhidden hidden gaze" (2004: 275). Political activists are defined by *intent* to do or change something, but the masking of the eyes states clearly that the Black Panthers

Figure 6.3 George Murray, Education Minister for The Black Panthers, addresses a rally of students in shades, 1969. (Photograph by Stephen Shames © Polaris.)

disallow their audience to fully read what that might be. For a group to do this en masse, in a uniform, indicates that this unknown intent is shared by the group (Carter's "communitas" gaze). It seems that this image consciously joins the fear of the modern warrior and the power of detachment from emotion to stereotypical fear of the black "other," with all the connotations of criminality and the "black beast" thrown in. Hughey's content analysis of the Black Panther newspaper indicates that what he calls the "counter-hegemonic gaze" was a major preoccupation of numerous articles, that there was a conscious effort to subvert the white patriarchal gaze "which tended to 'see' the black male as emasculated victim or monstrous, hypermasculine threat" (2009: online).

The other principle of the Black Panthers' approach to representation was the notion of self-determination. Hughey says they represented themselves as "industrious, productive, adaptable" and as "wielders of intellectual ideas" (2009: online), thus the established connotations of sunglasses were also of use to them. The recognition of black heritage, with an insistence on new forms of black identity seems also to have been the thinking behind the logo for a black arts movement begun in the 1960s called "Africobra," which featured a tribal mask with a pair of dark shades.

The "improvised" uniform (similarly to that of the early fighter pilots studied by Mentges) was unofficial, consisting of borrowed bits and pieces from other modes of dress. The choice to use shades demonstrates how, by the 1960s,

Figure 6.4   Flava Flav and Chuck D of Public Enemy, 1988. (Photograph by Kevin Cummins © Getty Images.)

dark sunglasses had accrued a complex range of meanings which had the capacity to suggest not only the general idea of detachment or transformation, but specifically where black people had come from (exclusion, demonization, stereotypes of darkness and night, pre-civilization), where they might wish to head (modernity, wealth, status, glamor, self-exclusion, or exclusiveness), and the heroic struggle or battle (connotations of military, armor) it would take to get there.

This continued to resonate through the latter decades of the twentieth century, and musical innovations like rap, hip-hop, and so on; Public Enemy, for example, made frequent visual references back to the Black Power movement, and bold and expressive sunglasses (for example Cazals) became a key aspect of a detached but deliberately "in your face" style for rap and hip-hop (see Morgado 2007).

The presence of sunglasses as a signifier of wealth and status in the "bling-bling" (their shiny lenses affording that all important sparkle or glint) of some 1990s hip-hop music videos (Murray 2004) demonstrated achievement against the odds but perhaps lent them additional connotations of a detachment toward women and an objectifying, voyeuristic gaze, where what "ought" to be a startling presence of pretty desperate "booty" very close at hand is met with blasé amusement. But the girls wear shades too—perhaps meeting (or not meeting) these gazes with similar knowing detachment.

The femme fatale

Indeed, another significant cultural figure in the construction of modern cool and its relationship with dark glasses is the femme fatale. Unlike the jazz musician or the black panther, there is no social "scene" or "ground" for the femme fatale — she is a product of fiction, and a lonely one, making it difficult to view her as in any way part of a "cool" subculture (in spite of the potential to see the femme fatale as a daughter of the powerful courtesans of the nineteenth century). She exists, in the flickering lights of the cinema projection, as the embodiment of the fear of female power in the modern world (Snyder 2001: 155). The femme fatale has been the focus of substantial critical attention, but she tends not to be recognized by those attempting to theorize cool per se. However, she is certainly an "innovator" in her substitution of means to reach the goals, and she displays a number of elements of the cool demeanor as we have considered it so far.

In film noir, the associations between the dark and the feminine occupy that space in opposition to healthy, democratic, bright modernity, making the femme fatale, too, a profoundly modern figure. The femme fatale's enduring attraction to audiences and critics alike also relates to her command of the activity of the eye. Laura Mulvey famously demonstrated the objectification of the female body for heterosexual male spectatorship in Hollywood cinema—but it has also long been acknowledged that the ability to draw the male gaze can be a source of power for female performers (Bruzzi 1997). The art of seduction has historically included the batting of eyelids, the fluttering of fans, the wearing of veils, and, as we have already seen, the wearing of masks. The appearance of Barbara Stanwyck in *Double Indemnity* (1944) in a pair of dark glasses in a supermarket is an early example of the use of shades to connote the "evil woman" in film. The associations with female sexuality and deviance are particularly strong in film noir and although "dark" uses of sunglasses do not occur much in film culture until the 1950s, the femme fatale's eye is frequently shaded, with either heavy lids, veils, long shiny fringes, hat brims, cigarette smoke, or the shade of venetian blinds. Masking the eyes could intensify the objectification of the female body, as suggested in Chapter 4, removing the woman's individuality. But in film noir, the woman is not passive enough to make this a preferred reading.

In *Double Indemnity*, Stanwyck's character uses sunglasses to attempt to "evade the gaze of the law;" the police are on her trail, but they also seem to feature as a signifier of her "inauthenticity" and "insincerity." Naremore describes the elements of manipulative masquerade in her appearance: "blatantly provocative and visibly artificial [with] lacquered lipstick, sunglasses and chromium hair';" "cheaply manufactured" (Snyder 2001: 159). In film noir, mirror shots abound, as Snyder says, functioning as a sign of duplicity and that "nothing is as it seems" (2001: 160), articulating anxieties about the potentially deceitful, cold charm of glamor (Gundle 2008; Wilson 2007).

Although these images are attractive, the shaded eyes of these women not only situate them in the grim alienation of the modern city at night, but in their refusal of the male gaze they resurrect the threat of castration to both the male "victim" within the film and the male film spectator. The femme fatale in sunglasses could potentially be seen as assuming the masculine position of the voyeur, since they deny certain emotional, vulnerable aspects of conventional femininity, and allow her to gaze undetected.

Discussions of the femme fatale have focused on the interpretation of her as a "woman." But it is interesting to consider her not only as a woman but also as a modern subject in relation to my discussion so far. She is virtually a machine (an idea rehearsed in *Bladerunner*, as discussed in Chapter 4) whose shaded eyes contribute to her cool in the senses of detachment, narcissism, and uncompromising style. Like the dandy, she is always polished, flawless, in clothing that speaks of a powerful ability to play the semiotic systems of fashion and glamor to create a convincing and impermeable image of self. Her modernity (again, going against the ascribed role for women to be guardians of tradition, hearth, and home (Sparke 1995)), is expressed through her ability to be blasé in the night spaces of the city, through independence and her competence with technology; since the femme fatale is frequently also armed with a gun.

The femme fatale is cool. She is a figure with a superior adaptation to certain challenging aspects of modernity. The mythic power of the femme fatale is in the seamless, detached mastering of contexts, relationships, and image within the modern environment and even outside of the law. She may be evil, and she may end up disgraced or even dead in order to uphold the law of the "good woman," but the value of cool is also upheld in these narratives, since her demise frequently occurs after a lethal "loss of cool"—becoming desperate, uncontrolled, emotionally overwrought—in the narrative's resolution. And this dangerous, rich, and complex mix of associations between the feminine, the masculine, the dark, the duplicitous, and the play of power within the alienation of the modern city can be economically conveyed in an image of a woman's shaded eyes. Her covered eyes frequently "express" pathological emotional detachment from "the act," as in *Leave Her to Heaven* (1945), where the femme fatale watches expressionless as she allows a small boy to drown in an "accident" she has engineered. A slightly different example might be in a neo-noir film like *Nikita* (1990), where Nikita's newly discovered emotional sensitivity must be masked from herself in order to fulfill her life-or-death obligation to act as an assassin. The femme fatale type in dark glasses has become a potent and enduring image of popular culture, advertising, and fashion; a sign of the powerful modern woman whose sexuality and ambition is not tamed by tender concern for others or conventional morals, and who uses glamor as a weapon to achieve her goals.

The extent to which sunglasses, by the early 1960s, could indicate a particular kind of sexualized femininity is also evidenced by the presence of sunglasses in the Lolita stereotype deriving from the film directed by Stanley Kubrick in 1962. Originally written by Nabokov and first published in America in 1958, the book, and its original cover, refrained from defining the appearance of the young girl in terms of any shared cultural codes of attractiveness, sexuality, or seductive power, and apparently this was Nabokov's express intent, since he was "not in the business of objective sexualisation" (Vickers 2008: 8). Kubrick's film, however, places Lolita herself far more squarely in the role of "fille fatale" (Hatch 2002); it was "her fault."

In Kubrick's film, Lolita wears sunglasses, which can be used to underpin her complicity or guilt by suggesting the femme fatale's "evil seduction" but also her apparent independence and self-control.

Figure 6.5 Sue Lyon licks a lollipop in the promotional poster for the film *Lolita* (1962). (Photograph by Metro-Goldwyn-Mayer/Getty Images. Photographer Archive Photos/ Stringer © Getty Images.)

Carter derives the idea of the "fleeting partial gaze," discussed in Chapter 5, from the way she looks over the top of the glasses, inviting the viewer in beyond the barrier of the glasses which work here as a metaphor for the possibility of transgressing the boundaries of the body. By the aesthetic of the appearance and disappearance of her eyes, Lolita gains Humbert's erotic gaze and beckons him to cross the threshold.

The film poster, photographed by Bert Stern 1962, adds a further layer of meaning to the image of Lolita in sunglasses—as Vickers says, his image is "an entirely bogus Lolita" (Vickers 2008: 8); her sunglasses are now heart-shaped and she suggestively licks a red lollipop. The connotations of the femme fatale merge with both the "cheap and tawdry;" the demonic, and notions of narcissistic, girlish pop culture—love hearts, dressing up and sweetie-eating, in an image with the memorable intensity of the quintessential pop image—red, shiny, close up. Like adverts, film posters are forced to reduce an epic voyage to a schematic map and an anchor; and doing so, this iconic image marks the emergence of sunglasses in the early 1960s as a visual sign of a precocious and potentially dangerous female sexuality, which also displays the cool of the nonchalant disregard for rules and traditional virtues suggested by frivolous sunglass forms in a complex and ambiguous layering of meaning.

Summary—outsider cool

I have necessarily focused here on a small range of examples, but enough to demonstrate how dark glasses became associated with a whole range of dark and "outsider" values with the potential to be read as heroic, from blindness, to black identity, to the avant-garde artist, the political activist, the criminal, and the femme fatale. These associations all developed roughly simultaneously with those of elite glamor, democratic leisure, and healthy modernity, moving from lighter frames and more feminine forms to the double dark of frames and lenses which became the iconic look of the 1950s and 1960s, perhaps even a type-form for sunglasses post war.

Cool as a conscious, politicized stance was seen in the self-presentation of the Black Panther movement. But comparing the cool traits previously explored with Merton's taxonomy of adaptations to anomie suggests that cool might be a useful adaptation for *anyone* in modern society who might feel that the goals and means provided do not match up.

The association between cool and violence, crime, deceit, and narcissism is evident in many of these images of shaded eyes, necessarily "glamorizing" these traits and behaviors. This has been seen as problematic by some of those studying cool as an attractive and persuasive force in modern life, suggesting that cool is at best impotent to change anything and at worst destructive and anti-social (Majors and Billson 1992). But Merton's point about the appeal of the "retreatist" in cultural representations hints at the possibility that it is not necessarily the power of violence, deceit, and self-love which is at the heart of the attraction of cool. Instead, it is the ability to successfully manage modernity, to somehow transcend the insignificance and instability of atomized existence.

In the next chapter I will consider this in more detail, looking at the intensification of the risks and instabilities of modern life as a justification for the increasing signifying potency of sunglasses and the increasing applicability of the contemporary cool demeanor to ever-widening sections of modern society.

7

HEADING FOR THE SHADE—THE SPREAD OF OUTSIDER COOL (1950s–PRESENT)

Introduction—sunglasses and outsider cool in the mainstream

Sunglasses were tactically used by people who were "outside" the goals and means of dominant society, as part of an articulation of a dissonant style which held an attraction just as great as that of those sunny images of "straight" success and leisure. This chapter will show how the more complex connotations of "outsider cool" became desirable and were appropriated by the "mainstream" in the 1950s and 1960s and beyond. Sunglasses could act as a sign of a "bettered self"—but they also started to signify a glamorously "battered" mode of existence, functioning as a barricade, the shade offered a kind of self-imposed exile, eyes perhaps as "downcast" as disdainful.

Macadams' history of cool quips that in the late 1950s and early 1960s, "hipsters" donned dark glasses not in the face of the bright sun of leisure and success, nor in the face of white patriarchal oppression, but "against the nuclear flash" (2002: 185). This brief remark highlights a more general anxiety, dissent, rebellion, and retreat key to the meanings of sunglasses since the Second World War. Indeed, by the end of the twentieth century, sunglasses were featuring in advertising as a sign of anxiety and exposure to risk, coinciding with increasing knowledge of the health risks of sunbathing, bringing latent connotations of darkness and death to the fore.

The outlook suggested by sunglasses here is bleaker. Here the "atom" is faced with the bomb, together with a more general sense of the self being "under siege," to quote Christopher Lasch (1984). The challenges brought by modernity are so extreme that sunglasses function less as brave, battle-ready armor, and more as barricade in a late or postmodern intensification of threats to mind and body. However, something of the heroic and the glamorous remains in these images as we shall see.

Specifically, this chapter will begin by looking at the appropriation of black jazz style and the sartorial codes of the "beat" and "beatnik" who employed sunglasses as an expression of dissent, which influenced subsequent subcultures and mainstream culture, as cool got co-opted in marketing after the 1960s. It will draw on Goffman's theory of "composure," and a variety of theories linked to broad questions of identity and risk which shed further light on the expansion and subtlety of cool in the latter decades of the twentieth century which made sunglasses such a useful, seductive, and widely-resonating symbol.

Post-war appropriation of black style

The appropriation of black style is a very evident and controversial aspect of twentieth century fashion history of which sunglasses are just a small part. The fetishization of blackness and black culture has been evident in the last two chapters; a fascination with "otherness" which might suggest the urban "interculturation" that informed the avant-garde, but which frequently also reproduced racist power relations. Beat writer Jack Kerouac remembers "wishing I were a negro, feeling that the best the white world had offered was not enough ecstasy for me, not enough life, joy, kicks, darkness, music. Not enough night" (Macadams 2002: 202). Dark glasses could be suggestive of this ecstatic night, of desire to be in that world, *their* world, rather than this world. Mailer's essay "The White Negro" (1957) is frequently cited as an example of this fascination with black cool. Dark glasses at night were a hallmark of the jazzman, and they did indeed go on to be a key signifier of beat style or the "beatnik" (Welters and Cunningham 2005).

The desire to appropriate black style has been motivated by different things — perhaps white, western culture has "lost" certain qualities which it identifies in black culture (such as spontaneity, pleasure, authenticity). Black culture's innovations could also be seen as superior, more original, and, therefore, another resource for white people to exploit. Cultural codes developed in the context of black experience have often been adopted as superficially "cool style" — Tate's book claims white culture has taken *Everything but the Burden* (2003).

Macadams demonstrates how black jazzmen like Davis and Gillespie got into the culture of the avant-garde intellectual, and how members of the white avant-garde might recognize admirable characteristics in jazz and align themselves more comfortably with the "unseen of the world" than the conformists or the ritualists of Merton's taxonomy (discussed in Chapter 6), or the "faceless strivers" (2002: 82). The 1959 off-Broadway play *the Connection* specifically addressed the idea of cool as a desirable attribute, displayed first by the black characters, then admired, and emulated by the whites. The poster for the play—which in this period may well have suggested a taboo "connection" between black and white—shows a black figure in the foreground, silhouetted in dark shades, with a white figure close behind in the same posture, his eyes in shadow. The play hinged around illegal drugs, and as heavy drug-use was common to both the jazz scene and the mostly white, avant-garde "beats," many drug-related nuances of cool and justifications for wearing sunglasses resonate. According to Larry Lypton in his 1959 beat generation novel, beats wore dark glasses because "light hurts the eyes if you are a pot-head" (Welters and Cunningham 2005: 161).

The beat generation; beat cool and sunglasses as sign of beatnik style

The beats had additional reasons to feel an affinity with "outsiderhood;" both Alan Ginsberg and William Burroughs were gay, beats often had alternative political and religious ideas, some experimented with Zen Buddhism, which Macadams says suited them as it was "indifferent to privilege, dogma, and attachment, in but not of the world" (2002: 180). Sunglasses could suggest depth and spirituality, as well as wiseness (or hipness) to the specific subcultural knowledge or to the modern world more generally, and a desire to cut yourself off, to refuse that game.

What beats wore, and the mood their clothing expressed, has been discussed in some detail by Welters (2005). Beats admired the style of jazzmen—Kerouac describes one hipster's clothing as worn in such a precise way as to invoke "exact sharpness and coolness" (Welters 2005: 152). But the beats seem to have had less conviction about maintaining this sharp exterior, preferring old, worn, casual clothing. This image began to emerge in the late 1940s, coexisting with the hipster style, but not deriving from it. What stands out in Welters' analysis is the idea of the clothing as "beaten," "worn out," "sad." This world-weariness connects with the sense of beat as "defeated," unwilling or unable to "make it"—up against the wall or going for broke (Charters 2001: 238). The beat context brings a complicated, "defeated" quality to sunglasses.

By 1950, Welters says the key elements of the beat wardrobe were in place; jeans, T-shirts (previously worn as underwear), horn-rimmed glasses, and dark glasses worn indoors (2005: 155). Black as a color is described in this context as "dark, dissident, different, a threat" (Breines in Welters 2005: 158).

Although Breines places black in opposition to the pastels and pearls of 1950s conventional femininity, black became a sign of the beat community's

Figure 7.1 "Beatniks" in shades, at favored hang-out, The Gaslight Café, Greenwich Village 1960. (Photograph by Fred W. McDarrah © Getty Images.)

opposition to mainstream society more generally. Dark glasses with black lenses signified a "dissident" outlook; a "darker" view. The generally unkempt look which accompanied the glasses suggested nonchalance toward proprietary and prevailing social rules of 1950s America; "I can't be bothered" to follow those rules, which "do not apply to me."

Broyard (1948) claimed dark glasses were worn "because the light offended [the] eyes" (Charters 2001: 45). Light here takes on the poetic meaning of unwanted or offensive surveillance. One striking photographic portrait of William Burroughs shows his face cast in a deep, diagonal shadow, also suggestive of a life "apart."

Sunglasses and the language of 1950s rebellion also connected in cinematic representations of teen rebels like *The Wild One* (1953) and *Rebel Without a Cause* (1955), films which also galvanized more widespread dissent among

American youth. Here the sunglasses are primarily connected to the outlaw and the motorcycle. These films helped to compound part of the beatnik style (Welters 2005: 164) as the outsider rebel of pop culture resonated with the beats in spite of being mainstream representations. Macadams says Burroughs was obsessed with "the self-sufficient image of the gun-slinging frontier man, the gangster" (2001: 112), for example. Beats consciously recognized black culture as superior in terms of "style and attitude," but equally there was a sense of admiration for other "outsider" types, which was felt not only by the avant-garde, but by the increasing number of people who were buying into the image of the cowboy, the gangster, even the femme fatale. As discussed in Chapter 6, Merton acknowledged the appeal of fictional characters who somehow manage to evade the rules of dominant society, which sunglasses might signify, but another highly attractive quality these "outsider" types demonstrate is exceptional "composure." Goffman's theory of composure is worth exploring in a bit more detail.

Cool and fatefulness

Goffman's fascinating essay "Where the Action Is" (1967) derives from observations of gamblers in the "outsider space" of Nevada casinos. The essay highlights certain special qualities associated with cool, found in those who engage in highly "fateful" (or risky) activities. First, he speaks of sensitivity to fatefulness becoming "blunted":

> When we look closely at the adaptation to life made by persons whose situation is constantly fateful, say that of professional gamblers or frontline soldiers, we find that aliveness to the consequences involved becomes blunted in a special way. (2005: 181)

Here Goffman connects the military with the gambler, but he goes on to include criminals, performers, professional sportspeople, "hustlers;" many types we have seen in previous chapters. Although mostly humans avoid danger, Goffman notes that some cannot avoid it or even seek it out, making a "practical gamble." Among these people, hierarchies develop based on the scale of fatefulness involved and the ability to manage it.

These activities are likely to excite anxiety, remorse, or disappointment (think of the bungled bank job, losing in a casino, the danger of the bullfight), all states Goffman noticed were carefully hidden by the performance of "composure:" "self-control, self-possession, or poise… a capacity to execute physical tasks (typically involving small muscle control) in a concerted, smooth, self-controlled fashion under fateful circumstances." He adds that composure also has "an affective side, the emotional control required in dealing with others" but concludes that the critical key is "physical control of the organs employed in discourse and gesture" (2005: 223–4). This can be critical in terms of betraying nerves and, therefore, a weak hand (in gambling, where we have already seen dark glasses used), or guilt (in the case of a criminal who must "act natural" when trying to escape from a crime scene or evade capture even when that "naturalness" slows them down), or a lack of talent (for a performer). You could consider the catwalk fashion show as one of these occasions, where the designer has gone out on a limb aesthetically, the models are implicated in it, all of their fates depending on the unpredictable reception of the clothes. Goffman notes it takes special levels of composure to be "under the observation of others while in an easily discredited role" (2005: 226). He also speaks of an "ability to contemplate abrupt change in fate—one's own and by extension, others'— without loss of emotional control, without becoming 'shook up'" (2005: 225) and the expression of this through "smooth movement" and dignity, which he defines as "bodily decorum in the face of costs, difficulties and imperative urges." To be composed is to be your own master (2005: 224). Critically, it is also considered by Goffman to be an index of character; "Evidence of marked capacity to maintain full self-control when the chips are down—whether exerted in regard to moral temptation or task performance—is a sign of strong character" (2005: 217). This connection between physical composure, management of "fatefulness," and strong character enables us to see more clearly the widespread attraction to the kind of cool often associated with outsiders and their frequently risky pursuits. These "risk managers" demonstrate "character" in the face of uncontrollable forces through "physical control of the organs employed in discourse and gesture" (2005: 217); the eyes being the supreme communicator (Botz-Borstein 2013: online).

Goffman briefly connects his points on composure with the new performance of cool in youth culture, which he realizes adds something "raffish" and "urban" to the traditional aristocratic ethic. In a footnote, he suggests that cool seems to be a defence not merely against involvement in "disruptive matters" but "involvement in anything at all—on the assumption that for those whose social position is vulnerable, any concern for anything can be misfortunate, indifference being the only defensible tack" (2005: 227). Goffman here acknowledges the potentially widespread value of this demeanor. Images of cool management of *specific* fateful events may be read as exemplars of ways of managing more *general* vulnerabilities; vulnerabilities which were perhaps becoming ever more apparent in the post-war context of potentially catastrophic scientific and technological advances, certainly to the beats.

Macadams said that dark glasses were worn for protection against the nuclear flash, but obviously this is a poetic suggestion. The dark glasses *stylized* doom, in an ironic rejection of the absurdly upbeat glow of the "American tan." Initially this style posed a political challenge; the early beat girl wardrobe prompted abuse from some on the basis that wearing black stockings almost certainly meant you were a communist (Welters 2005: 161). Macadams says that the beats exerted a worldwide influence; as "the shock troops in a cultural war that would continue for decades" (2002: 1801). But Welters also describes how the power of this symbolic dissent was defused. A cartoony stereotype emerged which enabled the beatniks to be ridiculed, and the style was subsumed into fashion—made commercial and offered for sale as a superficial image of "cool" without the underlying values of dissent. Sunglasses were part of this "rent-a-beatnik" get-up.

Beatnik cool was given a mass audience in *Funny Face* starring Audrey Hepburn (1957), where she hung out in black in cool Parisian nightclubs replete with crazy artists and intellectuals; and to some extent in *Breakfast at Tiffany's* (1961) which gave us the image of Hepburn in huge dark wayfarers which has proved irresistible to generations in its depiction of utter composure and vulnerability, reproduced endlessly on posters, accessories, and even furnishings.

Undoubtedly the "original" nuances of sunglasses as a sign of dissent are diffused and defused in these reproductions, following a similar trajectory to all subcultural styles. Some might argue, then, that the style is no longer "cool" in subcultural terms. But if, as Goffman says, the "socially vulnerable" might find "composure" a useful skill or a desirable trait, we might see the appeal of sunglasses as less a superficial novelty and more a symbolic form of protection against genuinely felt pressures affecting almost everyone, encouraging more of us to literally "head for the shades."

Sunglasses, identity, and risk in late modernity

Although in many ways post-war life has been relatively stable, authors note "background" anxieties based in the greater complexity of life and awareness of its potential disasters. Beck's theory of the *Risk Society* (1992) detailed the precarious interconnectedness of systems and processes that support industrialized societies, and the "generally invisible… often irreversible" (1992: 23) risks of the late modern era. Lasch, writing toward the end of the millennium, says people have "begun to prepare for the worst, sometimes by building fallout shelters [physical protection] …commonly by executing a kind of emotional retreat from the long-term commitments that presuppose a stable, secure and orderly world" (1984: 16). People are becoming more aware of what Nietzsche described long ago as "the uncanny social insecurity" of modernity. They understand that everything in our modern world is so interdependent that "to remove a single nail is to make the whole building tremble and collapse" (Frisby 1985: 31). Lasch identified a tendency toward "cosmic panic and futuristic desperation" (1984: 17), and a response to this characterized by "protective irony" and "emotional disengagement" (1984: 18). The nihilistic response of the dada dandies is perhaps echoed here on a much broader scale.

One particular "invisible, potentially irreversible" risk has created a new set of ideas around sunglasses—the threat of skin cancer. That most natural act, of walking out in the sun, feeling warm and happy—the source of health, well-being, modernity, and even glamor, was, by the 1990s, an invisible threat. Adverts of the 1920s showing bonnie babies playing happily in shafts of sunlight let in through glass claiming to let all the ultra violet rays through have been replaced by warnings to cover up, protect, seek shade. The traditional image of young children on the beach, seen in travel brochures, family photo albums, and so on had been the epitome of escape to nature; away from modern smog and humanity-sapping television. Parents are advised to provide children with sunglasses, hat, factor 50 sunblock, UV-proof body suit, and to "seek shade." A television advert for sun protection products (2006) depicted eerily still children's bodies on towels; their skin burnt a deep brown under a piercing, relentless sun. The advert received many complaints from parents upset by its suggestions of death. But now that sun exposure could mean death, in certain circumstances sunglasses could mean "holiday," "glamor," "protection," and "risk" all in one cool and profit-making package.

Sunglasses came to signify glamor, protection, and exposure to risk more generally. A 2003 advert for the Renault Mégane was especially blatant in its use of these ideas. Captioned "Stay Special," it featured a typically attractive, blonde woman, shielding her brow with her forearm as if from extreme heat or sunshine. Her eyes were closed, and her face expressionless, but graphic cross hairs of a gun positioned over her temple indicated that she was a potential victim. The languid pose, bare arms and loosely held shades suggested she was not fully prepared; not looking, nor braced. The text on the opposing page lists numerous intangible dangers she faced (for example, genetically modified foods, ultra violet rays), finally reminding us that there is a worse risk than this. Not a lone gunman, but a car crash that is someone else's fault. The emotive description of the Mégane's safety devices (including "anti-submarine" seats) reassures us that this risk could be reduced with a wise and stylish purchase. In the face of such risks, a *lesser* woman might decide not to drive at all. She is presented as cool, *because* she faces these risks.

Because sunglasses have so many positive connotations, including those of supreme emotional and physical composure, they can blur the distinction between the fearful (neurasthenic) and the heroic (blasé). In advertising especially, "negative" experiences can be suggested but with a positive gloss—an image of fear or grief could be simply depressing, but with a decent pair of shades, these states are romanticized, processed, and reshaped as eye-candy. A woman truly frightened of being shot or hurt in a car crash would not be appealing. The Renault ad (and others like it) brings together a strange mixture of fear and narcissism, in which the "self at risk" becomes aspirationally heroic in its ability to simply "stay beautiful" in the face of modernity's extreme pressures. Just like the hipster donning shades against the nuclear flash.

Another new layer of risk and set of potential meanings for sunglasses came from the growth of surveillance culture. Simmel and Benjamin noted the increase in the potential for "surveillance" in anonymous city streets, but toward the millennium, open plan offices, CCTV, speed cameras, webcams, and social networking sites intensified the sense of being watched and possibly recorded by potentially powerful, anonymous others. This is a subtle form of pressure, for as Rosen, author of *The Unwanted Gaze* notes "it is the uncertainty about whether or not we are being observed that forces us to lead more constricted lives and inhibits us from speaking and acting freely" (2000: 19). The panoptican works by giving the subject no option but to police him/herself in precisely this way, we internalize the all-seeing eyes, just like the Iraqis who surrendered to a flying eye in Virilio's illustration.

Again, this can relate to sunglasses in a number of ways. They can be worn in real life (along with a hoody or a baseball cap, perhaps) to mask identity where CCTV is operating. But they can also be worn—whether in real life or in imagery—to suggest the *idea* of evading surveillance. As hi-tech surveillance became a theme in popular culture around the end of the twentieth century, sunglasses became a handy signifier of it. Invasion of privacy might seem to be a negative thing, but to be observed by a hi-tech surveillance kit appears to be both frightening and somehow aspirational. Around the millennium, a protective aesthetic emerged in western fashion which repeatedly drew on the idea of the need to camouflage and protect, in the urban environment. One particularly striking image came from the branding for the British, mainstream, women's wear retailer Oasis. A model, alone in the urban night, was caught just slipping out of view in the grainy blue-gray monochrome of urban CCTV footage, a code familiar from news reports about missing or wanted persons. Of all the anonymous women caught by that camera, this one is significant. She is protected by a functional-looking coat, but clearly vulnerable; at least to the ultimate cool gaze of the mechanical, arbitrary voyeur. On every carrier bag and swing ticket, this image confirmed the glamor of being "at risk" of being seen.

Sunglasses and the mutable self

Perhaps the most pervasive risk to emerge from modernity though is the risk to a coherent sense of self. Where Simmel considered a "blasé or neurasthenic state" a likely consequence of modern life, writers of the postmodern era claim the increasing scale of psychic threat produces a generally defensive mentality. Lasch says "Everyday life becomes an exercise in survival... Under siege, the self contracts to a defensive core, armed against adversity. Emotional equilibrium demands a minimal self, not the imperial self of yesteryear" (Lasch 1984: 15). Besieged by instability and risk, retreat and detachment are necessary to survive. Rather than hoping for society to be improved, Lasch says people aim for a much more modest goal: to "hold one's own life together in the face of mounting pressures" (1984: 16), and this leads to a form of narcissism.

Consumer culture, encouraged by a "romantic ethic" which underpinned the pursuit of a more idealized self (Campbell 1987), fueled narcissism. Modernity made appearance more critical to identity. But Lasch's narcissism is motivated by the need to turn away from the uncontrollable complexities of the world "out there," again something sunglasses are ideally placed to signify.

In fact the whole issue of identity was becoming problematic in late or postmodernity; the self not merely flexible, but perhaps multiple or fragmented. For all the reflected glory of shades in the bright sun or flashbulbs of celebrity mecca, post-war images of celebrities in shades (usually hurrying, head down) also suggested identity crisis, disjuncture between public and private selves, or perhaps even embarrassment as the celebrity became less desirable through ageing, poor performances, or other "loss of cool." Contemporary celebrities know that the key to success is to keep their image moving—to mutate before the very eyes of their public. Since Madonna made "self-reinvention" and "multiple identities" a business strategy in the 1980s (Schwichtenberg 1993), just about every manufactured pop phenomenon does the same, and a significant industry of semiotically-skilled stylists and public relations professionals has evolved to support them. Madonna's performances were seen by some as suggestive of liberation and limitless potential, empowerment even; and compared with artists like Cindy Sherman, who made a spectacle of multiple versions of herself. Lady Gaga's changing image now rushes past seemingly at the speed of light (while she claims she was "born that way"), each new and more "extreme" look designed to fix the gaze of the paparazzi.

But, of course, it is not only celebrities who now experience multiple, mutable identity as the conditions of modernity have intensified. Fashion, consumer culture more generally, migration, education, advances in technology—in the last 20 years or so virtual culture has introduced a whole new arena for self-presentation, indeed a new scene of "micro" celebrity; while the sense of the self as potentially irrelevant and uninteresting expands and the gazes of others, wanted, unwanted, and unknown must be managed, both on and offline. The slipperiness of the self has indeed been a preoccupation of many late twentieth century writers and artists. Identity is now "liquid," contingent, and, therefore, subject to constant scrutiny and pressure. The freedom to aspire, to experiment with identity has become an imperative.

For Kenneth Gergen, author of *The Saturated Self* (1991), this is not solely a requirement of the fashion industry: "It is not the world of fashion that drives the customer... but the postmodern consumer who seeks means of 'being' in an ever-shifting multiplicity of social contexts" (1991: 155). We now habitually move between geographical locations for work, leisure, and family reasons, and inhabit family environments that may cross class, "race," cultural, and geographical boundaries.

Gergen describes a response to these conditions; "the pastiche personality, ... a social chameleon, constantly borrowing bits and pieces of identity from whatever sources are available and constructing them as useful or desirable in a given situation" (1991: 150). This is not merely a hybrid or fragmented self, but a departure from an authentic self altogether. People "manage" plural identities. Snyder calls this "high self-monitoring" (Gergen 1991: 154), adapting personality and demeanor to suit situations. The idea of sunglasses here merely reflecting back the viewer, suggesting a void, an absence of information—where the *greatest* revelations should be being made (i.e. in the eyes) makes it apparent that perhaps they are the ideal expression of the high, self-monitoring type, and the impossibility of an authentic self—identity as something you "put on," Zurchner says the "mutable self" is necessary to cope with the speed of cultural change, replacing the traditional goal of "stability of self (self as object)" with "change of self (self as process)" (Gergen 1991: 154). These are qualities which Gergen says might once have been condemned as "incoherence, superficiality, and deceit."

As we saw in Chapter 5, changes to identity and appearance have often been facilitated by sunglasses; all the artists/performers mentioned so far have used them, as did Claude Cahun, Samuel Fosso, and Nikki S. Lee; all artists whose work has been centered around the idea of a mutable self. A brief glance at Facebook or any other such site, reveals countless "selfies" of "ordinary" subjects hiding and showing themselves with sunglasses, some with multiple versions of the self (with sunglasses, without sunglasses, with the Lolita shades, with the hippy granny shades, with the reservoir dogs shades, and so on).

But my point here is how this fluidity, this background sense of the self as unstable, might impinge on consciousness in a way that adds to the symbolic potential of sunglasses. In a world of threat which strikes at the very coherence of existence, a thing which has the ability to suggest invulnerability, inner composure, and outer toughness has exceptionally wide potential resonance.

Gergen says we live a condition of widespread "multiphrenia;" "For every-thing we 'know to be true' about ourselves, other voices within us respond with doubt and even derision" (1991: 6). We also have less clear markers of success or well-being—survival is no longer enough. James says that media and consumer culture encourage a "maladaptive comparison" where those we compare ourselves to are unrealistic models, simulations perhaps (Pountain and Robins 2000: 152). Lasch says we all face "the danger of personal disinte-gration" (1984: 16). With this level of pressure on the self it is not surprising that it becomes a focus.

Narcissus gets bewitched by his reflection. Becoming enthralled to the illusion of the self, he can no longer see anything else. Literally, to show yourself wearing sunglasses in a profile picture implies concern about your appearance above communicating with others, or a desire to show a dandyish lack of concern for them as we have already seen. But equally, the "anti-gaze" of dark glasses (Carter and Michael 2004: 275) creates the effect that the wearer "does not want to know," as if the reflective interior surface of the lens were actually a comforting mirror, the exterior a "bullet proof" *barricade*.

In spite of Zurchner's belief in the value placed on mutability, a person who too readily and too wholeheartedly adopts trends is sometimes known as a "fashion victim." Not all rebrandings or celebrity reinventions work, because they are not "believable." So in fact, it is not only imperative to be capable of multiple adaptations, but to do this while upholding the notion of remaining somehow "true to yourself" or "self-possessed." This is the absolute essence of cool composure, also potentially expressed through the unflinching and resolute surface of the sunglass lens.

In this context it also pays to adopt an ironic stance, or at least an ambigu-ously detached relationship with the current choices, knowing they are always *temporary*.

Anti-mainstream cool

This mounting pressure on the self is something it was possible to be aware of, and to detach yourself from, in another articulation of cool. To some extent we could read beat culture in this way. In fact, as Thomas Frank's book *The Conquest of Cool* (1997) demonstrates, by the 1960s, "consumers" were becoming increasingly mistrustful of the onslaught on the sense of self created by modern advertising and the weight of corporate power. For Frank, hip and cool are defined primarily in the sense of being against the "establishment," against consumer culture, against the corporate, against the puritan. One of the reasons for the spread of cool as an attitude and as a desirable attribute was a growing awareness of the extent to which consumers were being manipulated and exploited by advertisers, as a beat or bohemian attitude informed a counter-culture in America which, taking a variety of forms, set to do battle with the corporations and mainstream values more generally. Cool here is a refusal of commercial culture, and consumer values. Numerous rebellious subcultures made a sartorial virtue of "not having the right stuff"—from the beats to the hippies, and later punks and goths. In spite of sunglasses being an iconic product of fashion, Hollywood, and mass consumption, their capacity for displaying disdain, refusal, and composure made them very handy for any counter-cultural bricoleur. Hippies had their "granny specs" which placed tinted lenses inside old, wire-rimmed frames—the first style to strike a clear note of retrospection. Punks came back at them with "X-ray" specs, wayfarers, and wraparounds in intense, artificial colors.

Frank demonstrates how, in the 1960s and beyond, corporate America diffused the counter-cultural threat by incorporating the languages of rebellion (verbal, visual, and sartorial) into the marketing of mainstream products and brands. The techniques in marketing included: ironic self-deprecation, where the product is shown damaged or defiled; a tendency to mock consumer culture more generally, use of counter-cultural imagery (Frank 1997: 238); and reference to more general notions of outsiderhood and otherness—"nonconformity, escape, resistance, difference, carnival, and even deviance" (Frank 1997: 133). Cool tactics for cool consumers wise to the usual tricks of advertising. Marchand says that advertising in this period "counselled consumers on maintaining individuality and purpose in a time that sought to deny individuality" (Frank 1997: 133). Frank, writing in the late 1990s, suggests that contemporary marketing methods were being drawn from the template of this period, with a view to "transform alienation and despair into consent" (1997: 235). What Frank describes is an endless game of cat and mouse, which perhaps only highlights the pressures on identity that modernity and consumer culture have brought with them, pressure to survive and to forge identity that isn't (or doesn't feel as if it is) merely mass produced from materials of little value in exchange for your money. In this context sunglasses were again picked up, becoming a short-hand for a complex package of desirable attributes, even for the dissenter.

So, someone who feels at odds with mainstream consumer culture could use a pair of shades at this point to identify with the outsiders and to show disdain for "straight society." An advertiser could then use them to convey that idea, in order to circumnavigate objection and show that this is a product or brand which is also at odds with mainstream culture, and, therefore, a way for them to "escape" (symbolically of course).

A perfect example of the way sunglasses have been used to convey the kinds of cool discussed in this chapter is an advert for fashion brand Moschino from 1999. The advert depicted a serious, blacker-than-black portrait of something between the femme fatale, the androgynous beatnik, and the mafia widow—masked by big, black shades. Perfect, glossy, polished, and detached with no smile, and a fishnet veil. But a scrap of paper in the corner sent a provocative "unofficial" message, in tiny type, to deconstruct the image; "You watch too much fashion—protect your eyes." Is this "Moschino himself," telling us we consume too much? It would seem so. But as this was an advert, it would seem his antidote to this over consumption was… more consumption; but of the right kind of thing, *Moschino* things. This suggests a sophisticated awareness of the idea of fashion as a threat, and confidence that this was an ironic joke which viewers would get and be prepared to be complicit in.

But, in a single image, it also revealed sunglasses as both a symbol of consumer culture and of protection against it. With all of the complexities that sunglasses introduce to communication—the lie, the double bluff, the narcissistic anti-gaze, higher knowledge, and its strong connections with all American glamor, fashion, speed, and modernity more generally, it is no surprise that they became useful in such tricksy representations—whether in advertising or in counter or subcultures, or in the increasingly blurred zones in between.

Summary—cool as composure

This chapter has shown how, post-war, sunglasses became a sign of a complex oppositional attitude with wide applicability, as the narcissistic detachment of the outsider was becoming a model for increasing numbers of people affected by anomie, risk, and the "impossibility" of stable identity. From the beat subculture onwards, sunglasses made a stylish show of refusal and disdain for mainstream values.

The intensification of modernity's threatening conditions added a new urgency to the display of composure. A layer of anxiety and tragedy was added to the potential meanings of sunglasses in later or post-modern popular culture (aided by the tragic fates of so many of the cool outsider jazz and beat heroes listed in Macadams' book, whose shaded eyes did ultimately hint at death by overdose, suicide). Sunglasses as a *barricade* came to indicate not the desire to be immersed in modern light, but to head for the shade and "hunker down" in the terms of Lasch's minimal self. Indicative of this is the literal change in the meaning of sunglasses in the context of sunbathing—sun and sun-bathing as "health-giving" gave way under the evidence of connection between skin cancer and tanning, but also the wider risks associated with the destruction of the ozone layer, which previously helped to filter ultra violet light. This added a level of medical urgency to the wearing of sunglasses. In certain contexts, sunglasses now indicated an invisible, unknowable threat.

However, image-makers could then choose to mobilize the connotations of glamor, risk, or any of the other associations attributed to sunglasses to indicate the supreme status of remaining composed in the face of such fatefulness, or even to help create anxiety about risks which their product could glamorously help the purchaser to negotiate, as with the Renault advert.

This use of sunglasses to suggest risk in advertising could even extend to those risks to self presented by consumer culture and its constant demands, as in the Moschino advert. Frank showed how, from the 1960s, and recurring strongly again in the 1990s, signifiers of "outsider" cool were increasingly used in advertising to reach the growing numbers of people wise to marketing's aspirational dogma. Eventually, the detachment and ironic stance suggested by sunglasses became common currency, further blurring the distinctions between "inside" and "outside."

I will reflect on what this study means for how cool can be defined—and how it relates to "inside" and "outside"—in the conclusion. But this also raises the larger philosophical question of the vanity of visual information. Does any of it mean anything anymore beyond the surface appeal? Is it all just "postmodern play?" If nothing else, sunglasses are magnificently qualified to signify just that—a superficial, nihilistic, late- or post-modern form of consciousness, which we will explore in the next chapter via the iconic image of a blonde man in dark glasses.

8
SEEING IN THE "ECLIPSE"—SUNGLASSES, COOL, AND THE ABSENCE OF MEANING (LATE 1950s–PRESENT)

The light is artificial and mirrors are provided, but not windows,
because the characters must be protected from bleak, bruising reality.
(CECIL BEATON 1956: 62)

Introduction

So, who is the blonde man in dark glasses? Maybe it's Lady Gaga. If this chapter is going to deal with sunglasses as a sign of the empty signs and signifiers of postmodern culture, and a hollow, metallic form of glamorous cool, then surely she (s/he if you prefer) is the ultimate example. Much-discussed pop provocateur of the third millennium, strutting her multi-phrenic "camp" and "counter cultural" stuff, just as you might think sunglasses would have started to lose their currency, up she popped, reveling in shiny, plastic, surfaces both rigid and liquid. Gaga's myriad sunglasses (the smoking glasses, the video glasses, the Minnie mouse-eared glasses) take the lexicon of the meanings of sunglasses and scramble them at surreally high speed. They are the ultimate signifier of dandyish self-determination and a complex, fragmented or multiple identity. But perhaps they also have the power to signify the profound detachment and emptiness which has been a common critique of postmodern culture (and of some of the theories used to explain it).

However, Lady Gaga's provocations—and her pre-occupations—owe a lot to Andy Warhol, who perhaps presaged the present culture of hyperreal media and celebrity. In many ways Warhol's person and work exemplify another layer in the geology of the meaning of sunglasses. Not only is he an iconic and influential figure of the pop movement of the 1960s for whom sunglasses were a "trademark"—according to Bockris, he was even buried in them (1998: 492)—but the mythology of his work and life indicates a slightly different form of cool which is neither inside nor outside, neither (and *both*) "in the light" and "in the dark," yet high status.

The ability of sunglasses to convey both sets of meanings not only guaranteed their wide appeal and but also helped to perpetuate it, as we saw in Chapter 7. But Warhol's use of sunglasses adds something new; not the oppositional cool of the jazz musicians or the beats, or the blatant masking of ill intent in the femme fatale, but the *absence* of critique, emotion, indifference to all distinction between truth and lie, a glamorous absence and emptiness. This will be the focus of this chapter, first looking at how sunglasses contributed to Warhol's position "inside" or "outside" the dominant culture, his image and demeanor, then moving on to consider his artistic vision, how and what he "sees" through those dark glasses.

Finally, we will look for sunglasses which connote this glamorous absence in other areas of popular culture, bringing on or celebrating the "eclipse" of meaning. In an eclipse, a dark circle passes across the fiery planet, briefly producing a dazzling ring of light at its circumference, and a black hole where the sun once was. This condition of "dazzling darkness" seems like an apt metaphor for the final shade of cool I am arguing sunglasses have been used to suggest; intense, powerful, glamorous, and—perhaps—chillingly empty.

Inside or outside?

Warhol's relationship to the "mainstream" or dominant culture is complex. On the one hand he was utterly motivated by and attracted to celebrity; the bigger the better, as manifested by his obsession with Liz Taylor. He sought and achieved fame in the mass media, and in the upper echelons of New York society. On the other hand, his social world, status as an artist, and homosexuality, among other things, linked him inextricably with the cool of the outsider, "deviancy," the underground; bohemia.

Lower bohemia (its outer reaches) was, according to Koch, the breeding ground for Warhol's gang of "superstars;" the "more or less inspired outcast[s]… intensely romantic… [with] hopeful dreams and a narcissism of doom… interesting people who see themselves as excluded from everything desirable except their own forbidden ecstasies" (1991: xi–xii). Koch describes "upper bohemia" as the world of celebrity—that successful, glamorous elite which is condoned and celebrated by the "system" yet which is "outside" mainstream society.

Forging links between upper and lower bohemia was Warhol's "central social enterprise" in the 1960s (Koch 1991).

Warhol could also be seen as "excluded" from another "dominant culture"; that of the prevailing modern artists of the period, the Expressionists, who early on had dismissed Warhol as "mindless, decadent, dehumanised, the enemy of art" (Koch 1991: xii). Warhol's response was not to try to break in to any existing scene, but to create a new one which confounded categorization. Warhol refused to take "responsibility" for meaning. Koch claims that Expressionist criticisms of Warhol's work contained "a hint of protest against the insult to them obscurely felt in Andy's presence," believing that Warhol's work was an unspoken "snub" or a form of vengeance, "born in his passivity" against the serious art scene, and that this was "central to Warhol's entire strategy as an artist in the world" (Koch 1991: xii).

Warhol took issue with his exclusion from the "middle bohemia" of the serious art scene by exaggerating the criterion of his exclusion in a cool tactic similar to that of the black male's adoption of dark glasses. *If you say I am superficial, I will make myself gloriously and visibly superficial*. His love of "upper bohemia;" the rich, fast, narcissistic, famous, *successful* bohemians might almost have been calculated as a provocation. For Warhol the "real men" of art were just as vain; "not the vanity of fame but of opinion" (Koch 1991: xi). This is a "refusal to refuse"—if art was about saying no to things, Warhol made a virtue of saying an indifferent yes to everything; "all is pretty" (Koch 1991: xiv). If art was about "expression," Warhol made it simply about the surface.

Warhol's image

Warhol's own image also indicated these complex and perhaps dandyish positions. First, however enamored he was of Hollywood, he certainly wasn't wearing his sunglasses to facilitate a celebrity tan. Like the hipsters, he disliked light.

He was pale, with a sickly "subterranean pallor" which hinted at that underground cultural milieu. Key photographer of the period Nat Finkelstein reminisces about "tricking" Warhol into going out during the day, saying to Andy "Here, let's see what you do in the sunlight" (Finkelstein 1989). He was even nicknamed "Drella" by Lou Reed of the Velvet Underground, derived from "Cinderella" and "Dracula" (both of whom only get out at night).

Inside, however, Warhol's world was a celebration of the super-shiny, with artificial light exaggerated by reflective surfaces. The lights of the cine projector, the flashbulb, the mirror surrounded him. His hair was sprayed silver, or dyed bright blonde, and the walls of the Factory (his studio, business headquarters, and social space for his entourage) were silver; there were silver, helium-filled pillows, girls in mirrored dresses which spoke of modernity, technology, and the future. Finkelstein remembers "cellophane… glass… plastic-wrapped bodies," "showers of silver foil to deflect the radar," "speed and delirium, reflected light of aluminium foil stars" (1989). In one sense these lights are the lights of modern glamor, just like the glittering cafés, department stores, portrait studios of the early twentieth century. In another, these are categorically lights of fame and the mass media. In spite of Warhol's reputedly terrible skin, he himself is often described by people who were around him (such as Nat Finkelstein and Stephen Koch), as "glowing," "shining" like the sun, sometimes as a mirror. This calls to mind the dandy; indeed Cecil Beaton's photographs of 1920s dandy Stephen Tennant used foil backdrops and mirrored surfaces, a common theme in discussions of the dandy highlighting narcissism, the cold play of surface and self-invention (Millar 2003: 3–4).

Incorporating sunglasses made a "mirror"—albeit an obscure one—part of his face.

As a pop artist in the 1960s, Warhol was confronting the arrival of a truly mass and increasingly disposable visual culture in the west. As a cheap, plastic, widely consumed symbol of the pleasures of consumption and the modern world, sunglasses are an ideal pop signifier. Warhol's media were mechanized processes, allowing multiple reproductions, advancing the speed of production and famously suggestive of the "cheap" and the "mass" in both form and content, depicting "stuff" like coke and tinned soup. Sunglasses were a daily part of his self-presentation; a highly visible and reproducible complement to the white, side-parted hair, jeans, Breton stripes, and black jacket, incorporating certain elements of the beat/beatnik wardrobe. Warhol claimed not to be very interested in clothes (Warhol 1975), but this look is a versatile "trademark" with high tonal contrast and well-defined form which makes it memorable, and media friendly. In contrast to Warhol's natural eyes, sunglasses, like a cartoon, exaggerated the eyes, creating impact in print.

Warhol's unswerving pursuit of media attention is recalled by Finkelstein: "Andy would do anything for publicity… eat Danone yoghurt… fuck King Kong if it paid" (1989). Like Gaga today, Warhol used his own celebrity and that of others as subject matter, famously (and perhaps paradoxically) fusing the pursuit of art and fame. Many photographs of Andy Warhol featured in Nat Finklestein's book *Andy Warhol—the Factory Years* feature dark sunglasses, and very few show any facial expression. The numerous writers who have discussed his enigmatic and contradictory persona all note his "affectless gaze," Koch calling him the "tycoon of impassivity" (1991: 29). Many shots are "snapped," seemingly spontaneous; but many, especially those with the Velvet Underground, are posed with Warhol in shades, square to the camera, or side-on; deliberately "expressionless" in body as well as face. Often the flash bounces off the dark lenses, emphasizing their impenetrability. In one well-known image by Finkelstein, Warhol remains behind the other band members, not touching anyone, his stiff pose resembling a waxwork or mannequin, deliberately at odds with the (nevertheless cool) languid posture of the others.

At least once, Finkelstein deliberately used sunglasses to signify Warhol's detachment, in a picture with Bob Dylan at the Factory. Dylan only visited once, seemingly just to be photographed (as the Velvet Underground disliked him). Finkelstein was critical of the vanity of this staged meeting; "I suddenly flashed that these people were there only for my camera. They were sitting together, but their existence was predicated on being recorded" (1989). He seems to have used the shades as a means of visualizing this idea:

I … put the spots directly on them, obliterating all shadow and background… Did these people want exposure, boy, would I give them exposure: all the exposure that the floods [lights] would allow. I told Andy and Bobby to put on shades and look directly into the camera. I told Gerard to look at the side… None related to the other, and I shot them that way. (Finkelstein 1989)

Finkelstein damned them as "children of darkness, vivified by my lights" (1989)

The blank-faced square to camera pose, evident in Finkelstein's double portrait with a tambourine (1966), almost has a regal quality, suggestive of stamps, coins, and royal portraits, but also of criminal mug shots and passport photographs where recognition is all. As Carlyle said, dandies want to see and be seen and to be known for what they are—their own greatest invention. The dandy aspires simply to be "a visual object or thing that will reflect rays of light. Your silver or your gold… he solicits not; simply the glance of your eyes… [Do] but look at him and he is contented" (Carlyle in Millar 2003: 3–4). This is the anti-gaze. There is no hint of personality, no purposely "relaxed" demeanor, no musical instrument. Warhol's writings indicate a quirky sense of humour, charm, wisdom, and intelligence. But these images made no attempt to "express" Warhol's "personality." The glasses suggest, "I see nothing, I know nothing. Just look at me." The silver rings of the tambourine loom out of the darkness in the image, resembling the lights of a backstage mirror, the flames of a circus hoop, crown, or halo. Finkelstein selected that particular photograph as representative of the Factory years, saying "it says all about that period… Warhol in the spotlight, in the centre" (1989).

This image celebrates Warhol, but there is an evident emptiness about it, the eyes create those hollow sockets of the skull, drawing your eye into and away from them by virtue of high tonal contrast between the very light skin and the very dark frame and lens. The effect of doubling the image (two very similar photographs are placed side by side in Finkelstein's "double-portrait") is reminiscent of Warhol's own doubled or multiplied prints of iconic celebrity images—instant destruction of the "aura" of authenticity (Benjamin 1999) on the one hand, while proof of the superhuman presence of the reproduced image on the other.

Sunglasses signify the status or admirable personal qualities of the star, while refusing or denying those special qualities. It is all aesthetics. This was confirmed by Warhol when he provocatively sent *someone else* in his place on a lecture tour in 1967, appropriately decked out in leather jacket and sunglasses. He is quoted in a newspaper as having defended this action with the line "He was better than me" (Warhol Museum 2004: 134); the copy exceeding the original. The sunglasses were a cheeky prop in this knowing game of authenticity and inauthenticity, both the marker of authenticity and the cover-up for the lack therof.

Images of Warhol in shades also resonate with the idea of protection against modernity's onslaught on the senses. Indoors, surrounded by the business of the Factory and the intense artificial light, he appears empowered to be stoic in the midst of a man-made visual onslaught, compounded by being surrounded by artworks which themselves speak of the proliferation of attention-seeking graphics and imagery. The Velvet Underground literally demonstrated the same idea; they wore their sunglasses on stage—not, they claimed, because they were "trying to look cool," but because they were playing in a chaotic, hi-tech, visual environment; "We just played while everything raged around us without any control on our part" (Morrison in Bockris and Malanga 1983: 36). This included "blinding" light shows and Warhol's films projected onto and behind them. Their display of being blasé, unperturbed by this, again suggests that superior adaptation to the sensory demands of modernity and makes them look "cool." The influence of the Velvet Underground on the predominantly white, rock star image has been far-reaching, with generations of subsequent bands adopting a remarkably similar demeanor, look, and, of course, the very dark, often wraparound shades. The wearing of black accompanies this look, with its alluring associations of "night" and its denial of emotion, anchored by every low-key instrumentation and deadpan vocal delivery in the Velvet Underground's musical aesthetic.

Factory cool

The power of this "neo-stoic" composure, hinted at in the semi-regal posture, the lack of expression, the generally minimal behavior, has been commented on by biographers and scholars of Warhol's work. The Factory was in some way analogous to the royal court, with extremely subtle behaviors articulating a hierarchical system. The Factory was "open to anyone," according to Warhol (Warhol Museum 2004), but, as Koch remarks, Warhol was "the stilled surface of power... a reversed mirror of wanting" (1991: xvii). The eyes, instead of being active, expressive, and vulnerable become a "stilled surface," and the mutual gaze is transformed into "a reverse mirror" of power. La Bruyère, a courtier, expressed neatly the hierarchical significance of "open-ness of face," saying:

> Let a favourite observe himself very closely, for if he keeps me waiting less than usual… if his face is more open… if he listens to me more willingly or accompanies me further to the door, I shall think he is beginning to fall and I shall be right. (Mennell 1989: 85)

La Bruyère's comment demonstrates the importance of a cool demeanor in maintaining status, but also how subtle the articulations of power might be. In the Factory "When Warhol arrived, usually in the late afternoon, one's whole house of cards might fall if the master didn't smile his 'oh, hi' as he drifted by" (Koch 1991: 7).

But court life had a clear set of behavioral rituals and rules in comparison with the informality of the Factory, which seems to have added to Warhol's ability to evade and exert power with what was essentially a very slight presence. The Factory may have been a place where everyone was welcome, but no-one was specifically *welcomed*. People drifted in and out, took up residence, seemingly independently of Warhol's invitation. Warhol allowed it to go on around him, financed it, invisibly orchestrated it, but if they had not been invited, how would a visitor initially gain Warhol's attention? Fields, a Factory veteran, said, "If you weren't sure what was going on, it was very important to behave minimally, let other people wonder what was on your mind" (Macadams 2002: 42). It was not OK to assume that you were welcome, but perhaps also Field means that you had to create your own mystique to be deemed worthy of Warhol's attention. This would make sunglasses a useful prop in social environments where cool rules, as a way to weigh up the situation without being seen to be "needy," and to circumnavigate any embarrassing moments of unreciprocated eye contact.

Dandy Warhol

Warhol's ability to affect other people's status is another characteristic he shared with the dandy. He was self-made, not just from outside the aristocracy as the regency dandies were, but the son of a Polish, immigrant coal-miner. Koch describes the incredible power of Warhol's quiet arrival at a party, where, without any show of "entrance" the whole busy scene was instantly energized (Koch 1991: 21). This anecdote is virtually identical to Barbey d'Aureville's description of Beau Brummell's arrival at a society gathering (2002: 80).

However, unlike the dandies, Warhol worked, and he had money; but from a dandyish profession where individual style expressed through a variety of means was all. In a sense he was able to achieve more robust status because conditions allowed him to commodify the activities of the dandy, frequently through technological means. His image was not just perfected for social life and for print to function as publicity, he also sold it in portrait form, and his appearance at events was exchanged for money (even when it wasn't him).

In dandyism (as it had been with the cavalier), the impression of superiority was partly based on the appearance of effortlessness, another of those traits seemingly ubiquitous to cool. Warhol's stillness and lack of expression, as well as his low-key, "beat," sartorial style, indicated an unwillingness to make an effort. His artwork did the same. Finkelstein comments that Warhol had a very strong work ethic, but that "he hid this very carefully, creating the myth that his products just kinda (*sic*) appeared… He didn't want to get paint on his hands" (1983). Similarly, Koch reveals "it was a closely held secret…that he was a constant habitual reader of books; in fact, he was one of the best-read visual artists of his generation" (1991: xvii). The Warhol Museum holds some ephemera from his creative process, for example, hand-cut stencils used for the lettering on some of the soup cans (2004), which look strikingly earnest and earthy in contrast with the slick flatness of the finished prints, an almost touching visual equivalent of the secret notebooks used by dandies to practice and polish their "off-the-cuff" wit.

Final prints are (deliberately?) mis-registered (it takes a lot of effort to register a screen print without unintended gaps or overlaps); films use the most basic of techniques. Warhol does not push the media; he goes with it. As Koch says, "Warhol never, under any circumstance, tried" (1991: xvi). Photographs show him working in the studio, wearing his sunglasses, suggesting nonchalance toward his craft and detachment from his art. This apparent lack of effort makes the quality of the outcome all the more powerful a sign of excellence or personal style.

But there are some more significant differences to the dandy's demeanor. It would be hard to describe Warhol as displaying "sheer nerve" or "unconquerable self-assurance" (Burnett 1981: 52). Nor does anyone describe his eyes as "extraordinarily penetrating" (Lister in Walden 2002: 111). This would seem distinctly ardent in comparison to Warhol's cool. To affect a superior posture displays a confidence and a presence that seems too positive to be Warhol. It seems the regency dandy's occasional "glacial indifference," or the "calm and wandering gaze which … neither fixes itself nor will be fixed" (Lister in Walden 2002: 111) is likely to have been a deliberate performance of "ignoring," explicitly showing lack of respect. Warhol was just impassive, hardly there at all; you might not notice you were being ignored.

Warhol did have relationships with others but he was seemingly not keen on intimacy, using not only his sunglasses, but also the phone, his tape recorder, and Polaroid camera as what Koch calls "baffles" (tricky "involvement shields") in social situations; for example, if a conversation became intimate, he would get out his camera to take a portrait, cutting the emotion dead. The almost constant use of camera to snap social situations has now become fairly normal among users of mobile devices—perhaps we are all that bit more detached as a result. Warhol is quoted as saying, "I think once you see the emotions from a certain angle, you can never think of them as real again" (Warhol in Koch 1991: vi). Some writers suggest he had no empathy and no sense of responsibility, oscillating between vulnerable and childlike and monstrously inhumane (as Finkelstein said (1989) he was like a black widow spider "fucking them over, sucking them dry and spitting them out"). What connects these two extremes is the profound sense of detachment. Here the connotations of the soul-less, the "evil" resonate with how Warhol was often perceived. The sometimes tragic fates of the others within the Factory were "nothing to do with him."

This may seem extreme, but in wider society, emotions were seen as increasingly inconvenient to progress. Stearns says that by the 1960s, open emotionality could be a sign of "embarrassing vulnerability" (1994: 230); indeed of immaturity. (Emotions could be discussed, but that was preferably done in a detached and "unemotional" way.)

But Warhol's cool also connects directly with the idea of risk. Warhol said it was "too hard to care." Koch says Warhol was fearful to a point that was "scarcely credible" (1991: 26). Warhol's cool was not Goffman's composure, strong character shown by smooth movements in fateful situations (unlike the dandy), but the narcissism of Lasch's minimal self. Looking out at the spectacular Manhattan night, he said to Koch, "Think about everybody down there getting held up" (1991: 26). For all Warhol's ability to be seamlessly in tune with the modern world, he also displayed the neurasthenic tendencies of the overstimulated urban dweller, his sunglasses as much a shiny barricade as anything else. Koch links this state of mind to his art and his obsession with fame:

> [Warhol's] glamour is rooted in despair, meditating on the flesh, the murderous passage of time, the obliteration of the self, the unworkability of ordinary living. Against them he proposes the momentary glow of a presence, an image, anyone's, if only they can lap out of the fade-out of inexistence into the presence of the star. (1991: 12)

Warhol's shaded vision

So, Warhol's gaze in sunglasses can be perceived as the anti-gaze, but it is not *only* this. We know he sees something; he is an artist who records his observations and proposes something to look at, a "view of the world." How Warhol "sees," will shed further light on how sunglasses might be perceived in this context.

Many portraits of Warhol show him behind a camera, emphasizing the established idea of him as an observer, or operative of a mechanical eye. The commercial medium of screen print also created a distance between the "artist" and the "work." Koch identifies a defining paradox in Warhol's work; "the obsession… with human presence" which "he invariably renders as a cool velvety, immediate absence" (1991: 29). In the famous screen-printed portraits of Marilyn and Liz Taylor, the ink is thick, flat, and crisp-edged; both immediately arresting and uninformative. No trace of human gesture appears in the manipulation of paint, there is no attempt to "capture" something "within" the star, innumerable shades and tones of skin and hair are reduced to just a few colors. Kuspit locates Warhol's work in the discourse of the fragmented self: "Broadly speaking, Warhol's work symbolizes the postmodern rejection of the unconscious dynamics of the self… and its replacement by the idea that the self is a social construction." It is "a sphinx without a secret" (2005:35). Behind the enigmatic surface, there is nothing.

Koch says Warhol "is a way of looking at the world… a style that renders the presence of the real absent… that castrates the gaze" (1991: 30–1). Warhol's sunglasses obviously suggest this. Koch also says Warhol's gaze "dulls" the way human vision ordinarily darts about in order to perceive space. There is a neat conceptual rhyme here with the function of tinted lenses—which distance the viewer from the environment, evening contrasts and flattening space. Koch describes the movie camera as a "dead unblinking eye" and the way it is used in Warhol's films, to display a spectacle of stillness, as in *Sleep*. How can an eye that evidently looks (because it keeps a record of that looking) be described as "dead"? It can be described as dead because this is an eye that perceives without discernment, without an aspiration to knowledge; recall here Warhol's knowing assertion against the Expressionists that "All is pretty" (Koch 1991: xiv). Perhaps it perceives without discernment also because of the sheer volume of imagery, that compression of background and foreground in Schivelbusch's "panoramic perception" (1986).

Ultimately, the lack of confidence in knowledge implied by Warhol's glamorously blank vision, and the sunglasses which symbolize it, is perfectly captured by Michel Serres: "the eyes of the all-seeing God… have been transferred to the plumage of a peacock, where sight looks blankly on a world from which information has already fled" (Jay 1993: 593).

Beyond Warhol

Even at the time, Warhol's work was not alone in implicating sunglasses as a signifier of "ecliptic" cool. Jean-Luc Godard's 1959 film À *Bout de Souffle*

Figure 8.1   Kissing in shades: lovers in *À Bout de Souffle* (1959).

(*Breathless*) became renowned as the epitome of a new cinematic cool. In its highly stylized "light" treatment it has also been seen as a very early example of a "postmodern" aesthetic of play. The trailer featured a series of near stills, crudely introducing each character, and voiced over with a label; for example, "the nice man," "the cruel girl." Many of these little takes from the film show characters in sunglasses: "the little American girl," "the villain," "the novelist," "the photographer," which demonstrates the range of connotations for sunglasses at this point, but also invoking the discourses of play and disguise, what is meant and not meant which permeate the film. Sunglasses also appear as the voiceover states "lies," and, finally, "the devil in the flesh" as the two ambivalent lovers lay kissing, *both* in their sunglasses—negating the conventional notion that this act requires either an intensely emotional mutual gaze or eyes closed. Kissing in sunglasses is not easy—they are physically cool to be able to do it without clumsiness—but equally the sunglasses imply vanity, insincerity, a different kind of "devil in the flesh." The film is regarded both as a "trashy pastiche" of film noir and other American crime thrillers and as "the moment when self-consciousness dawned in the cinema" (Lucas 2007: 104).

   This playful self-consciousness is expressed in the constant putting on and taking off of the sunglasses, amidst light or heavy conversational remarks. They pose, gazing into mirrors, practicing their various "looks;" even down to

Belmondo looking imitatively into the face of Humphrey Bogart on a poster. The main characters are described as "jazzy, show-off kids… unimpressed, defiantly insolent," and ideas of emotional disengagement permeate the film. The dialogue is casual, and there is what Thompson describes as an "artful, cool dodging of any feeling or monumental embrace" (Thompson 2000: 29). Where strong emotions are referred to, for example, in Seberg's ambivalence toward Belmondo's love, a detached delivery and a thoughtful pose indicate that this is an intellectual rather than emotional dilemma, which allows her to project an enigmatic image. The idea that we might see these characters, these dilemmas, as anything other than entertaining poses is made ridiculous.

Quentin Tarantino's films of the 1990s and beyond provide another context in which sunglasses become symptomatic of problematic emptiness. Since *Reservoir Dogs* (1992), which featured the much-copied title sequence of gangsters nonchalantly walking en masse, looking sharp in black suits, ties, and sunglasses, Tarantino's work has invited speculation as to the complex moral universe of his films and the equally complex position the spectator is placed in, where the spectator's detached voyeurism is telegraphed and magnified, as extreme violence and death are often spectacular but "incidental." Tarantino himself is frequently depicted in promotional material in them, perhaps unsurprising for the subject of serious books titled *The Cinema of Cool* (Dawson 1995) and *Cool Men* (Fraimen 2003). Tarantino not only depicts and draws on the visual clichés of "outsiderhood" in his films (for example, with frequent references to the cool of the blaxploitation movies of the 1970s) he is also mythologized as a director with "geeky" characteristics—a former "loner in a video shop"—outside of the mainstream cool of American glamor. Slightly unconventional-looking, with

Figure 8.2 Quentin Tarantino as Mr Brown in *Reservoir Dogs* (1992).

a frantic, intelligent, and therefore "nerdy" speech (in the terms of pop culture), sunglasses do give Tarantino some of the outward signs of glamor, cool, and success, helping to justify his importance, while also invoking the questions surrounding his authorial intent or responsibility—which are frequently raised in relation to the "meaningless" violence in his films (Tarantino is also the subject of a book entitled *The Tarantinian Ethics* (Botting and Wilson 2001)). Given that Tarantino's work also emphasizes the performative nature of identity and indeed cool ("Let's get into character" says one of the gangsters before a "hit" in *Pulp Fiction* (1994)) sunglasses are deployed as a signifier of this as well as the infinite play of meaning in a world of "free-floating signs" in "rhizomatic" culture.

Distinctions between high, low, inside, and outside have been challenged by the innovations of postmodernism as well as the incorporation of the cool attitude, hence controversial photographers like Terry Richardson are now employed to create images to sell prestige brands like Tom Ford at Gucci, merging the aesthetics of pornography and advertising, suffusing the imagery with hard, cold glamor; detached and deflecting. In the campaign of 2008, sunglasses accompanied other trappings of the hedonistic lifestyle—champagne on ice and cigarettes—for a group of male and female models lying naked and near-naked in the sun, baring armpits and genitals. Their sunglasses enabled us to be voyeurs; suspecting their eyes are closed behind them, or at least, the sunglasses denied their singular personhood, objectifying them as mere bodies. Their almost hairless flesh was rendered as rigid, smooth, and glossy as the lenses of the sunglasses; ironically, *impenetrable*. Viewers of such an image may barely have batted an eyelid—we all know it does not literally mean that these models are porn-stars, nor that these products are for those who even believe porn is acceptable. It doesn't mean anything; it is "just an advert."

This recognition of how sunglasses might exemplify or signify a cultural condition of "emptiness" or "vanity" in some specific images raises a broader question as to whether we can read meaning in contemporary images of sunglasses at all. At this point we return to Lady Gaga—would a detailed analysis of one of her videos or some of her key looks tell us something about what sunglasses mean in pop culture today? Does any one of those images "matter?" Warhol might say not.

Lady Gaga's performance is also characterized by the shiny hardness of her surfaces: her own flesh, prosthetic shoulder blades, metal, plastic, leather, pvc, and, of course, the heavy usage of myriad forms and styles of sunglasses, which are frequently kept on during interviews. The emotion coded into the vocal performance and some of her utterances is consistently contrasted with bodily and sartorial codes of the mechanical. The occasional softening of voice, admission of vulnerability, and opening of the eyes is choreographed to be rapidly and seamlessly followed by the deadpan removal of access.

Figure 8.3 The tough reflective surface of Lady Gaga, at a party in
Toronto, 2009. (Photo by George Pimentel/WireImage © Getty Images/WireImage.)

Layer upon on layer of clothing, costume, make-up, prosthetics, and accessories are added and removed in a performance beyond the straight sexual purpose of burlesque (to create desire for her body). The content—the multiple references to outsider/avant-garde "heritage," to gender play, to machinery and technology, to media and to the vain workings of celebrity—are almost irrelevant. This could be read as a camp celebration of surface *as* substance; or it could be read as an extreme strategy to fix the blasé gazes of overstimulated audiences. Most of all, it is an irresistible display of narcissistic invulnerability.

Summary—ecliptic cool

This chapter has explored another shade of cool for sunglasses—described as the "ecliptic." Images of Andy Warhol and his artworks reveal qualities which go beyond those already considered in relation to modern, techno, "insider," or "outsider" cool, though certain elements of all can perhaps be seen, along with the emphasis on effortlessness and detachment common to so many articulations of "cool." Significant parallels with the dandy may be drawn, however his minimal and fearful behavior could in no way be described as an uncomplicated performance of unconquerable self-assurance (Burnett 1981), which brings the element of the neurasthenic and the tragic, making sunglasses as much a fearful barricade as proud and confident armor. Warhol's detachment was enhanced by almost constant use of other technological involvement shields (the camera, the phone), leading some to conclude that he was amoral, incapable of intimacy or empathy. Considering Warhol as "soulless" invokes the connotations of evil, absence, and death attached to sunglasses. Another defining quality of "ecliptic" cool is that absence of commitment to meaning or knowledge, an unwillingness to take responsibility for meaning.

Koch suggested that Warhol's glamor was "rooted in despair" (1991); a solution to loss of belief in old ways of knowing and feeling in the world. This "glamor" is the power of a cold, shiny, sumptuous surface. Michael Serres' illustration of the blind peacock with glamorous plumage indicates an abdication of the possibility of knowing which resonates with postmodernist notions that image is all there is.

Warhol, Godard, Tarantino, Richardson, Gaga—though different, all present sunglasses as a self-conscious sign of the vanity of the image. But in spite of the loss of literal meaning, the ethic of cool can be seen in them all. They act as metaphors for something sunglasses are happy to stand for—impenetrability, confidence, and composure—redemption through cool.

9
SUNGLASSES AND COOL—CONCLUSIONS

This chapter concludes the book, but it does not, of course, conclude the "story" of sunglasses. As we might expect from the current "mashed up" and "remixed" fashions of the past, present, and imagined futures, sunglasses are now stylistically "all over the place," these styles are used in earnest, in irony, avoided as a sign of "inauthenticity," selected and used to "authenticate" a look, worn by just about everyone (perhaps rejected by some who wish to avoid clichés of cool, but not as many as we might expect). A teenage T-shirt brand, David and Goliath, places two cute cartoon ice-cubes on a T-shirt. One with shades, one without. The first one says, "I'm cool." The one in the shades replies, "I'm cooler." Huge, black, Jackie O style glasses dominate the cover of a trend brochure for high fashion knit company Stoll entitled "Faux Real," alongside big power bouffants and deceptive knits masquerading as wovens. A 2010s brand of sunglasses, "Shwood," has replaced shiny plastic with the warmth and honesty of wood for their frames, in a minimal counter-attack to the glitzy shouting of the big brands. The wood used is alive with history, too, coming from eco-friendly forest clearances and barrels used to age artisanal whisky. The frames are classic, the lenses still dark—this is perhaps a new way for sunglasses to refuse the apparent superficiality of the dominant culture. Vintage sunglasses allow a whole range of potential for recontextualized and reconfigured meanings, as within steampunk or by kitsch jewelers Tatty Devine. For everything I have included, there are masses of interesting specific examples I have had to leave out. But I have tried to ensure that the themes and examples explored in each chapter, do add up to a comprehensive catalog of the principle ingredients in the meaning of sunglasses in popular culture, as they developed in the twentieth century, which are being "remixed" and "replayed" today.

Modernity, speed, and technology

Before sunglasses, certain changes were taking place which created an environment in which they could become functionally and symbolically useful. The city, as an exemplar of modern life, was a place of new opportunities for display, self-fashioning, and casual voyeurism, as well as new levels of sensory and psychological stimulation which threatened to swamp the individual, and from which some kind of protection was required. This initially came in the form of a "blasé attitude," and various behaviors designed to cut down on interactions with others. Culture was becoming increasingly visual and style increasingly powerful, as evidenced by the social success of the super-cool dandy. These changes created a world in which sunglasses could become a mass commodity, be useful as protection, as a display of style, and as a sign of an urbane ability to be unperturbed by modernity's challenges.

Although *sun*glasses did not appear in fashion images until well into the twentieth century (in the 1930s), a forerunner of sunglasses entered the European and American markets in the early twentieth century which made it into fashion images by the 1920s. "Goggles" for driving, cycling, and rail travel supplanted the connotations of weak sight attached to dark glasses with the status of engagement with the most advanced and exclusive forms of travel and leisure, as well as with speed. At the same time, speed created a new form of perception characterized by detachment from place, as everything became blurred. Sunglasses thus became a sign of the exhilarating power of modern mechanized speed, and the "cool" consciousness and controlled body required to engage with it, bringing a sometimes shocking sense of masculinity to early images of women in such goggles. Such images also hinted at the new rapidity of change in society generally, and in fashion specifically, adding to those pressures already felt in the modern environment and therefore, the value of unflinching eyes.

As a product of modern technology, goggles and sunglasses became a sign of the hi-tech body, and the technical rationality needed to work it. First World War fighter pilots, with their ugly goggles and laid-back superiority were a very early group to be dubbed "cool." For warriors, security forces, and competitive sportspeople, sunglasses could be an advantage, signifying to others a physical and mental superiority deriving from a lack of emotion, and hinting at support from the latest technologies.

Post-war, sunglasses were an ideal accessory for all kinds of popular representations of sub- and super-human creations—prosthetics, aliens, cyborgs, and robots—where they could visualize the enhanced knowledge and powers of the "future human," mask *inhuman* eyes, or hint at a cold, hi-tech heart inside, or even the "mechanised somnambulism" of "industrialised consciousness";

nuancing the human/machine binary in any number of ways. Ultimately sunglasses became a sign of involvement in modern speed and technology, and superior adaptation to those forces; emotional and physical preparedness, as well as the superior detachment facilitated by those technologies. An up-to-date pair of shades could then stand for a superior ability to adapt to change in the modern world more generally.

Light, dark, and shade

Modernity also brought with it a proliferation of natural and artificial light, and sunglasses, shedding their connotations of weakness, became a sign of life in that light, which operated as a metaphor for success within the promises of modernity. From the Riviera set getting a naughty tan in the 1920s, through to the jet set and the off-duty celebrities of Hollywood, by the 1930s, sunglasses were selling en masse as "sunglasses," and with the idea that they symbolized a fast, modern, glamorous life of ease, attractiveness, and significance, which, through the 1950s, became crystallized as a critical sign of celebrity, success, and the freedom to play with identity. Life in this particular "fast lane" involved further forms of detachment and exclusion well expressed by sunglasses: the rejection of traditional manners and styles, and politics (American casual set against European class), the "tourist gaze" which saw places as "mere backdrops," and the seductions of the inaccessible movie star and the star's attempt to hide from the unforgiving and relentless gaze of the public and the paparazzi. The sparkle of reflected light off glass and plastic also emerged as a sign of modernity and of a certain kind of glamorous cool which both attracts and deflects. Attracting the eye, it guarantees attention, but that attention is also held at bay by an aesthetic of impermeability.

However, at roughly the same time, meanings of sunglasses were being produced which majored not on their role as protector from light, but on their capacity to create instant dark. Associations of blindness, darkness, and night were mobilized especially when sunglasses were worn in the dark, as they were by black jazz musicians in the nightclubs of the early 1940s, a group credited with innovating the use of the word "cool" in the United States, and a major influence on the development of cool as an ethic. Here, sunglasses quietly communicated a defiant self-possession, disrupting the white, patriarchal gaze, as it continued to do for the Black Panther movement in the 1960s, also making suggestions of modernity, the avant-garde, and the military in a show of modern, black empowerment; a use of sunglasses which merged with connotations of glamor in "pimp" aesthetics and the aesthetics of hip-hop later in the century.

Gangsters in the urban, American nightclub also adopted sunglasses, as sunglasses became suggestive of the underground with its "shady" dealings.

Film noir in the 1940s picked up on this, and the fear of the modern woman, using sunglasses to indicate the femme fatale's monstrous artifice and the seductive power of her emotional control, going on to become a sign of "dangerous" female sexuality through their ability to manipulate—and frustrate—the male gaze.

Mid-century theorists of "deviance" identified various forms of detachment which demonstrate the "retreat," "rebellion," "innovation," and "self-segregation" which are survival tactics used by those excluded from succeeding "inside" straight society, including the avant-garde who create "an auxiliary set of values." This sense of stylish self-exclusion and alternative knowledge was neatly expressed by dark glasses in numerous music subcultures thereafter.

The adoption of black styles by white hipsters and the literary "beats" of 1950s America extended to their use of dark glasses, suggesting admiration for cool, black culture, and an "anomic" rejection of mainstream society and its values. The social and aesthetic connections between jazz and the beats were strong, and included a cool demeanor which derived from the use of illegal drugs—something which could initially be masked (and later hinted at) by the wearing of dark glasses. Some jazz musicians achieved fame and notoriety, making them models for others beyond their group, and beat(en) style and attitude also captured the imaginations of many others in that period. Sunglasses became a trademark of the retreat away from "doing the right thing" to "doing your own thing," and getting kicks while you could, in whatever way you could as increasing numbers of people became conscious that the "goals" they were set "did not match the means" provided. They became a badge of the "dark" worldview of the beatnik, rejecting traditional femininity, mainstream fashion, and consumer culture.

In this period, sunglasses' "deviant" connotations appealed not merely as novelty, and not necessarily out of desire to "be bad," but because the threatening conditions of modernity were intensifying. Increasing awareness of self as an atom—and of the bomb—made the supreme emotional and physical composure evident in the behavior of "those whose situation is constantly fateful" as Goffman put it, widely appealing. Shades helped to articulate generalized rebellion in Hollywood films like The Wild One (1953), giving an additional push to the role of sunglasses as a signifier of increasingly mainstream dissent.

In consciously stylizing a beaten world-weariness, dark glasses here ironically continued to suggest that these are the people really immersed in and facing up to modernity's challenges, and finding a way to seem on top of it.

Furthermore, in the decades which followed, sunglasses became a more literal sign of risk, as simultaneously, the pressures, complexities, and risks of modern life became more pervasive and far-reaching, as noted by Beck (1992). The threat of the bomb was one thing—but what about skin cancer? The ultimate, natural source of life and the sign of modern success was now something to turn away from. Sunglasses became a sign of a new, fearful retreat or barricade, and appeared in advertising as a sign that there is something out there to be afraid of. But again, they managed to turn this into a somehow desirable state of immersion in modernity, and, at any rate, a state which could be improved by buying whatever product it was pushing.

In the latter decades of the twentieth century the very notion of the self as potentially coherent or stable was breaking apart. Sunglasses here were liberators, facilitating the realization of a rainbow of selves, but also announcing the complex dandyish articulations of surface/depth, real/fake and truth/lie in such dress-up. But "Who could you be?" was also inevitably "Who should you be?;" hence, this freedom was also viewed as another layer of potential anxiety and pressure in the struggle to maintain a coherent identity—ironically making sunglasses something to retreat behind as well as show off in. And speaking of irony, in masking the "tone of voice" in our eyes—they could be a permanent get-out clause—I might not mean what I say. Here sunglasses could, by stilling those vulnerable, liquid pools, stand for a preparedness for an onslaught on the vulnerable human mind and body which derived from urban life, technology, and fashion to strike at the very possibility of knowing or possessing the self.

The final "shade" of cool for sunglasses is perhaps the bleakest, bringing together the coldest elements of cool from all the other shades and compacting them into one icy expression of a nihilistic absence of meaning. The work and persona of Andy Warhol defiantly stated that there was nothing behind the lenses. The cold push-me/pull-you attraction and deflection of glamor is not armor for the modern world, it is the only thing of value in it. This is the ultimate, narcissistic detachment from all responsibility for feeling, knowing, and acting. With sunglasses becoming iconic for directors like Godard and Tarantino, and performers like Lady Gaga, those associations have continued. The fear that possibly there is no meaning left in a world full of signs, a hall of mirrors, makes sunglasses here a sign of a postmodernist apocalypse, put to work in the stylization of millennial panic in pop culture at the end of century. In 2000, Alexander McQueen placed sunglasses on a skull, a now widely-copied motif combining the romantic, gothic sensibility with the superficial "icy butterflies" of glamor. Futile sovereign of a futile, *modern* world.

In luxury fashion branding, an aesthetic of tough gloss, rigid and uniformly smooth sheeny flesh, is accompanied by a death mask of blank shades which speaks of a total and utter impermeability. In all of these images, the literal meaning (of brains accidentally blasted out on the TV, or a simulated scene of gang rape advertising shirts) "means" nothing; *except* the celebration of that total detachment.

What comes through consistently in all of the research is how, in shading the eyes, sunglasses have the potential to articulate some of the most significant issues and widely experienced "problems" in modern culture: the relationship between seeing and knowing, the gaze and appearance, the struggle for survival and a coherent identity in mass society, rapid developments in technology and fashion. Sunglasses offer connotations both of immersion in the latest forms of modernity, and preparedness for its onslaught.

Analysis of images from such a range of cultural and historical contexts has also revealed a remarkable variety of meanings and functions for sunglasses which helps to explain their widespread and continued use: a masquerade, tough armor, neurasthenic barricade, castrator, blindfold, mirror, "death mask," screen, veil, magnet, and commodity fetish. The wearer of sunglasses could also be seen to represent a variety of modern types: the "star," basking in the glow of modern success; the alienated "atom" floating and anonymous in a city street; subcultural "style surfer," "cyborg," even Serres" blind (but glamorous) "peacock." This range of possible meanings and functions makes sunglasses ideally suited to visualize the conditions of modernity and the search for significance and status within it, whether seen as tragic or heroic. These conditions are enduring, intensifying, and widely shared. I think this is why, in spite of saturating all markets, sunglasses have retained their currency.

Since twentieth century culture has been highly visual, sunglasses' ability to nuance the gaze and visualize such a variety of "inner" states in an immediate way has made them an extremely useful tool for image makers of all kinds. Carter and Michaels" communitas gaze, anti-gaze, unhidden hidden gaze, fleeting partial gaze, Hughey's counter-hegemonic gaze, Urry's tourist gaze, the panoptic gaze, an ironic gaze—and perhaps more could be identified—are all highly economic visual expressions of attitude and power relations.

At the same time as communicating all of these states, in concluding we should not gloss over the obvious fact that these glasses (and their representations) are themselves a commodity. They could be seen as the ideal symbol of Thomas Franks" idea that if cool was once set against white patriarchy and capitalism, it has been colonized and conquered. In certain powerful contexts sunglasses may have been worn as a sign of real and urgent refusal or rebellion—but they may now "stand for" those refusals and rebellions which only involve the consumption of signs.

It is also quite important to stress that the categories explored in each of the chapters are frequently seen in combination. For example, Springer's analysis of cool in *The Matrix* (2005) prioritizes the way it presents a specifically black form of style and composure. A military "autocrat" like Qaddafi employed sunglasses as a sign of status and glamor as much as technical rationality, and wraparound sunglasses worn in the context of surfing combine the cool of speed, the bodily control and detached focus of the sportsperson, the hedonistic glamor of beach life, and the rebellion and retreat of a "deviant" subculture.

Modern cool

Considering sunglasses as a sign of cool opens up the "deep" significance of such a "superficial" object, but it also brings together, and perhaps extends, the definitions of cool in late twentieth/early twenty-first century popular culture.

Basing the study on sunglasses prompted a search for cool in a wider variety of places than have generally been studied for their coolness; it certainly involved considering seemingly quite disparate forms of cool together—connecting the European aristocrat with black politics, subcultural "street style" with polished celebrity glamor, the technical rationality of the cyborg, and the poise of the fashionista. The consistency of cool behaviors, attitudes, and aesthetics in these varied examples was remarkable and telling, as were the numerous connections with modernity. The broadest accounts of cool (Pountain and Robins 2000, Macadams 2002) focus on the influence of a cultural avant-garde, heavily influenced by black survival tactics. Frank sees it as a counter-cultural movement against capitalism (1997). Stearns (1994) sees cool as the change to emotional culture necessary to facilitate the smooth workings of modern society's systems and processes. Mentges' account focuses on cool as a form of heroic preparedness for the "culture of technical rationality" (2000). Can cool really be a "requirement" of and a "rebellion" against "dominant society"?

What draws all the examples I've looked at together, in spite of their different and sometimes seemingly opposed positions within culture, is the profound connection with the idea of a *superior adaptation to modernity*. The control of mind and body suggested by sunglasses in so many different modern contexts *demonstrates self-possession in the face of extreme encounter with modernity's challenges to the self*. This achievement is undoubtedly more difficult and therefore perhaps all the more heroic, for some. The cool culture of black Americans, for example, which holds such influence, and left such a great cultural legacy, has been forged in exceptionally challenging conditions.

Adaptation to modernity is a way of looking at cool which does not *depend* on rebellion against capitalism, or against white oppression and which manages to incorporate the ubiquitous connections with technology without primatizing it. Neither does it depend on the idea of simply "being in fashion," or "having the latest kit" (both popular understandings of "cool"). Being perceived as "on top" or "ahead of" trends in fashion or technology could indicate composure in the face of change; but so could a defiant display of indifference or opposition to such dictates (indeed the dynamic of fashion depends on someone "rejecting" what currently passes for "the latest thing"). Neither is it determined by a bleak, nihilistic, or ironic position. It can incorporate all of those things, but would not be dependent on any of them. And while cool may be a demeanor more readily adopted in youth, nor is this form of cool *dependent* on age, as some studies suggest. Competence in reading and wielding the precise signifiers of modern cool for "the people that matter" is obviously crucial (see Lui 2004); but these could be people of any age. What is not cool is to look (to the people that matter) as if you are running to catch up. Like the geek, to some extent the older person has that ability to demonstrate disdain for those other (in this case, younger) people who slavishly follow fashions or other rules perceived to be "dominant," or who lack certain knowledge.

Cool is also often viewed as an illusory and ineffective form of rebellion and self-possession, because adopting a "cool pose" and working the signifiers of cool does not change anything (Pountain and Robins 2000). In fact, the pursuit of cool can lead to profoundly anti-social and self-destructive behaviors (Majors and Billson 1992). As an aspirational model, perhaps images of cool tend to foster irresponsibility and narcissism. My conclusions do not necessarily contradict this theory but they do suggest that what attracts mass audiences to images which suggest cool, ironic nihilism, narcissism and "deviance," might rather be the fact that these are exaggerated and highly visible models of enviable composure in modernity.

Inhabitants of the late or postmodern world contend daily with the demands of technology and fashion, the anomic properties of a life lived increasingly alone in pursuit of increasingly unattainable goals, in an overwhelming sea of conflicting and often useless information, which also populates the back (if they are lucky, the forefront if they are not) of their minds with incalculable, irreversible risk. In this context, any person who can adapt to these conditions, while displaying composure, self-possession, and dignity, shows an enhanced capacity for survival which translates into prestige. The ability of sunglasses to suggest this composure is the base note of their appeal in popular culture.

Further studies

Looking at sunglasses and cool in this way has also raised a number of issues which I have not had space to elaborate on here but which are ripe for further investigation. There is obviously potential to perform numerous ethnographic studies which could offer a counterpoint of lived experience to the interpretations of images here; especially interesting might be an ethnography of sunglasses/goggles in competitive sport or at different lifestages. Another very obvious opportunity exists here in relation to sunglasses as a signifier in more specific contexts globally.

There are some other themes which kept bubbling to the surface in this study. The first is the relationship between gender and cool. Unconventional femininity was often marked by the way the gaze was blocked or enacted with sunglasses, but most often, studies of cool are focused on maleness and masculinity. Focusing on gender, sexuality, and cool could also provoke an investigation of camp. Another theme which might benefit from focused study is the relationship between glamor and the model of "modern cool" I am proposing. Perhaps a related question is how this model of cool intersects with theories of taste and fashion. There are also more general questions about materials, aesthetics, and cool.

Being uncool, including how to be cool

There are a lot of ways to be uncool with sunglasses in real life and in images. You have to be pretty cool to get it "right;" sunglasses are always part of those complex webs of signification in visual and material culture. The internet is awash with "uncool" sunglass images, some of them accompanied by labels and aphorisms mocking these perceived "errors of judgment."

The rejection of wearing sunglasses as an obvious "attempt" to be cool could be read into the trend for "geek" spectacles (recently widespread, but traceable back to Jarvis Cocker, Morrissey, Elvis Costelloe, Buddy Holly…). These are typically empty-frames or plain lenses, only partially invoking all those "uncool" connotations of weakness. But of course being uncool isn't necessarily uncool, because to reject rules perceived to be dominant, or to make a virtue of what might exclude you, indicates that detached self-possession and composure. This is why the term "uncool" is now sometimes used as a term of approval, and the specs with chunky frames have (naturally) become known on the internet as "hipster glasses." At the same time, T-shirts appear announcing to all with an ironic wink "I wear sunglasses at night"—the behavior currently deemed most genuinely uncool by those who make their opinions about such things felt in cyberspace. Other T-shirts appear stating "I was uncool before uncool was cool." As a signifier of cool with so many functions and reference points, sunglasses continue to be deployed in these battles.

But of course all these people are staking a claim for cool in the terms I have described here. Each makes a counter-attack on the ownership of cool, disdainfully stating, "I am beyond the reach of "your" rules, I am already one step ahead," just like every other cool group before it.

André Breton used the top hat to symbolize modernity, Fred Miller Robinson claims the bowler for the same job. If the position is vacant for late or postmodernity, sunglasses are surely in with a chance. In the digital age, we've placed yet more layers of glass and plastic between ourselves and the world with a multitude of screens and "windows" behind or beyond which we place images of ourselves in sunglasses. Perhaps when we look back, we'll see sunglasses as a symptom of—and a solution to—the problems of the twentieth century, the ultimate symbol of the age.

REFERENCES

Books

Acerenza, F. (1997) *Eyewear,* Chronicle Books, San Francisco.

Aperture. (1991) *Aperture no.122: The Idealising Vision,* Aperture Foundation, New York.

Ash, J. and Wilson, E. (1992) *Chic Thrills,* Pandora, London.

Augé, M. (1995) *The Non-Place,* Verso, London.

Baudelaire, C. (1964a) [1869], *Le Spleen de Paris,* Librairie Générale Française, Paris.

—(1964b) [1863] *The Painter of Modern Life and Other Essays,* Phaidon, London.

Baudelaire, C. (ed. and trans. Charvet, P. E.) (1972) *Selected Writings,* Penguin, Harmondsworth.

Baudrillard, J. (1988) *Selected Writings,* Polity Press, Cambridge.

Bauman, Z. (1992) *Intimations of Postmodernity,* Routledge, London.

Beck, U. (1992) *Risk Society: Towards a New Modernity,* Sage, London.

Benjamin, W. (1985) [1938] *Baudelaire,* Verso, London.

—(1999) *Illuminations,* Pimlico, London.

—(trans. Eilund, H. and McLaughlin, K.) (2002) [1927–40] *The Arcades Project,* Harvard University Press, London.

Berman, M. (1982) *All that is Solid Melts into Air,* Simon and Schuster, New York.

Bockris, V. (1998) *The Life and Death of Andy Warhol,* Fourth Estate, London.

Bockris, V. and Malanga, G. (1983) *Up-tight: The Velvet Underground Story,* Omnibus Press, London.

Botting, F. and Wilson, S. (2001) *The Tarantinian Ethics,* Sage, London.

Brassai. (1976) *The Secret Paris of the 1930s,* Pantheon, New York.

Braudy, L. (1986) *The Frenzy of Renown: Fame and its History,* Oxford University Press, Oxford.

Breward, C. (2003) *Fashion,* Oxford University Press, Oxford.

Bruzzi, S. (1997) *Undressing Cinema,* Routledge, London.

Bruzzi, S. and Church-Gibson, P. (eds) *Fashion Cultures* Routledge, London.

Bukatman, S. (2003) *Matters of Gravity: Special Effects and Supermen in the Twentieth Century,* Duke University Press, London.

Burnett, T. (1981) *The Rise and Fall of a Regency Dandy: The Life and Times of Scrope Beardmore Davis,* John Murray, London.

Butler, J. (1999) *Gender Trouble,* Routledge, London.

Campbell, C. (1987) *The Romantic Ethic and the Spirit of Modern Consumerism,* Blackwell, Oxford.

Caponi, G. D. (ed.) (1999) *Signifyin', Sanctifyin' and Slam Dunking,* University of Massachusetts Press, Cambridge, MA.

Charles-Roux, E. (2005) *Chanel: Friends, Fashion, Fame,* Thames and Hudson, London.

Charters, A. (2001) *Beat Down to Your Soul; What was the Beat Generation?,* Penguin, London.

Corson, R. (1967) *Fashions in Eyeglasses,* Peter Owen, London.

Dahl-Wolfe, L. (1984) *A Photographer's Scrapbook,* St. Martin's, London.

Dawson, J. (1995) *Quentin Tarantino: The Cinema of Cool,* Applause Theatre Books, Montclair, NJ.

Deregowski, J. B. (1984) *Distortion in Art: The Eye and the Mind,* Routledge and Kegan Paul, London.

DiCorcia, P.-L. (2001) *Heads,* Pace Wildenstein, New York.

Dinerstein, J. (2003) *Swinging the Machine: Modernity, Technology, and African American Culture Between the Wars*, University of Massachusetts Press, Massachusetts.

Dowalisky, M. (1961) *Modern Eyewear: Fashion and Cosmetic Dispensing,* Professional Press Inc., Chicago.

Ellison, R. (1965)[1947] *The Invisible Man,* Penguin, London.

Entwistle, J. (2000) *The Fashioned Body,* Polity Press, Cambridge.

Entwistle, J. and Wilson, E. (eds) (2001) *Body Dressing,* Berg, Oxford.

Evans, M. (1996) *Sunglasses,* Hamlyn, London.

Ewen, S. (1992) *Channels of Desire,* University of Minnesota Press, Minneapolis.

Di Fate, V. (1997) *Infinite Worlds,* Virgin, London.

Featherstone, M. and Burrows, R. (eds) (1995) *Cyberbodies/Cyberspace/Cyberpunk: Cultures of Technological Embodiment,* Sage, London

Finkelstein, N. (1989) *Andy Warhol – the Factory Years,* St Martin's Press, New York.

Fraimen, S (2003) *Cool Men and the Second Sex,* Columbia University Press, New York.

Frank, T. (1997) *The Conquest of Cool,* University of Chicago Press, Chicago.

Frisby, D. (1985) *Fragments of Modernity,* Polity Press, London.

Futurismo (Ex cat.) (1972) *Futurismo 1909–1919,* Northern Arts and Scottish Arts Council.

Gateward, F. and Pommerance, M. (2002) *Sugar, Spice and Everything Nice: Cinemas of Girlhood,* Wayne State University Press, Detroit.

Gelder, K. and Thornton, S. (1997) *The Subcultures Reader,* Routledge, London.

Gergen, K. (1991) *The Saturated Self,* Basic Books, New York.

Giger, G. (1989) *Giger's Alien,* Titan Books, London.

Giles, D. (2000) *Illusions of Immortality: A Psychology of Fame and Celebrity,* Macmillan, London.

Gillis, S. (ed.) (2005) *The Matrix Trilogy: Cyberpunk Reloaded,* Wallflower Press, London.

Goffman, E. (1963) *Behaviour in Public Places,* Free Press, New York.

—(2005) [1967] *Interaction Ritual,* Aldine Transaction, New Brunswick, NJ.

Gold, H. (1994) *Bohemia – Digging the Roots ofCcool,* Simon and Schuster, London.

Globus, D. (2000) *Louise Dahl-Wolfe: A Retrospective,* Harry Abrams, London.

Graves, R. and Hodges, A. (1961) *The Long Weekend – England between the Wars,* Four Square Books, London.

Greer, L. and Harold, A. (1979) *Flying Clothing,* Airlife, Shrewsbury.

Grundberg, A. (1989) *Brodovitch: Master of American Design,* Harry Abrams, New York.

Gundle, S. (2008) *Glamour: A History,* Oxford University Press, Oxford.

Hamilton, P. and Hargreaves, R. (2001) *The Beautiful and the Damned: The Creation of Identity in Nineteenth Century Photography,* National Portrait Gallery, London.

Handley, N. (2011) *Cult Eyewear,* London, Merrell.

Haraway, D. (1990) *Simians, Cyborgs and Women,* Routledge, London.

hooks, b (2003) *We Real Cool: Black Men and Masculinity,* Routledge, London.

Hovenden, F. Janes, L. Kirkup, G. and Woodward, K. (eds.) (2000) *The Gendered Cyborg: a reader*. Routledge, London.

Howe, P. (2005) *Paparazzi,* Artisan, New York.

Hudson, J. (1992) *Wakes Week: Memories of Mill Town Holidays,* Alan Sutton, Stroud.

Huxley, A. (1974) *The Art of Seeing,* Chatto and Windus, London.

—(2004) [1923], *Antic Hay,* Vintage, London.

Hvattum, M. and Hermansen, C. (2004) *Tracing Modernity: Manifestations of the Modern in Architecture and the City,* Routledge, London.

Jay, M. (1993) *Downcast Eyes: The Denigration of Vision in Twentieth Century French Thought,* University of California Press, Berkeley.

Koch, S. (1991) *Stargazer: The Life, World and Films of Andy Warhol,* Marion Boyars, London.

Kracauer, S. (1995 [1927], *The Mass Ornament: Weimar essays,* Harvard University Press, Cambridge, MA.

Lartigue, J.-H. (1978) *Diary of a Century,* Penguin Books, London.

Lasch, C. (1984) *The Minimal Self,* W. W. Norton, New York.

—(1991) *The Culture of Narcissism,* W. W. Norton, New York.

Lehmann, U. (2000) *Tigersprung: Fashion in Modernity,* MIT Press, London.

Lencek, L. and Boskev, G. (1998) *The Beach: A History of Paradise on Earth,* Penguin, London.

Lingis, A. (1994) *Foreign Bodies,* London, Routledge.

Lipow, M. (2011) *Eyewear: A Visual History,* London, Taschen.

Lista, G. (2001) *Futurism,* Terrail, Paris.

Lui, A. (2004) *The Laws of Cool: Knowledge Work and the Culture of Information*, University of Chicago Press, Chicago.

Lussier, S. (2003) *Art Deco Fashion,* Victoria and Albert Museum Publications, London.

Macadams, L. (2002) *Birth of the Cool: Beat, Bebop and the American Avant-garde,* Scribner, London.

Mailer, N. (1957) *The White Negro*, City Lights Books, San Francisco.

Majors, R. and Billson, J. (1992) *Cool Pose: The Dilemmas of Black Manhood in America,* Simon and Schuster, New York.

MacLuhan, Marshall. (1964) *Understanding Media: The Extension of Man,* Prentice Hall, New York.

Mazza, S. (1996) *Spectacles,* Chronicle Books, San Francisco.

Mennell, S. (1989) *Norbert Elias: An Introduction,* Blackwell, Oxford.

Merton, R. K. (1967) *Social Theory and Social Structure,* The Free Press, New York.

Millar, J. (2003) *Brighton Photo Biennial,* Photoworks, Brighton.

Mirzoeff, N. (1999) *An Introduction to Visual Culture,* Routledge, London.

Museum of Modern Art (1967) *Lartigue,* Museum of Modern Art, New York.

Nietzsche, F. (trans. Hollingdale, R.) (1983) *Untimely Meditations,* Cambridge University Press, Cambridge.

Paulsen, W. (1987) *Romanticism, Enlightenment and the Blind in France,* Princeton University Press, Princeton.

Peretti, W (2007) *Nightclub City: Politics and Amusement in Manhattan,* University of Pennsylvania Press, Philadelphia.

Pountain, D. and Robins, D. (2000) *Cool Rules: Anatomy of an Attitude,* Reaktion Books, London.

Pringle, H. (2004) *Celebrity Sells,* John Wiley and Sons, Chichester.

Redhead, S. (2004) *Paul Virilio: Theorist for an Accelerated Culture,* Edinburgh University Press, Edinburgh.

Robinson, F. R (1993) *The Man in the Bowler Hat,* University of North Carolina Press, Chapel Hill, NC.

Rojek, C. (1993) *Ways of Escape,* Macmillan, London.

Rojek, C. and Urry, J. (eds) (1997) *Touring Cultures,* Routledge, London.

Rosen, J. (2000) *The Unwanted Gaze,* Random House, New York.

Rushing, J. H. (1995) *Projecting the Shadow,* University of Chicago Press, London.

Sabau, L. (ed.) (1998) *The Promise of Photography,* Prestel, London.

Schickel, R. (2000) *Intimate Strangers: The Culture of Celebrity in America,* Ivan R. Dee, Chicago.

Schivelbusch, W. (1986) *The Railway Journey,* University of California Press, Berkeley.

—(1995) *Disenchanted Night,* Berg, Oxford.

Schwichtenberg, C. (1993) *The Madonna Connection,* Westview Press, New York.

Simmel, G. (ed. Wolff, K. H.) (1964) *The Sociology of Georg Simmel,* Collier-Macmillan, London.

—(ed. Levine, D.) (1971) *On Individuality and Its Social Forms,* University of Chicago Press, London.

Smith, M. and Morra, J. (eds) (2006) *The Prosthetic Impulse,* University of Massachusetts Press, Cambridge, MA.

Sparke, P. (1995) *As Long as It's Pink,* Pandora, London.

Stearns, P. (1994) *American Cool,* New York University Press, New York.

Sterling, B. (ed.) (1988) *Mirrorshades: A Cyberpunk Anthology,* Ace, New York.

Svendsen, L. (2006) *Fashion: A Philosophy,* London, Reaktion Books.

Tate, G. (2003) *Everything but the Burden: What White People are Taking from Black Culture,* Harlem Moon, Broadway Books, New York.

Tester, K. (ed.) (1994) *The Flâneur,* Routledge, London.

Thomas, H. and Ahmed, J. (eds.) (2004) *Cultural Bodies: Ethnography and Theory,* Wiley Blackwell, London.

Timms, E. and Kelly, D. (eds) (1985) *Unreal City: Urban Experience in Modern European Literature and Art,* Manchester University Press, Manchester.

Tomlinson, J. (2007) *The Culture of Speed: the coming of immediacy,* Sage, London.

Turner, L. and Ash, J. (1975) *The Golden Hordes,* Constable, London.

Twain, M. (1996) [1895] *The Million Pound Bank Note,* Oxford University Press, Oxford.

Underhill, P. (2011) *Why We Buy: The Science of Shopping,* Simon and Schuster, New York.

Urry, J. (1990) *The Tourist Gaze,* Sage, London.

Veblen, T. (1994) [1899] *The Theory of the Leisure Class,* Penguin, New York.

Vickers, G. (2008) *Chasing Lolita,* Chicago Review Press, Chicago.

Virilio, P. (1978) *La Dromoscopie ou la lumière de la vitesse,* Editions de Minuit, Paris.

—(1997) *Pure War,* Semiotext(e), New York.

—(1999) *Politics of the Very Worst,* Semiotext(e), New York.

Walden, G. (2002) *Who is a Dandy?,* Gibson Square Books, London.

Ward, P. (1997) *Fantastic Plastic,* Book Sales Inc., Minneapolis, MN.

Warhol, A. (1975) *The Philosophy of Andy Warhol (from A to B and Back Again),* Harcourt Brace and Co., London.

Warhol Museum. (2004) *365 Takes,* Thames and Hudson, London.

Welters, L. and Cunningham, P. A. (2005) *Twentieth Century American Fashion,* Berg, Oxford.

White, C. (1970) *Women's Magazines,* Michael Joseph, London.

Wilson, E. (1985) *Adorned in Dreams: fashion and modernity,* Virago, London.

—(2003) *Bohemians: The Glamorous Outcasts,* Tauris Parke, London.

Winship, J. (1985) *Inside Women's Magazines,* Pandora, London.

Articles

Arnold, R. (2002) "Looking American," *Journal of Fashion Theory*, vol. 6 no. 1: 45–60.

Balsamo, A. (2000) "Reading Cyborgs, Writing Feminism," in Kirkup et al. (eds) *The Gendered Cyborg*, Routledge, London: 148–158.

Banham, R. (1967) "Shades of summer," *New Society*, June 29, 1967: 959.

Barbey d'Aureville, J. (2002) [1845] "The Anatomy of Dandyism," in Walden (2002) *Who is a Dandy?,* Gibson Square Books, London.

Bauman, Z. (1994) "Desert spectacular," in Tester (ed.) *The Flâneur*, Routledge, London: 138–57.

Becker, H. S. (1963) "The Culture of a Deviant Group – the Jazz Musician," in Gelder and Thornton (eds) (1997) *The Subcultures Reader*, Routledge, London: 55–65.

Bennet, R. (1963) "The magic of glasses," *Vision: supplement to the Optical Practitioner*, Winter: 26–27.

Bliven, B. (1925) "The flapper," *The New Republic*, September 9, 1925: 18.

Blumer, H. (1969) "From class differentiation to collective selection," *Sociological Quarterly*, x: 281.

Botz-Bornstein, T. (2013) "Veils and sunglasses," *Journal of Aesthetics and Culture*, vol. 5, online.

Boyd-Whyte, I. (2004) "Modernity and Architecture," in Hvattum and Hermansen (eds) (2004) *Tracing Modernity: Manifestations of the Modern in Architecture and the City*, Routledge, London: 42–55

Brown, J. (2005) "New look's double act" *Drapers – the Fashion Business Weekly*, August 20, 2005: 24–6.

Broyard, A. (1948) "A Portrait of the Hipster," in Charters (2001) *Beat Down to Your Soul*, Penguin, London: 43–9.

Buck-Morss, S. (1986) "The *flâneur*, the sandwich man and the whore: the politics of loitering," *New German Critique,* Fall, no. 39: 99–140.

Campbell Warner, P. (2005) "The Americanisation of Fashion: Sportswear, the Movies and the 1930s," in Welters and Cunningham (eds) *Twentieth Century American Fashion*, Oxford, Berg: 79–98.

Carter, S. and Michael, M. (2004) "Here Comes the Sun: Shedding Light on the Cultural Body," in Thomas and Ahmed (eds) *Cultural Bodies: Ethnography and Theory*, Wiley Blackwell, London: 260–82.

Clark, N. (1995) "Rear-view Mirrorshades: The Recursive Regeneration of the Cyber Body," in Featherstone and Burrows (eds) (1995) *Cyberbodies/Cyberspace/ Cyberpunk: Cultures of Technological Embodiment*, Sage, London: 113–31.

Craik, J. (1997) "The Culture of Tourism," in Rojek and Urry (eds) *Touring Cultures,* Routledge, London: 110–39.

Daily Mail (2007) "Pdiddy and the princes: the night William and Harry met rap royalty," July 2, 2007, online.

Dickinson, (1938) "A critical analysis of new absorptive glass – Ray-Ban," *The Optician*, August: 417–18.

Dinerstein, J. (1999) "Lester Young and the Birth of Cool," in Caponi (ed.) *Signifyin', Sanctifyin' and Slam Dunking,* University of Massachusetts Press, Cambridge, MA: 239–78.

Edwards, K. (1987) "Effects of sex and glasses on attitudes towards intelligence and attractiveness," *Psychology Reports*, vol. 6 no. 2: 590.

Edwards, O. (1989) "Shades of meaning," *American Photographer*, vol. 23, July: 57–9.

Ewen, S. (1992) "Marketing Dreams," in Tomlinson (ed.) (1992) *Consumption, Identity and Style*, Routledge, London: 41–56.

Ewing, W. (1991) "Perfect surface," in *Aperture: The Idealising Vision*, no. 122, December: 6–23.

Farren, A. and Hutchison A. (2004) "Cyborgs, new technology, and the body: the changing nature of garments," *Journal of Fashion Theory*, vol. 8 no. 4: 461–75.

Fer, B. (2007) "Night," *Oxford Art Journal*, vol. 30 no. 1: 69–70.

Fisher, T. (2013) "A world of colour and bright shining surfaces: experiences of plastics after the Second World War," *Journal of Design History*, vol. 26 no. 3: 285–303.

Flick, C. S. (1949) "Goethe, man of vision," *Vision*, Autumn: 29–31.

Gafforio, L. and Ceppi, G. (1996) "Revolutions in Sight," in Mazza (ed.) *Spectacles,* Chronicle Books, San Francisco: 28–42.

Goldberg, V. (2000) "Louise Dahl-Wolfe," in Globus (2000) *Louise Dahl-Wolfe: A Retrospective*, Harry Abrams, London: 16–24.

Gray, H. (1995) "Black masculinity and visual culture," *Callaloo*, vol. 18 no. 2: 401–5.

Greenaway, P. (2007) "Night," *Domus*, no. 909: 70–1.

Greenslade, R. (1999) "Good Will Hunting," *Guardian*, August 9, 1999: 8.

Hamel (trans. Newell, J.) (1955) "Historical note on tinted lenses," *The Optician*, October: 349.

Handley, N. (2005) "D-spectacles, horseshoe spectacles and protective railway spectacles," *Opthalmic Antiques*, no. 92, July: 5–8.

Harcombe-Cuff, P. (1912) "The Use of tinted glass" and "The use of spectacles in gambling," *The Keystone Magazine of Optometry*, vol. 4, no. 8: 637.

Hatch, K. (2002) "Fille Fatale," in Gateward and Pommerance (eds) *Sugar, Spice, and Everything Nice: Cinemas of Girlhood,* Wayne State University Press, Detroit.

Hennessy, S. (1999) "Goody U2 shoes…the thing about Bono is he actually means what he Says," *Observer*, February 21, 1999: 27.

Heyl, C. (2001) "When They Are Veiled In Order To Be Seene," in Entwistle and Wilson (eds.) (2001) *Body Dressing,* Berg, Oxford: 121–42.

Hughey, M. (2009) "Black aesthetics and panther rhetoric," *Critical Sociology*, no. 35: 29–56.

Jelbert, S. (2000) "Pop: the wages of sincerity," *Independent*, May 5, 2000: 13.

Keystone Magazine (1910) May 1910: 489.

Kuspit, D. (2005) "From Max Ernst's "Oedipus Rex" to Andy Warhol's "Marilyn Monroe," or why the sphinx no longer has a secret," *Art Criticism*, vol. 20: 33–48.

Lucas, T. (2007) "Inside Room 12," *Sight and Sound*, vol. 17 no. 12: 104.

Maffei, N. (2009) "Both natural and mechanical: the streamlined design of Norman Bel-Geddes," *Journal of Transport History*, vol. 30 no. 2:141–67.

—(2013) "Selling gleam: making steel modern in postwar America," *Journal of Design History,* vol. 26 no. 3: 304–20.

Manufacturing Optician. (1966) "Sun-specs: the big volume business sector," (U.S.), July: 67.

Mauri, P. (2007) "About the dark," in *Domus*, no. 909: 63–5.

McVeigh, B. (2000) "How Hello Kitty commodifies cute, cool and camp," *Journal of Material Culture*, vol. 5 no. 2: 225–45.

Mentges, G. (2000), "Cold, coldness, coolness: remarks on the relationship of dress, body and technology," *Journal of Fashion Theory*, vol. 4 no. 1: 27–47.

Mercer, K. (1987) "Black Hair/Style Politics," in Gelder and Thornton (eds) (1997) *The Subcultures Reader,* Routledge, London: 420–35.

Morgado, M. (2007) "The semiotics of extraordinary dress – a structural analysis of hip-hop style," *Clothing and Textiles Research Journal*, no. 25: 131–54.

Morel, J. (1937) "Venetian summer," *Harper's Bazaar*, September: 62–3.

Moxey, K. (2008) "Visual studies and the iconic turn," *Journal of Visual Culture*, vol. 7 no. 2: 131–46.

Murray, D. C. (2004) "Hip hop vs. high art: notes on race as spectacle," *Art Journal*, vol. 63 no 2: 5–17.

—(2007) "Kehinde Wiley – splendid bodies," *NKA*, Fall, no. 21: 90–101.

Optician, The (1936) "Spectacles for everybody," *The Optician*, June: 331.

Park, R. E. (1915) "The City: Suggestions for the Investigation of Human Behaviour," in Gelder and Thornton (eds) (1997) *The Subcultures Reader,* Routledge, London: 16–27.

Parkhurst-Ferguson, P. (1994) "The *Flâneur*: On and off the Streets of Paris," in Tester (ed.) *The Flâneur,* Routledge, London: 22–42.

Pearson, G. (1983) "Victorian Boys, We Are Here!," in Gelder and Thornton (eds) (1997) *The Subcultures Reader*, Routledge, London: 281–92.

Pountain, D. and Robins, D. (1999) "Cool rules, anatomy of an attitude," *New Formations*, no. 39: 7–14.

Radner, H. (2000) "On the Move," in Bruzzi and Church-Gibson (eds) *Fashion Cultures,* Routledge, London.

Saville, D. (2005) "Dress and Culture in Greenwich Village," in Welters and Cunningham (eds) *Twentieth Century American Fashion*, Oxford, Berg: 33–56.

Sawyer, M. (1997) "On tour with the disco vicar," *Guardian*, March 2, 1997: 12–14.

Shields, R. (1994) "Fancy Footwork: Walter Benjamin's Notes on Flânerie," in Tester (ed.) *The Flâneur,* Routledge, London: 61–80.

Simmel, G. (1964) [1903], "The Metropolis and Mental Life," in Simmel *The Sociology of Georg Simmel*, Collier Macmillan, London.

—(1964) "The Philosophy of Money," in Simmel *The Sociology of Georg Simmel*, Collier Macmillan, London.

—(1971) [1908] "The Stranger," in Simmel *On Individuality and Its Social Forms,* University of Chicago Press, London.

Snyder, S. (2001) "Personality disorder and the film noir femme fatale," *Journal of Criminal Justice and Popular Culture*, vol. 8 no. 3: 155–68.

Springer, C. (2005) "Playing it Cool in *The Matrix*," in Gillis (ed.) *The Matrix Trilogy: Cyberpunk Reloaded*, Wallflower Press, London: 89–100.

Spurling, B. (1953) "Spectacles to be proud of," *Vision*, Summer 1953: 33–4.

Squires, C. (1980) "Slouch, stretch, smile, leap," *Artforum*, November, no. 19: 47–50.

Terry, R. (1989) "Affective responses to eyeglasses: evidence of a sex difference," *Journal of the American Optometric Association*, vol. 60 no. 8: 609–11.

Terry, R. L. and Stockton, L. (1993) "Eyeglasses and children's schemata," *Journal of Social Psychology,* vol. 133 no. 4: 415–38.

Thompson, D. (2000) "Godard: that breathless moment," *Sight and Sound*, vol. 10 no. 7: 28–31.

Thornton, S. (1995 [1997]) "The Social Logic of Subcultural Capital," in Gelder and Thornton (eds) (1997) *The Subcultures Reader*, Routledge, London: 200–12.

Virilio, P. (1998) "Photo Finish," in Sabau (ed.) *The Promise of Photography*, Prestel, London: 19–24.

The Wellsworth Merchandiser (1920) "Style in eyewear," vol. 8 no. 2: (n.p.).

Welters, L. (2005) "The Beat Generation," in Welters and Cunningham (eds) *Twentieth Century American Fashion*, Oxford, Berg: 145–67.

Williams, L. (2007) "Heavy metal: decoding hip hop jewellery," in *Metalsmith*, vol. 27 no. 1: 36–41.

Wilson, E. (2007) "A note on glamour," *Journal of Fashion Theory*, vol. 11 no. 1: 95–108.

Wright, P. R. (1920) "By a noted war correspondent," *The Wellsworth Merchandiser*, vol. 8 no. 2: 31.

Zdatny, S. (1997) "The boyish look and the liberated woman," *Journal of Fashion Theory*, vol. 1 no. 4: 367–97.

Additional sources

Internet

De Silva (2007), "Who could you be?" www.duffyshanley.com (accessed January 13, 2001).

Drewry, Richard (1994), "What man devised that he might see" www.eye.utmem.edu (accessed January 1, 2001).

Foster Grant (2009), "Foster Grant" www.fostergrant.co.uk (accessed January 7, 2009).

Meinhold, B. (2009), "Solar glasses can power your gadgets" inhabitat.com, (accessed July 14, 2009).

Mintel (UK), June 2012, "Executive summary – sunglasses (UK)" mintel.com (accessed January 9, 2012).

Mori, M. (trans. MacDorman, K. and Minato, T.) (1970), "The uncanny valley" in *Energy* vol. 7 no. 4: 33–35, www.movingimages.info (accessed January 7, 2012).

Oakley (2009), oakley.co.uk (accessed July 14, 2009).

—(2013), oakley.co.uk (accessed March 14, 2013).

Vision (1948) *Vision: supplement to The Optical Practitioner* Summer 1948.

Magazines

The Face 1992–2001)
Good Housekeeping (1957–61)
Harper's Bazaar (1928–38)
Marie Claire (France) (1937–39)
Stoll, "Faux Real" *Trend Collection* A/W 2012/13
Vogue Magazine (U.K.) (1922–present)
Woman's Journal (March 1929)

Patents

Lawrence, S. S. (1905) *Improvements in Eye Protectors* American Patent No. 8275:
    patents online (accessed November 16, 2008).
Spill, F. (1929) *Method and Apparatus for Manufacturing Frames for Sunglasses*
    American Patent No.1739696: patents online (accessed October 5, 2011).

Optical journals

Amoptico (U.S.) (1911–16)
American Journal of Optometry (U.S.) (1930–49)
The Keystone Magazine of Optometry (U.S.) (1910–12)
Manufacturing Optician (U.S.) (July 1966)
The Optician (U.K.) (1910–60)
The Optician: Special Supplement on Sunglasses (U.K.) (1939)
The Optician: Special Supplement on Sunglasses (U.K.) (1967)
Rodenstock Clear Vision catalogue (U.S.) (c. 1960)
"Vision" supplement to *The Optical Practitioner* (U.K.) (1947–64)
The Wellsworth Merchandiser (U.S.) (1916–25)

Conference papers

Hackney, F. (2003) "That Dangerous Modern Problem" *Design History Society
    Conference: "Sex Object."*
Harris, L. (2003) "Women and Cars" *Design History Society Conference: "Sex Object."*
McMahon, K. and Morely, J. (2011) "Innovation, Interaction and Inclusion: heritage
    luxury brands in collusion with the consumer," *International Foundation of Fashion
    Technology Institutes (IFFTI) Conference Proceedings: Between Heritage and
    Innovation,* Institut Français de la Mode, Paris: 69–78.

Unpublished

Wilson, G. (1999) "The Psychology of Specs and Shades" for Brook Wilkinson on behalf
    of Dolland and Aitchison.

Films

À *Bout de Souffle* (1959) dir. Jean-Luc Godard.
Bladerunner (1982) dir. Ridley Scott.
Breakfast at Tiffany's (1961) dir. Blake Edwards.
Charlie and the Chocolate factory (2005) dir. Tim Burton.
Cool Hand Luke (1967) dir. Stuart Rosenberg.
Desperately Seeking Susan (1985) dir. Susan Seidelman.
Django Unchained (2012) dir. Quentin Tarantino.
Double Indemnity (1944) dir. Billy Wilder.
Fear and Loathing in Las Vegas (1998) dir. Terry Gilliam.
Funny Face (1957) dir. Stanley Donen.
Great Escape (1963) dir. John Sturges
K-Pax (2001) dir. Ian Softley.
La Dolce Vita (1960) dir. Federico Fellini.
Leave Her to Heaven (1945) dir. John Stahl.
Legally Blonde (2001) dir. Robert Luketic.
Leon (1994) dir. Luc Besson.
Letty Lynton (1932) dir. Clarence Brown
Lolita (1967) dir. Stanley Kubrick.
Marie Antoinette (2006) dir. Sofia Coppola.
The Matrix (1999) dir. Wachowski Brothers.
Metropolis (1927) dir. Fritz Lang.
Minority Report (2002) dir. Steven Spielberg.
Nikita (1990) dir. Luc Besson.
Pulp Fiction (1994) dir. Quentin Tarantino.
Rebel Without a Cause (1955) dir. Nicholas Ray.
Reservoir Dogs (1992) dir. Quentin Tarantino.
Skyfall (2012) dir. Sam Mendes
Smash His Camera (2010) dir. Leon Gast.
The September Issue (2009) dir. R. J. Cutler.
Terminator (1984) dir. James Cameron.
Trainspotting (1996) dir. Danny Boyle.
The Wild One (1953) dir. Laslo Benedek.

Archives

British Optical Association Museum

The Wellcome Institute

The College of Optometrists
42 Craven Street
London WC2N 5NG
Wellcome Collection
183 Euston Road
London NW1 2BE, UK

INDEX